Freud on Madison Avenue

Freud
on
Madison
Avenue

Motivation Research
and Subliminal Advertising
in America

Lawrence R. Samuel

PENN

UNIVERSITY OF PENNSYLVANIA PRESS

PHILADELPHIA · OXFORD

Published by
University of Pennsylvania Press
Philadelphia, Pennsylvania 19104-4112

Printed in the United States of America
on acid-free paper
10 9 8 7 6 5 4 3 2 1

Library of Congress Cataloging-in-Publication Data

Samuel, Lawrence R.
Freud on Madison Avenue : motivation research and subliminal
advertising in America / Lawrence R. Samuel.
p. cm.
Includes bibliographical references and index.
ISBN 978-0-8122-4251-5 (hbk. : alk. paper)
1. Motivation research (Marketing)—United States--History. 2.
Subliminal advertising—United States—History 3. Advertising—
United States—Psychological aspects—History. 4. Consumer
behavior—United States—History. I. Title.
HF5415.34.S26 2010
659.101'9—dc22
2009048472

The conscious mind may be compared to a fountain playing in the sun and falling back into the great subterranean pool of subconscious from which it rises.

—Sigmund Freud

Contents

Introduction

About ten years ago I found myself staring up at the ceiling of a meeting room in a Boston hotel. Lying around me were twenty or so other people in comfortable clothes, thinking about our very first encounter with money. Leading the session, if you could call it that, was a moderator for Archetype Discoveries Worldwide, a consultancy run by Clotaire Rapaille. The moderator was attempting to induce me and my fellow subjects into a primal state in which the "reptilian" part of our brains would take over, enabling us to reveal key, otherwise unavailable insights about the role of money in America. I don't remember anything particularly interesting emerging from the three-hour session, although I do recall briefly falling asleep.

While researching this book, I came across an interesting comment made by Ernest Dichter in his autobiography. "It probably would be a good idea, in trying to understand people, to go back to the very first money they ever acquired and to find out what they did with it," Dichter wrote in 1979, a full twenty-one years before my experience.[1] Sheer coincidence? The parallels between Dichter and Rapaille were, upon closer inspection, downright eerie. Rapaille was working with many of the same clients Dichter had, and covering much the same territory by interpreting the "collective unconscious" of different cultures for Chrysler, Procter and Gamble, DuPont, and many others. Whether he was "a sage or a charlatan," as *Fast Company* magazine wondered in 2006, was unsure, but there was no doubt that the velvet-suited, Rolls Royce–driving Frenchman was striking a chord similar to the one the frugal Austrian had struck during his long career. While Dichter leaned heavily toward Freudian theory, at least early in his career, Rapaille added Jung to his psychoanalytic mix, a potent combination. "Cracking the code" was the essence of Rapaille's deliverables, and multinational companies that wanted to do business in the global economy were eager to learn what made a particular society tick. In fact, Rapaille claimed that he had worked with half of the

Fortune 100, charging \$125,000 to \$225,000 a pop, numbers that surpassed even Dichter's considerable success.[2]

There were more similarities between the two gurus. Besides being happy to pay him big bucks, clients were often in awe of Rapaille, a lot like how a couple of previous generations of executives had been entranced by Dichter's ability to wax poetic on any subject imaginable. "I never believe what people say; I want to understand why people do what they do," Rapaille told *Fast Company*; his marathon group analysis was the way to achieve that, much like Dichter's reliance on the depth interview. Toss in a few commonalities in their personal lives—a scary brush with the Nazis in World War II, a mansion in Westchester, and a deep appreciation for the American Dream—and you might start thinking that Clotaire Rapaille could be one of Dichter's younger brothers in French disguise. "The thing that makes Clotaire so striking to me is how closely he modeled his whole pitch on Dichter and how well his technique works on marketers," observed Douglas Rushkoff, one of the few people to recognize the overwhelming weirdness of it all.[3]

Also like Dichter, not too surprisingly, Rapaille had his critics. Richard A. Shweder, professor of cultural anthropology and psychology at the University of Chicago, described Rapaille's appeal as "the soft porn of irrationalism" and is highly skeptical of his ability to crack any code except that to make a lot of money.[4] While I share this sentiment, having been woefully unable to access my personal primal state, I am pleased to see that the spirit of motivation research lives on. Rather than an embarrassing episode in business history, which it very well may have turned out to be (particularly because of its relation to the black sheep of the family, subliminal advertising), Rapaille's wild success suggests that motivation research is still considered a valuable market research technique. That it is viewed as leading edge, even radical, is icing on the (Freudian) cake.

The corporate world's importation of Freudian psychological techniques a half-century ago thus continues to resonate despite the retirement of the term "motivation research." Long before focus groups—those interminable gatherings in which M&M-popping marketers sitting behind one-way mirrors watch people tell all or at least some—motivation research was *the* way to glean information from consumers. Besides the Dichter doppelgangers, it is "consumer insights" and "account planning" that are now probing consumers' inner psyches, without the insidiousness associated with these kinds of qualitative research. Anthropologic and ethnographic research also seem more popular than ever, the idea being that, as Yogi Berra had once expressed it, "You can observe a lot by watching." Trend spotters and "cool hunters" spend inordinate amounts of time on the hipper streets of Los Angeles and New York (and, increasingly, Shanghai and Mumbai), immersing themselves in what ahead-of-the-curve kids are wearing, listening to, and talking about. Spying on shoppers too is a prime way to learn, as Paco Underhill put it in *Why We Buy*, as he and his clients believed there is no substitute for good old undercover surveillance when it comes to gaining intelligence. Again, we can thank Ernest Dichter more than anyone else for all this. As Barbara Stern wrote in her aptly titled article "'The Importance of Being Ernest": "His introduction of motivation research is so fully assimilated in the field that it has changed the very grammar of marketing—the common language that underlies disciplinary thought. MR [motivation research] is now part of the marketing community's specialized language or 'code,' a system of verbal conventions mastered by all users as a common tongue for research communications. . . . Whether or not he is mentioned by name, his revolutionary ideas are embedded in the research language. . . . Dichter is 'there' by proxy."[5]

Freud on Madison Avenue tells the story of motivation research, the journey beginning in, of all places, a Viennese laundry in 1930. Over the next few decades, motivation research would become the darling of Madison Avenue, its psychoanalytic roots spreading like kudzu across the American landscape. Its orbit involved politicians, religious leaders, and, most important, a colorful cast of characters wearing bow ties and black glasses with lenses as thick as Coke bottles, the men in gray flannel suits rather incongruously embracing Freudian psychology in order to—as Vance Packard, its most ardent enemy, put it—"get inside the consumer's subconscious." By the time the postwar era was over, motivation research had not just altered the trajectory of American business but injected psychology directly into the nation's bloodstream, playing a key role in the rise of the individual or self. Motivation research foreshadowed some of the "mind expansion" philosophy (and trippy chemical goings-on) of the counterculture as well as helped shape many other subsequent movements with a psychological bent, including self-help in the 1970s, New Age in the 1980s and 1990s, and today's pervasive therapeutic culture. By "building into products the same traits that we recognize in ourselves," as Packard described it, advertisers helped forge the more me-centered society that has flourished ever since.

The field of market research, of which motivation research was part, had far less dramatic beginnings. Market research (marketing or consumer research if you prefer) can be traced as far back as 1879, when the New York ad agency N. W. Ayer did a survey for a potential client interested in a list of newspapers in areas where threshers were sold. Via what Tom Standage called "the Victorian Internet" (the telegram), the agency quickly got the information (and the advertising account). Political polling, a close cousin of market research, started even earlier, in 1824, when the *Harrisburg Pennsylvanian* asked residents of Wilmington, Delaware, if they planned to vote for John Quincy Adams or Andrew Jackson for the upcoming presidential election.[6] Jumping ahead a half-century or so, Claude C. Hopkins was "the first advertising professional to develop a deliberate, conscious notion of the marketing problem," thus seeding the idea of the need for market research in the late nineteenth century, argued Pamela Walker Laird. Cyrus K. Curtis, founder of the *Ladies' Home Journal* and later the *Saturday Evening Post*, established a department of "Commercial Research" in 1910, notably, using the information to sell more advertising.[7]

It was advertising agents, continued Laird, who "added new directions to commercial communications by learning to research markets and to seek out consumer reactions to products as well as to specific advertisements and overall campaigns," but with "inchoate" market analyses gradually replacing industrialists' questionable judgment. Driven by intense competition for accounts (and their clients' intense competition for sales), advertising specialists experimented with market analysis for products like Crisco and Uneeda Biscuit in the first decades of the twentieth century. "In the new century, the importance of planning and research reached general acceptance," wrote Laird, the larger goal being to rid business of guesswork. It was facts, including "the laws of the human mind," as adman Earnest Elmo Calkins expressed it in 1915, that were now considered essential to creating "scientific advertising," ushering a new, more psychological age in American business.[8]

As national, standardized brands began to dominate the American marketplace after World War I, finding out what consumers thought and how they behaved emerged as a full-fledged pursuit. "Pressed to develop ever more elaborate and effective sales campaigns, by the 1910s advertisers began studying consumers themselves," observed Charles McGovern, with more extensive and specific knowledge of consumers likely to lead to greater powers of persuasion.[9] The nation was, after all, a much different place from what it had been before the Great War, enthralled with anything and everything considered "modern." Companies went to school on the government's wartime progress in forecasting and budgeting, and adopted questionnaires used by the military for screening for marketing purposes. Borrowing techniques from social sciences such as sociology, anthropology, and ethnography, a new generation of researchers (notably Archibald Crossley, who developed the first formal surveys in 1919) began to apply their trade to the business world, fully aware that big companies were becoming increasingly interested in bringing logic, rationalism, and efficiency to their rather improvisational process in order to eliminate "waste." The explosion of new products, advertising, and media through the 1920s created the perfect climate for the new field to thrive, as marketers reoriented themselves from production to selling. With the publication of William J. Reilly's *Marketing Investigations* in 1929, which formalized survey research methodology, and Percival White's 1931 *Marketing Research Techniques*, a manual for researchers in the field, the discipline of market research was now a legitimate one.[10] Interestingly, research was an area of business in which women were generally welcome, mostly because they could more easily gain access to other women's homes to interview them. At ad agencies, these researchers were most likely to work on "women's products," their gender considered a plus when it came to what many viewed as the mysterious world of the female body.[11]

In the late 1920s and early 1930s, agency employees, especially copywriters, were encouraged to "mingle" with the masses, as Roland Marchand discussed in his classic *Advertising the American Dream*, a way to keep in touch with "Everyman." (Coney Island was a popular place for New York admen to find "the masses.") Formal research studies segmented the population by occupation and income but fell well short of providing any real subjective information. "Their many attempts to understand and gauge consumers' tastes, habits, and behavior led admen to a specific, if crude sociology," wrote McGovern, with income brackets researchers' most important classification system.[12] Marchand described the methods of the typical ad agency survey of the late 1920s as "slapdash," and using friends of employees as a "representative" sample was not uncommon. The "adman's wife" played a prominent role in representing the average consumer, of course, not exactly a scientific methodology.[13]

With both behavioral psychologist John B. Watson and Paul T. Cherington (the "father of market research," according to some historians) on its staff in the 1920s, J. Walter Thompson was tops among American ad agencies when it came to market research. (Equally impressive, Edward Steichen, the photographer, was head of the art department.) Cherington, who had previously taught at Harvard Business School, led a staff at JWT that investigated consumer attitudes and purchasing habits in a wide variety of product categories. Cherington's staff often went door to door, asking "Mrs. Consumer" about her preference in brands, design, and price. With his firm belief that it was the consumer who ruled the marketplace, rather than the manufacturer, Cherington was way ahead of his time, his thinking current, if not ahead of the curve, even today. The role of marketers was not to manipulate consumers, as many experts (including Watson) held, but "to please and satisfy the public," with research integral to figuring out how to best do that. Cherington also challenged the dominant research methodology of the 1920s—speaking to shoppers in retail settings—siding with those who believed that data gathering through surveys represented a more scientific approach. Cherington's "ABCD" consumer classification system, based on his department's quantitative research, was an early form of market segmentation, this too putting him and JWT ahead of the pack when it came to positioning clients' products and creating advertising campaigns.[14] "Market research and behavioral psychology became the bedrock of Modern ad agency practice," wrote Regina Lee Blaszczyk, with big businesses like General Motors and Procter and Gamble turning hard data into "scientific" marketing strategies.[15]

Rather than slow it down, the Great Depression pushed market research ahead, as marketers recognized its ability to make budgets work harder and smarter. George Gallup's joining Young and Rubicam as director of research in 1932 provided more credibility for the still nascent field, and his opinion poll quickly became a primary source for advertisers to learn what was on the public's mind. Housewives across the country were relentlessly quizzed on every subject imaginable, often by persistent researchers going door to door, a process that one executive at Gimbels department store called "X-raying the consumer." Benton and Bowles was another agency blazing the trail of market research in the 1930s, using the "man in the street" school for a bevy of brands for its client General Foods, including Hellmann's mayonnaise, Baker's chocolate, Post Toasties, Jell-O, and Maxwell House coffee.[16] The U.S. Department of Commerce, pursuing its goal to get the country back on its economic feet, also got into the market research act, "cross-sectioning" cities in order to help marketers tailor their products and services to regional and local tastes. Another researcher, Elmo Roper, soon joined George Gallup as a leading "opinion man," and his own survey results were eagerly gobbled up by sales-oriented clients like CBS Radio and *Good Housekeeping*. Continual progress was made through the 1930s in statistical methodologies and sample design, all part of American business's obsession with "scientific" sales management. By the time the American Marketing Association formally recognized the field with its own conference in 1937, textbooks in market research were being used in colleges across the country, further evidence that this still rather mysterious discipline was not simply a fad that was going to disappear.

General Motors' customer research of the early 1930s was a very ambitious effort for the times, the huge company considering it nothing short of an "operating philosophy." GM mailed questionnaires to more than a million of its car owners and, with a 20 percent or so return rate, got back a boatload of information related to issues like style, price, and engineering. Interestingly, in these early research days, people seemed to love it that GM took the time and effort to send them a letter and that such a big company was interested in their opinion. GM cleverly made the questionnaire folksy rather than formal, realizing that the research program could not only be a source of information but also have, as *Fortune* described it, "propaganda value." GM's customer research was soon elevated to a public relations effort, with questionnaires designed to create consumer goodwill, send an anti–New Deal message, and, ultimately, generate repeat sales. GM even alluded to the program in a trade advertising campaign with the headline "An Eye to the Future—An Ear to the Ground," the ear to the ground being the company's eagerness to listen to what consumers had to say.[17]

Compared to where it would be in twenty years, however, Depression-era market research was undeniably primitive. "Market research measurements in the 1930s were crude and commonly wrong," wrote Martin Mayer in his 1958 bestseller, *Madison Avenue U.S.A.*, blaming "quota samples" based on dated and regionally insensitive census data for many of the problems. Market research on children was particularly rudimentary between the wars, noted Lisa Jacobson, with even simple interviewing of kids not practiced until the late 1930s.[18] Understandably, then, market research was not viewed as a particular priority in the business world. "In those days we had a hell of a time convincing the people in our own agency to pay any attention to us, let alone the clients," recalled Garrit Lydecker, who had worked for Gallup at Y&R in the thirties. In 1943, Lester Frankel of the Census Bureau (who would go on to work for legendary researcher Alfred Politz) developed the "area probability" sample, which introduced the rather new field of statistics to market research, making possible far more accurate results than could be obtained via quota guesstimating. Bad interviewing (and interviewers, since they were often recruited from the ranks of the unemployed) was another issue that made market research in the 1930s sometimes not worth the paper it was printed on. Interviewers often steered subjects toward a particular answer or, if they were in a real hurry, simply invented one. By the late 1950s, however, training programs had been introduced to the field, as had control procedures to ensure that the interviewer had actually been on the job versus at the drive-in.[19]

As important in lifting market research from a business equivalent of medical leeching was the gradual revelation that consumers often didn't know what they were talking about. "It was not for some time that analysts of the reports realized they were being fed malarkey by the people of America," wrote Mayer of market researchers of the 1930s. The problem was either poorly designed questionnaires or subjects intentionally or unintentionally providing information that was something other than the truth. Many people simply weren't aware of what they purchased, much less why, and they gave the wrong answer to even the easiest of questions (e.g., "What brand in product category X do you use?") more often than one would think possible. (No longer trusting consumers, researchers would occasionally check their pantries and medicine cabinets.) Finally, consumers' desire to be "helpful" was making prewar research about as reliable as astrology as a predictor of future behavior. And even if the research was accurate, few marketers knew what to do with it, which is where the social and behavioral sciences made their grand entrance.[20]

Just as market research went back to the days of the horse and carriage, attempts to get inside consumers' heads had a long history. Walter Dill Scott's landmark textbook of 1903, *The Psychology of Advertising*, explored the topic, and a book published in 1919, *Advertising: Its Principles and Practice*, not only included a section called "Psychological Factors in Advertising" but also mentioned that several ad agencies had a psychologist on their staffs. Many other agencies "resort[ed] to the psychological laboratories for the purpose of having special researches and tests planned and conducted, either in the laboratory or in the field," the book stated, an early sign of the wholesale importing of expertise from the social sciences that was to come. The rise of market research after World War I brought a concerted interest in using psychology to try to understand the consumer, part of America's first serious brush with the inner recesses of the mind. As company and agency executives would latch onto motivation research after the next world war, marketers in the 1920s were quite smitten by the arrival of behavioral psychology. "The then new approach of Behaviorism was seized upon by advertisers and agencies who saw no bounds to their capability to engineer desires to sell their goods," wrote Eric Clark, a foreshadowing of what would occur on an even grander scale a generation later.[21] In his 1924 *Principles of Merchandising*, for example, Melvin T. Copeland identified both rational and emotional motives among consumers, arguing that there were two sides to the behavioral coin. The latter have their origin in "human instincts and emotions and represent impulsive or unreasoning promptings to action," Copeland explained, listing no fewer than twenty-three such motives (emulation, ambition, proficiency, and so on) in the textbook."

These were all baby steps compared with the giant leap that psychology-based market research would make in the 1930s, however. "Qualitative" thought—viewing something in terms of its character rather than its size or quantity—had been around since Aristotle or even earlier, the right brain yin to the left brain yang of mathematics and statistics. In fact, most of history has been qualitative, as Rena Bartos observed, as have other disciplines like literary criticism, sociology, and psychology. Still, the concept was largely alien to American businessmen steeped in rational, scientific thinking, with marketers relying almost exclusively on quantitative surveys and questionnaires to find out what consumers thought. This would all change when a few Viennese psychologists brought what were called "in-depth" interviewing techniques to the United States in the 1930s, their methodology directly lifted from psychoanalytic and Gestalt theory and practice (what social anthropologist Clifford Geertz would later call "thick description"). The exporting of this approach—motivation research—not only raised advertising and marketing to an entirely new level of sophistication in the postwar years but also provided ordinary Americans with firsthand experience in Freudian and Adlerian psychology, whose long-term effects are hard to overestimate.[23]

Although motivation research would eventually veer off into a disparate number of directions as more practitioners got into the (lucrative) game in the 1950s and 1960s, its core remained psychoanalytic theory. Nothing happened by chance in the human mind, according to the founding father of psychoanalysis, Sigmund Freud, and therefore consumers' minds had to be probed for the less than obvious. Not only was each "psychic event" meaningful in some way, argued Freud; each one was determined by those preceding it, suggesting that there was a certain logic even to the irrational. Unconscious thoughts were as significant, frequent, and normal as conscious ones in the universe of psychoanalysis, making them just as valuable to marketers as to therapists in terms of understanding people's behavior.[24]

It was ironic that psychologists of Freud's own time considered his theories strange, whereas they became popular with experts and laypeople alike in postwar America. "Thought" was strictly a conscious concept to psychologists a century ago, whereas for Freud much of the activity of the human mind was unconscious. Such unorthodox views made Freud persona non grata at universities until the 1930s, when psychoanalysis finally began to be taken seriously. Academics in other social sciences—cultural anthropology, sociology, even social psychology—were particularly hostile to psychoanalysis, their scorn receding only when they were thrown together in interdisciplinary military departments during World War II. Soon after the war, clinical psychology began to be widely taught at universities, with shrinks galore hanging out their shingle in the early fifties to tackle Americans' many problems. David Riesman's 1950 *The Lonely Crowd* helped to bridge the historical divide between sociology and psychoanalysis, the best seller doing a lot to take the latter out of the booby hatch. Even business, which had viewed Freud and his preoccupation with sex as irrelevant at best, started warming up to psychoanalysis at mid-century, with motivation research doing a lot of the matchmaking.[25] "As more and more psychiatrists, psychologists, physicians, and anthropologists plunged into the hurly-burly of the advertising offices," noted Edith Witt in 1959, "the difference between an adman and a behavioral scientist became only a matter of degree."[26]

Although such a thing was probably the last thing on Freud's own mind, the revolutionary form of psychology that had developed in Austria in the late nineteenth century fitted like a glove with American-style marketing some fifty years later. Freud had focused on the self, after all, and what better resource than consumer culture to create a unique personality and stand out from the crowd? Freud's theory of need gratification, whereby the relative satisfaction of one's needs as a child shapes one's adult personality, was also something marketers were very happy to learn about, knowing their ad agencies could figure out ways to complete (or compensate for) what was missing from consumers' lives. Abraham Maslow's theory of needs, first published in 1954—when excitement around motivation research was beginning to peak—also came in handy, offering marketers another model by which to better understand and more effectively sell products to consumers.[27]

It was Freud, however, to whom motivation researchers looked first to get deep into consumers' minds, where the reasons for their sometimes inexplicable behavior resided. His concept of the unconscious, with its hidden desires that shaped people's behavior, was a particularly powerful idea for marketers to embrace and exploit. Rationalization, the process by which conscious or unconscious acts were made to appear rational, was another psychiatric concept marketers could easily relate to. Projection, an unconscious mechanism people used to cast off their weaknesses onto others, would turn out to be an ideal motivation research technique, as would free association, which Freud used to extract unconscious feelings and thoughts. Freud was, in short, a godsend to Madison Avenue, his radical views just what the doctor ordered to advance consumer culture by allowing postwar Americans' ids to run free.[28]

Freud himself couldn't have chosen a better place for his theories to thrive than in midtown Manhattan in the 1950s. Like other ripples in the placid surface of the Eisenhower years (the Beats, bebop, Jackson Pollock, the Kinsey Report, and Elvis, to name a few), motivation research revealed the underside of the not-so-nifty fifties. In a pervasive atmosphere of peer pressure, conformity, and keeping up with the Joneses, psychoanalysis was not surprisingly having a field day, the fear of being somehow "abnormal" perhaps at an all-time high. It was this profound anxiety of not being in control, of losing one's mind, that provided a perfect breeding ground for motivation research and its sidekick, subliminal advertising, to strike a cultural chord and for Freudian thought to resonate so strongly. Other cultural factors—the triumph of a new medium specifically designed to promote consumerism, the trust in "experts" and the love fest with "research" of all stripes, the realization that politicians could and should be marketed as brands, and, of course, the baby boom—helped pave the way for various forms of hidden persuasion to flourish and, at the same time, be considered truly terrifying.

It was the backdrop of the Cold War, however, that turned a mere market research technique into a cultural phenomenon. Reports of mind control and brainwashing by the Communists were widely believed, with J. Edgar Hoover's 1958 *Masters of Deceit* and the 1959 novel *The Manchurian Candidate* only adding fuel to the fire. Through the Korean War, the McCarthy hearings, and the launch of Sputnik, fear and paranoia ran amok in the United States, and the Red Scare made many in postwar America hypersensitive and emotionally vulnerable to both real and imaginary outside threats (including the movies *The Blob*, *Them!* and *The Thing from Another World*). Subliminal advertising, an offshoot of motivation research that reared its ugly head in 1957, was literally a craze, with people afraid they might lose their minds from exposure to it. "For many, subliminal advertising confirms their worst fears about advertising," wrote Jack Patterson in 1958, Americans seeing what he called "a psychological sneak attack" as "another, more terrible weapon in Madison Avenue's arsenal for overpowering the human will."[29] Madison Avenue's new interest in consumers' subconscious was thus of deep concern, to say the least, with admen's potential ability to make people buy things they didn't really want or need or, much worse, elect Soviet sympathizers into office, a nightmare of epic proportions. In an age of startling scientific achievements—from the Salk vaccine to Tupperware—why wouldn't a new, diabolic kind of communication be possible?

Within the business community, however, the timing was especially good for what one writer called "psychic hucksterism" to take hold. There was a general feeling among executives that marketing and, specifically, market research had to be retooled after the war, that creating a new and improved American Way of Life relied upon new and improved investigative tools and techniques. Firms like A. C. Nielsen, Roper, and the Gallup Organization had provided sales tracking services and public opinion polls since the early

1930s, but such methods were just not able to provide the answers to the kind of questions marketers were increasingly asking (and sometimes, as in the case of "Dewey Defeats Truman," just plain getting wrong). The information provided by "nose counters" or "sample men," as they were often called in the trade, was fine but incomplete, a whole other side of consumers' brains not yet tapped. It was necessary, gray flannel suiters were realizing, to go around consumers' rational sides (and their defenses) to find the inner "truths" that would lead to great advertising. It would be the "depth boys," as motivation researchers were nicknamed (after their favorite tool, the psychoanalysis-based depth interview), who knew the best indirect route to take in order to discover the most valuable insights.

If research in the 1930s and 1940s thus focused on the market—how consumers were behaving—more research in the 1950s and 1960s was dedicated to why they behaved in such a way. Motivation research was devoted almost entirely to the "whys" of consumer behavior, its practitioners digging deep for root causes rather than being satisfied with whatever had risen to the surface. By "search[ing] out the levers that can motivate change in brand image and brand preference," as Albert Shepard, executive vice president of Ernest Dichter's Institute for Motivational Research (IMR) described it, marketers had a better chance of being in the right place at the right time with the right products or ads.[30] "Motivation research x-rays its way into man's psyche," George Christopoulos, associate editor of *The Biddle Survey*, more viscerally put it in 1959, thinking that the intimate relationship between American business and motivation research had only just begun.[31]

X-raying people's psyches relied heavily on the indirect or projective techniques that were part and parcel of motivation research. Such techniques, versus the direct-as-possible approach of traditional research, were "disguised," meaning it was believed that respondents weren't really aware of what their answers meant. Also, projective techniques were often designed to have respondents describe what someone else would think, do, or want in a particular situation, their own feelings and desires "projected" onto this fictional person. Last, the open-ended nature of motivation research's indirect and projective techniques were intended to reveal respondents' "true" attitudes, the findings free from the emotional baggage that came with surveys and questionnaires. Once the usual suspects of human fallibility—fear, self-consciousness, hubris, insecurity—were purged from research methodology, the real picture of an individual thus came through crystal clear, motivation researchers told clients increasingly likely to sign up for studies through the 1950s. The tools at these researchers' disposal were indeed impressive, ranging from sentence completion, word association, narrative projection, picture frustrations (illogical illustrations) and adaptations, free association to symbols, story association tests, description of others, thematic apperception test adaptations, shopping lists, error choice, and the Rorschach test. After analyzing the "data" uncovered in hundreds of interviews using these tools came the tricky part—interpreting the results and drawing out the business implications. Compared to the design, execution, and hand- or machine-tabbing of your typical survey, motivation research was thus a more ambitious undertaking but, hundreds of clients felt, well worth the additional investment, both financial and intellectual.[32]

The intersection of business and the behavioral sciences would prove to be an immensely powerful one in postwar America, an alliance (unholy to some) that supercharged consumer culture. With their advanced degrees and fancy jargon, psychologists and psychiatrists, many of them European Jewish immigrants, brought brains to American corporations and Madison Avenue, adding an intellectual component that simply wasn't there before the war. For most marketers, the idea of having direct access to consumers' ids was extremely exciting, something now hard to fully appreciate. With this secret weapon, marketers believed they had found the skeleton key that could open Americans' minds, the possibility to now answer their ultimate question, "What do consumers want?" "Rather than starting with the product and proclaiming its virtues," wrote Stephen Fox in *The Mirror Makers*, motivation research "began with the buyers and what they wanted, even if they did not know what that was."[33]

In an era of increasingly look-alike, act-alike products, the barriers to competition dramatically lowered after the war, and motivation research offered a powerful way for marketers to differentiate their brands. Improvements made to machinery during the war allowed manufacturers to more easily knock off successful brands, creating a "me-too" climate in many product categories. In categories in which products already seemed pretty similar sans packaging—cigarettes, whisky, and detergent, say—the need to make brands stand out was that much greater. With a new and improved marketplace full of interchangeable, mostly unnecessary things, there was greater pressure to assign brands a unique "personality" if they were to survive. For more and more marketers, it wouldn't be facts that would or could create their brand's personality but rather emotions that reflected those of consumers, a major shift in how products were sold. Emotions, not reason, were now the biggest factor influencing consumers' choices, with repressed drives the most powerful motivators of all.[34]

As the intersection of perception and the construction of reality, psychology was the perfect means to facilitate this decision-making process, its principal role being to match brands up with consumers by finding common emotional ground. Building brand loyalty thus became more critical in the 1950s, marketers believed, and one of the best ways to achieve this was to add "personality" to products. Procter and Gamble was the king of this kind of marketing strategy, personifying its brands of soap based on motivation research. Camay was a glamorous woman, for example, while Ivory was both mother and daughter, representing the essence of purity (the daughter apparently immaculately conceived, a skeptic might conclude).[35] Motivation research was particularly good at rescuing unpopular products and unsuccessful brands such as prunes ("dried out, worn-out symbols of old age," Dichter famously found) and Marlboro cigarettes ("sexually maladjusted," said research), and psychology provided the key .

More than that, however, it was felt that the nation's well-being—indeed, its very survival—depended on keeping the wheels of capitalism spinning as fast as possible, one of our primary weapons to keep the Soviets at bay. Keeping the good times rolling was necessary at virtually any cost, with consuming as much as possible a kind of patriotic duty. In fact, the ability for Americans to consume as much as our factories could produce was viewed by the military-industrial complex as the ideal scenario for a democracy to thrive, making motivation research a dream come true for economists and other wonks. Detroit automakers' goal was to have Americans trade in their cars every year for a new one, with serious talk about the possibility of "three cars in every garage." Yet even this abundance was simply not enough. There was a need for "psychological obsolescence" to complement existing product obsolescence, and advertisers looked to motivation research as the device that would make American consumers even better ones. Indeed, production began to outpace consumer demand in the early 1950s, a serious concern not only in economic terms but for national defense as well. It was clear that something really big was needed to keep factories humming at capacity and consumers spending as much money as possible. "Rather than cut back, [marketers] are asking the psychologists how they can induce the consumer to buy more," wrote Joseph Seldin for the *Nation* in 1955, a new "psycho-economic" age in which emotions ruled purchase decisions, allowing America to remain the greatest country on earth.[36]

Many of those outside the orbit of Madison Avenue, however, were a lot less joyous now that admen (they were always admen, even when they were women) possessed the skeleton key to people's brains. Critics believed that American business had an unfair advantage, now that shrinks' ability to spot consumers' weaknesses and irrationality gave marketers, in essence, "insider information." And for more left-leaning critics, it wasn't the Kremlin but rather Madison Avenue that ordinary Americans should worry about as the real enemy in our own backyard (or at least on our living room television sets) now that it had the atomic bomb of marketing tools. It would be one critic, Vance Packard, who most successfully articulated why the public was at great risk. "No popular critique of advertising moved the public, or changed their view of that essential corporate craft, as deeply or enduringly as Vance Packard's *The Hidden Persuaders*," wrote Mark Crispin Miller in his introduction to the fiftieth-anniversary reissue of the classic book, observing that the best seller "encouraged a new mass attentiveness to all of modern marketing." Admen were always suspect ("as popular as smoker's cough," Miller quipped), but now they were downright dangerous, endowed with powerful devices aimed directly at consumers' minds. Motivation research and subliminal advertising turned the battle between marketers and consumers into a war, with consumers feeling that they wouldn't be able to resist these new rapacious methods of persuasion.[37]

The cultural climate in the late 1950s was ripe for conspiracy theories, making *The Hidden Persuaders*, with its claims that psychology was being used against Americans, the perfect book for the time. The 1950s were "the heyday of the era of Freud, Jung, Adler, Reik and Reich, where everybody had his analyst or quoted Ernest Dichter," wrote Tom Wolfe, the latter the one that was really shaking things up. [38] "*The Hidden Persuaders* succeeded not by offering a true picture of advertising, but by itself tapping a deep unconscious motive: for a freedom-conscious America, a fear of being manipulated by dark, unseen forces," wrote Stephen Fox in his history of advertising, *The Mirror Makers*. For Packard, motivation research was not the disease but a symptom, a warning sign that Western society was, in a word, "sick." "The book revealed more about the public mentality, and about public attitudes toward advertising, than about advertising itself," Fox concluded.[39]

In his book, Packard made it clear who, when it came to hidden persuasion, should be considered Public Enemy Number One: Ernest Dichter. Before Dichter, what Franz Kreuzer and Patrick Schierholz called "announcement advertising" was the norm, with factual argument the prevailing method by which to promote products.[40] Dichter turned ad agencies into psychology labs, bringing the social sciences into what were basically factories of communication.[41] With his depth interviews, Dichter was the first person to seriously challenge the Claude Hopkins school of "reason-why" copy that had dominated advertising since it was recognized as a legitimate field. "His research provided advertising with a kind of radar to find its way through the darkness of the collective subconscious," wrote Marcel Blenstein-Blanchet, founder of the ad agency Publicis.[42] What was often lurking in the darkness that Dichter shone a light on was, in a word, sex. As Thomas Cudlik and Christoph Steiner flatly put it, Dichter "brought sex into advertising," a big factor in his becoming the first "star" of the field.[43] It wasn't sheer coincidence that the three studies which made Dichter famous (for Ivory soap, Plymouth, and *Esquire*) had to do with sex. "Man . . . is more strongly motivated by the pleasure principle than by the principle of reality," said Dichter, convinced that, when it came to human motivation, the libido ruled.[44]

Dichter's combination of psychoanalytic theory and pragmatic optimism was a powerful one-two punch in postwar America, making him sort of a cross between Sigmund Freud and Norman Vincent Peale. (Dichter was even more optimistic than the famously positive futurist Herman Kahn, who was a good friend and occasional collaborator.)[45] Dichter's grounding in European philosophy, with its narrative, humanistic approach, was balanced by a distinctly American brand of "positive thinking," a transatlantic blend very appealing to the general public curious about psychology. Psychology wasn't new in the late 1930s, when Dichter came to America with his doctor's bag of tricks, of course, but the use of it to influence consumers' behavior certainly was. "All purchase motivations were already present [but] Dichter unearthed what was hidden, analyzed it, and made it usable for the consumers," thought Kreuzer and Schierholz.[46] By freeing the id from the chains of reason—what Dichter would later call the "strategy of desire"—

American consumers could gain "moral permission" to enjoy the good things of life, something they weren't very good at because of their deeply engrained puritanical ethic. Freud's "pleasure principle" as interpreted by Dichter and applied to the world of consumer goods violated the principles of the superficially wholesome 1950s, certainly not as sensational as the Kinsey Reports but shocking nonetheless. Dichter's positive take on hedonism, what Cudlik and Steiner called a "prescription for social and individual therapy," was in retrospect very much ahead of its time, foreshadowing the self-indulgences of the 1960s and 1970s.[47]

Barbara Ehrenreich and Bill Osgerby have each commented on Dichter's fundamental tenet that consumers needed moral permission to enjoy, in Osgerby's words, a "hedonistic approach to life." "After the privations of the Depression and the war, Americans were supposed to enjoy themselves—held back from total abandon only by the need for Cold War vigilance," wrote Ehrenreich in *The Hearts of Men*. *Playboy* magazine was the most visible example of this new, morally sanctioned and justified consumer ethic.[48] "To sustain an economy increasingly dependent on consumer demand, a break had to be made with value systems that emphasized thrift and conservative reserve," Osgerby stated in his 2001 *Playboys in Paradise*, specifically that "the new economic imperatives of postwar America demand[ed] a code of acquisitive consumerism and personal gratification." And gratification is what Americans got, argued Osgerby, as the youth market and a more style-conscious, leisure-oriented middle class set the tone for a "morality of pleasure" and "ethic of fun," beginning in the 1950s.[49]

Working within the framework of this morality of pleasure, Dichter drew upon a startling array of sources to work his magic, borrowing ideas from literature, art, and folklore to interpret contemporary consumer culture. He was a true universalist, believing that the key to human behavior resided in individuals, not nations. Dichter was intent on identifying what he termed the "soul of things," fully believing that the stuff of everyday life held "psychic content." There were thus no "lifeless" things, everything around us having symbolic meaning inside or underneath its materiality. As in fairy tales or myths, things in real life were emotionally inscribed, teeming with social or cultural significance. Wood, then, wasn't just a material but for Dichter a "symbol of life," glass something that represented uncertainty, ambiguity, and mystery. Products and brands carried particular power, he argued, functioning as extensions of consumers' unique personalities. Shoes were not just objects to protect one's feet but represented strength and independence (as in Cinderella), one's hair representative of potency and virility (à la Samson and Delilah). In a consumer society like America, it was up to people to choose "correct" things and activities in order to convey the kind of status one wanted, Dichter thought, this now well-accepted idea not just new but a bit disquieting a half century ago.[50] Marina Moskowitz has shown how powerful the concept of the "standard of living" had already become in the United States by the 1920s. As "the yardstick by which middle-class Americans measured their material well-being," the standard of living was a way for citizens to be part of the national culture, something that Dichter was keenly aware of. Community, after all, was at the heart of consumerism, the possession of certain things a marker of identity for both oneself and others.[51]

By the time of his death in 1991, Dichter's contribution to American business and the entire motivation research phenomenon were largely forgotten, casualties of our historically challenged times. More recently, however, Dichter and motivation research are increasingly being recognized for the huge impact they had—and continue to have—in American culture. "Ernest Dichter was a pioneer who influenced the course of advertising in the half-century after World War II, a time when reappraisal of marketing thought took place, and the intellectual environment welcomed new and unorthodox ideas," wrote Barbara B. Stern, crediting him with accelerating the shift from marketer to consumer and from quantitative to qualitative research.[52] While Dichter, who ironically suffered from insecurity his whole life, would have appreciated such acclaim, he saw what he was doing in very simple terms. In his later years, in fact, Dichter often called himself the "Columbo" of human motivations (after the television homicide detective), considering himself not much more than "a psychological sleuth and Sherlock Holmes" trying to solve a particular mystery of human behavior.[53]

Freud on Madison Avenue tells the story of motivation research chronologically, from its birth in Vienna in the early 1930s through its decline in the early 1960s, its revival in the 1970s and 1980s, and its ultimate transformation into the consumer insights and account planning research methodologies of today. The spine of the story relies on contemporary magazines and newspapers, both popular and trade, drawing from journalists' writing of "the first draft of history." Literature in the field, both books and journal articles, is used to frame the story and provide context. Most of the book's sources are, however, "period," as, while I'm as big a fan of oral history as anyone, I felt it was important to capture events as they occurred, for accuracy's sake. I love hearing personal anecdotes about the glory days of Madison Avenue but, taking a cue from the old man himself, who said that we often reshape memories into something else, I tend to take fifty-year-old reminiscences with a large, and perhaps Freudian, grain of salt.

1

The Psychology of Everyday Living

Have you ever noticed . . . that people never answer
what you [ask]?
—G. K. Chesterton, "The Innocence of Father Brown"

One day in Vienna in 1930, the owners of a new laundry asked Paul Lazarsfeld, a psychology instructor at the city's famed university, to help them increase their business. Many Austrian women were reluctant to send out their laundry, the instructor learned, as they thought that doing so reduced their role as proper hausfrau. In interviewing existing customers, the psychologist learned that women who did use the laundry often first sent out their wash when an "emergency" occurred, such as a child becoming sick or houseguests unexpectedly dropping in. Once experiencing the joy of having someone else do their wash, however, the women were usually hooked, and became regular customers. This particular insight led the psychologist to suggest that the owners of the laundry send a letter describing the services of the business to every household in which a family member had recently died, knowing that the bereaved would find it difficult to do their own wash. The owners of the store tried the idea, and business instantly picked up, lighting a spark under a new kind of research that over the next few decades would revolutionize global consumer culture.[1]

The Accidental Researcher

Paul Lazarsfeld's clever, if ethically ambiguous, use of what he called the "psychological approach" to studying consumer behavior revealed the indisputable value of what would soon be called motivation (or motivational) research. Although he is hardly a household name, Lazarsfeld was one of the most important figures in the history of advertising and marketing, and his approach to gleaning information from consumers is much like the way it is still done today. Pioneering "the analysis of the complex web of reasons and motives that determines the goal strivings of human actions," Lazarsfeld was, according to Lewis A. Coser, "the father of sophisticated studies of mass communication." A disciple of Alfred Adler (his mother was a prominent Adlerian psychotherapist), Lazarsfeld absorbed the ideas of this most sociological of Freud's followers, creating a new, hybrid form of social science in the process. His most famous study, *The Unemployed Workers of Marienthal*, completed when he was a young man in Vienna, was an early attempt to quantify sociological fieldwork, a once radical pursuit that he would be obsessed with for the rest of his career.[2]

Although a devout socialist, a quite typical affiliation among Viennese intellectuals between the wars, Lazarsfeld ironically found himself in the market research business when he needed to fund his Wirtschafts Psychologisches Institut (Psycho-Economic Institute), a center studying economic problems in Austria. "We were concerned with why our propaganda was unsuccessful," the former member of the Socialist Student Movement remembered years later, "and wanted to conduct psychological studies to explain it."[3] With its depth interviews and analysis drawing from sociology, psychology, and psychoanalysis, the institute almost accidentally found itself doing what were probably the most progressive market studies in the world in the 1930s. These studies were the beginnings of motivation research, something that one of Lazarsfeld's students—Ernest Dichter—would bring to the United States and, in the process, change the course of American business.

Lazarsfeld's inauspicious work with the Viennese laundry in 1930 would soon lead to much bigger things. That same year, Lazarsfeld offered to help a group of Americans in the city "promote the use of applied psychology among business" and conducted a series of interviews with people regarding their preferences of soap and what was perhaps the first survey of radio listeners. Regarding the latter, Lazarsfeld was interested in, as Anthony Heilbut wrote, "what kind of people listened to what kind of programs for what kind of reasons," this another seedling that would sprout into motivation research. "The commercial applications were evident," Heilbut noted, and marketers of perfume and chocolate were eager to apply Lazarsfeld's findings. Working-class radio listeners in Austria preferred both strong perfume and chocolate, Lazarsfeld discovered, speculating that the reason for this was that their economic condition made them "starved for pleasure." This kind of neo-Freudian interpretation would define motivation research over the next few decades as intellectual descendants of Lazarsfeld kept Viennese psychology alive and well.[4]

After arriving in the United States in 1933 on a Rockefeller Foundation fellowship, Lazarsfeld chose to make America his home as the Nazis rose to power in Europe. (The success of his Marienthal study, with its socialist agenda, had attracted the attention of the police, another factor contributing to his decision to leave Austria while he could.) As a self-proclaimed "Marxist on leave," Lazarsfeld's arrival in the States in the thirties was particularly fortuitous, his own politics matching up nicely with FDR's New Deal progressive reforms. After a brief stint at the University of Newark (now Rutgers University), Lazarsfeld started working for an up-and-coming executive at CBS, Frank Stanton, who would eventually become president of the network. With Stanton, who also had a Ph.D. in psychology, Lazarsfeld found himself doing the same kind of radio research in New York that he had done in Vienna, spelling out his mission in a 1935 article cowritten with Arthur Kornhauser. Via "a systematic view of how people's marketing behavior is motivated," the psychologist turned market researcher wrote in "The Analysis of Consumer Actions," companies could "forecast and control consumer behavior," an idea nothing less than revolutionary in the mid-1930s. Lazarsfeld, admittedly more interested in exploring new methodologies in the social sciences than in selling products or candidates, nevertheless had become not just an agent of consumerism but one of its leading visionaries.[5]

Lazarsfeld's introduction of psychology-based, in-depth market research made a giant splash in a field in which counting bodies was the height of sophistication. Within a year of his arrival in the States, Lazarsfeld recalled, "the small fraternity of commercial market research experts got interested in my work" and invited him to talk at meetings and serve on committees of the brand-new American Marketing Association. In addition, the AMA asked Lazarsfeld to write several chapters for a new textbook it planned to publish, *The Techniques of Marketing Research*. One of the chapters contained references to depth psychology and is thus credited as the official beginning of motivation research.[6] The man who was, according to Heilbut, "a product of refined European learning who hustled himself a position in the marketplace," soon landed a job with the Rockefeller-subsidized Office of Radio Research at Princeton (which moved to Columbia University in 1939 and five years later was renamed the Bureau of Applied Social Research). There Lazarsfeld, along with a team of notable psychologists (including his second wife, Herta Herzog, another Adlerian, and Theodor Adorno of the Frankfurt school), reigned for decades, surveying radio listeners for ad agencies and sponsors.[7]

Again, with his move to Princeton, Lazarsfeld was in the right place at the right time. Market research was in a decidedly crude state and interest in surveying radio listeners was just beginning, making advertisers very receptive to innovative methodologies directly lifted from the social sciences. The kind of systematic interviewing done in classic sociological studies like Robert and Helen Lynd's *Middletown* and Lloyd Warner's *Yankee City*, for example, was exactly what was needed to advance market research beyond simple "nose-counting."[8] "Our idea was to try to determine . . . the role of radio in the lives of different types of listeners, the value of radio to people psychologically, and the various reasons why they like it," Lazarsfeld explained. The whopping salary of $7,000 that came with the Princeton job was an offer he couldn't refuse. At the university, he consulted with some of the leading psychoanalysts of the day (including Karen Horney and Erich Fromm) to satisfy his curiosity about the role of radio in their patients' lives. "Can Freudian theory elucidate the entertainment value of radio and account for some especially successful programs?" Lazarsfeld asked the noted analysts; this convergence of social research with psychoanalytical case studies was unheard of in 1937.[9]

Lazarsfeld wasn't the only one in the 1930s using psychological theory to solve marketing problems, however. In 1935, for example, Donald Laird identified what he considered "irrational" behavior among purchasing agents, claiming that their tough negotiating was not so much about saving money for their company as a way to boost their own egos.[10] A couple of Lazarsfeld's colleagues, Hadley Cantril and Rensis Likert, were also "important links between academic culture and the applied research of business and government," according to Jean Converse, and the three constituted a powerful troika of "survey research entrepreneurs." Unlike most other academics in the social sciences, these men were eager to venture outside the ivory tower, finding the emerging world of polls and surveys quite valuable to their work. While Cantril focused on polling and Likert would go on to develop his famous rating scale, Lazarsfeld stayed true to his roots in the Viennese school of motivation research, applying Freudian and Adlerian theory to the real world of consumer behavior. At the core of the school's thinking was what was referred to as "psychologically correct" questioning to identify the role that unconscious motivations played in buying things—hence "motivation research," or what Converse described as the exploration of "underlying motives, observation of involuntary actions, and free association of ideas and concepts."[11]

As his principal heir in the Viennese school, Ernest Dichter, would do on a much grander scale, Lazarsfeld brought an intellectual component to market research that was missing from the field in the 1930s and 1940s. Consumers' purchase decisions were as complex as any, he felt, entirely worth studying in detail. Lazarsfeld's 1935 article "The Art of Asking Why in Marketing Research" became a classic, a convincing argument that standard questionnaires were simply not revealing why consumers did the things they did. In the article, Lazarsfeld identified what he called "buyer behavior determinants of the first degree," which included not just a product's attributes but also consumers' emotional likes and dislikes. There were also "buyer behavior determinants of the second degree," consisting of the reasons for consumers' likes and dislikes, which were unknown.[12] Lazarsfeld, however, was determined to discover them. "A careful collection of opinions is far superior to pseudo-scholarly tabulations of the type of statistics which have only a remote relationship to the special problem under investigation," he wrote in another article a couple of years later, rebranding himself as a sociologist rather than a psychologist, because the former was more like a market researcher. At Columbia, students felt "they were in on the ground floor of an enterprise that believed it was about to remake social science, if not the world," remembered one of them, Seymour Martin Lipset, who, like many on Lazarsfeld's team, would go on to become a giant in the field.[13]

Although Lazarsfeld's trailblazing work in market research was remarkable enough, an even bigger contribution may have been his role in bringing together the previously separate worlds of academia and business. In a 1941 talk to the National Association of Broadcasters, Lazarsfeld made it clear that "communication research [was now a] joint enterprise between industries and universities," a way for academics to fund their work and an opportunity for American companies (like his clients CBS and the ad agency McCann-Erickson) to achieve their ambitious objectives. "The great innovation was the decision that contract work would be permitted," he wrote decades later, speaking of his bosses at Princeton and Columbia, "a real turning point in the history of American universities."[14] Lazarsfeld's own work focusing on identifying commonalities among people who shared opinions—to find out not just what individuals thought but if they formed a social group of some kind—was the stuff of marketers' dreams. Out of this kind of leading-edge

research came, for example, Lazarsfeld's notion of "opinion leaders," that certain people shaped the views of the "masses"—this more than a half-century
before Malcolm Gladwell's *The Tipping Point*.[15] "Thanks largely to his work,
mechanical systems of observation could chart everything from voting preferences to tastes in mouthwash and deodorant," concluded Heilbut, the ac-
cidental researcher forging an entirely new way to understand the American
consumer.[16]

The Public Pulse

An entirely new way to understand the American consumer would turn
out to be exactly what American business needed after World War II. Much
less than knowing consumers' unconscious reasons for buying or not buying things, business executives had precious little understanding of the most
basic marketing issues, the first being whether there was a market at all. Immediately after the war, some corporations became determined to discover
how big the postwar market for consumer goods would be, "a question that
keeps many a manufacturer awake at night," as *Business Week* described it
in 1946. While companies retooled to "turn guns into butter," as the saying
went, shelves remained mostly empty, giving marketers no information about
how much product companies should make or how much they might sell.
Economic and social conditions were quite different after the war, making
prewar numbers unreliable, managers believed.[17]

One company, for example, Silex, went the extra mile to try to figure
out how many coffeemakers it should make, doing some innovative market
research in Peoria, Illinois, which was then considered the most average of
American communities. (Peoria replaced another Midwestern town, Muncie,
Indiana—the subject of Robert and Helen Lynd's two Middletown studies—
as what Charles McGovern called "a divining rod of dominant public sentiment.")[18] Silex flooded Peoria with all the coffeemakers it could produce and
then waited to see how long consumers would keep buying them, the key
question being whether sales would be good not just during the expected initial "boom" period but for months after. Most companies believed Americans
would buy anything and everything they could for some time after the war,
having been deprived of most consumer products for half a decade. The company happily learned that sales of their coffeemakers kept percolating for the
duration of their market test, news that "should cheer other manufacturers
who are wondering how substantial their present order backlog really is."[19]

Silex wasn't the only company pursuing some interesting market research soon after the war to figure out what to do next. In 1947, for example, Ford gave consumers the chance to design a new car on paper (something more typical of today's "relationship marketing"), even asking them what they would pay for their dream automobile. Learning that consumers now wanted a lot more choices when it came to styling, colors, comfort, and safety than they did before the war, Ford realized it had a major gap between its research and sales departments and decided to do something about it. H. D. Everett, Jr., was quickly snatched up from Time, Inc., recruited to head up a seventeen-person research department at Ford created to "keep a finger on the public pulse." Besides farming out work to a number of suppliers, the market research department within the sales department also partnered with academics who were doing intriguing studies related to the driving experience. Anthropologists and anatomists at the University of Michigan were studying dashboard design, for example, and researchers at Northwestern University were looking into how and when drivers became fatigued. Ford was especially interested in how research findings differed by gender, fully aware that automobiles were designed for men and that, as *Business Week* reported the company's thinking, "maybe they should be changed to suit women too." Women from the Detroit area were brought to Dearborn to weigh in on issues of style and comfort, quite a radical step at the time given the accepted belief up to that point that automobiles were strictly a masculine domain. One research finding in particular—that husbands may have been the primary breadwinner but wives held the power to veto new car-buying decisions—no doubt shaped Ford's rather sudden interest in appealing to the interests of the woman of the house.[20]

Silex and Ford were more the exceptions than the rule, however, with most managers picking up where they left off before the war and using their familiar tools of research. In the thirties, market researchers had gleaned loads of information from consumers about everything from automobiles to zippers, which gave them a good handle on product sales, market share, and media ratings. By far the biggest fish in the market research sea in 1950 was A. C. Nielsen, and its $45 million in annual revenue was nearly six times that of its nearest competitor and constituted almost a quarter of the entire industry. Arthur C. Nielsen had begun issuing his indices of consumer sales in the early 1930s and hadn't looked back, his company zooming to become the top dog in the field with its purchase data and radio ratings that many companies depended on. Much of Nielsen's success had to do with its being among the earliest users of business machines, the company's three thousand electronic tabulators and calculators whirring away. Nielsen had already ordered from Remington Rand one of the first Univacs, a vending-machine-sized contraption able to tumble numbers at what was considered lightning speed.[21]

Marketers also had at their disposal Gallup's and Roper's opinion polls, which had shown that Americans were willing to share their feelings on a variety of issues, even the touchy subjects of politics and religion. The first Kinsey Report, published in 1948, proved that Americans would speak at length about the most intimate details of their lives, something that boosted market researchers' confidence that they would get answers to their many much less intrusive questions. "Doorbells are being rung every day to find out which products people are buying," Newsweek reported in 1948, as the ramping up of the field caught the attention of the mainstream press and the American public. "The odds are getting better all the time that when the doorbell rings, a well-trained young lady will be standing there to say, 'We are making a survey,'" the magazine added, and the number and range of questions being asked grew as more organizations decided to invest in market research. In addition, more new products were being tested in homes before they were rolled out to the masses, with different elements of the marketing mix, such as packaging and advertising, carefully scrutinized through research. Market research was gradually getting more sophisticated after the war, slowly moving beyond the simple "counting of noses."[22]

What perhaps was most interesting about the growth of the field was that it was taking place with little or no practical or ethical standards. How information was gathered and interpreted was left totally up to the organization and the individual, allowing plenty of room for highly questionable conclusions. Even market researchers, whose very jobs depended on being industry experts, had no real idea what was going on in their own field, as conducting the research was scattered among hundreds, perhaps thousands of companies, ad agencies, and consultants. The strongest, most obvious evidence that the field had some major bugs to work out was when opinion pollsters universally picked Dewey to beat Truman in the 1948 presidential election. As a result, many businesspeople wondered if the market researchers they had hired were applying the same sort of principles when making forecasts for them. Gallup had been off by 4.5 percent and Roper a lot more than that, the latter explaining that his firm's last poll was in September of that year and, with a Dewey landslide seemingly imminent, he had seen little reason to do another. (Roper had had much better luck with the previous three elections, coming within 1 percent of the popular vote for FDR in 1936, 0.5 percent in 1940, and 0.2 percent in 1944, this trifecta making him nationally famous.)[23] Alfred Politz, who was then rapidly becoming the most trusted market researcher, thought the "Dewey Defeats Truman" fiasco would ultimately be good for the field, saying, "It will help get rid of the charlatans."[24] Politz wasn't the only one convinced that market research needed an overhaul, however. "All agree that it is high time the market-research business got together with itself and decided on a set of standards of practice to ensure honesty and high scientific fidelity in their work," *Newsweek* wrote a few months after the worst blunder in opinion polling, one of the few things that people in the field did agree on.[25]

The 1948 opinion poll fiasco, not to mention the rather sluggish evolution of the field, were reasons enough for market researchers to realize they had a serious problem on their hands. By mid-century, researchers were acutely aware that there was something missing from their field—specifically, that only one side of their big brains was working. "As marketing people, some of us have been so damnably busy quantifying that we have forgotten about qualitative research," admitted Steuart Britt of McCann-Erickson, the main problem being that "we have plenty of marketing facts—but unfortunately we have little psychological information." Plenty of material was available on how much of a given product was sold to whom and when but precious little on why, something postwar marketers found increasingly disquieting. Very soon, Britt's wish for more "psychological information" would come true, as marketers looked to Vienna to find the answers to their many questions.[26]

A Third Ear

It would not be Lazarsfeld, however, but one of his students who would realize the full potential of motivation research and, in doing so, rewrite the rules of how American business did business. Also trained as a psychologist in Vienna, Ernest Dichter arrived in the United States in 1938, ultimately churning out a flood of books, articles, and studies for clients, all grounded in his particular brand of Freudian thought. His positive view of consumer culture, that the material world allowed individuals to more fully express themselves, differed from that of many if not most social critics who were unhappy about, as one put it, the nation's millions of status seekers. (Dichter's pro-capitalist values also differed from those of Lazarsfeld, who was willing to work with clients in order to fund his work but would always remain a Marxist at heart.)

Dichter's upbeat take on the dynamics of consumer culture was unquestionably a reaction to or backlash against his own childhood experience, which
was decidedly non-upbeat. Born in Vienna in 1907, the oldest of three sons,
Dichter (who later changed his first name from Ernst to Ernest) had to leave
school at the age of fourteen to support his family. The turmoil of World War
I and the rise of Nazism instilled in him a longing for individual and social
stability and prosperity. (Like thousands of underfed Viennese children, Dichter had been sent to Holland during the war, one of many experiences that
led to his lifelong insecurity.) Working in his uncle's department store as a
window decorator as a teenager, he was exposed to and enchanted by the universe of consumer goods, observing the psychic and even sexual power they
seemed to hold over the well-to-do. His father's failure as a salesman made his
interest in the good things of life even more intense, this outsider-looking-in
view no doubt shaping his life's work.[27]

Dichter ("poet" in German, rather fittingly) considered his red hair—
something rather unusual in Austria—another major source of insecurity. "I
was an outcast, and on top of that I was not a particularly good athlete," he
remembered in his 1979 autobiography, *Getting Motivated*. Combined with
the poverty he experienced as a child, Dichter's carrottop gave him what any
Freudian shrink would diagnose as an inferiority complex and a set of neuroses from which he would never fully recover. This deep-rooted, lifelong insecurity afforded him a special ability to see it in others, however; his almost
preternatural powers of perception were one of the main keys to his success.
"Because of these doubts I became critical of myself, and I watched continuously to see whether people around me would discover this insecurity," he explained, thinking that "self-observation leads inevitably to an increased skill
in observing other people." Dichter's Jewish background too certainly played
an important role in his development; he would weave stories and parables
into his ten- to forty-page typewritten reports in the spirit, so to speak, of rab-
binical tradition. While he would turn out to be an atheist, Dichter was in fact
sometimes called the "Messiah" of market research, an anointed savior ushering in a new age of prosperity for American business and the nation itself.[28]

Once able to resume his education, which had been interrupted by the
war, Dichter studied with Karl and Charlotte Buhler at the University of Vienna, soaking up their views of humanistic psychology and its emphasis on
the self-motivated individual (Lazarsfeld too had studied with the legendary
couple). Dichter was also strongly influenced by the general cognition theories and philosophical thinking of Moritz Schlick and the Viennese Circle of

the 1930s, these ideas adding to his rich intellectual stew. Lazarsfeld's methods of empirical social research too had a deep impact, the professor's interest in why somebody did or didn't choose to buy something contributing to Dichter's fascination with the role of motivation in people's lives. Dichter was one of Lazarsfeld's two star pupils, the other being his future second wife, Herta Herzog, who would also go on to great success in motivation research in America.[29]

As Gerd Prechtl observed, the social, political, and cultural climate of Vienna in the early decades of the twentieth century was ideal for a mind like Dichter's to blossom, the collapse of the Austrian monarchy and the rise of modernism allowing more liberal thinking than was previously possible. Jewish intellectuals in particular were able to find their voice, forging a holistic approach to the social sciences that offered a refreshing and exciting alternative to the earlier era's rigid academic boundaries.[30] Peter Scheer has argued that psychoanalysis in particular was a distinctly Jewish phenomenon, that with the acceptance of Jews by universities in the late nineteenth and early twentieth centuries their knowledge could "finally [be] phrased in academic language." With its focus on desires and motives, psychoanalysis served as the natural framework for motivation research, allowing Viennese Jews like Lazarsfeld, Herzog, and Dichter to see its implications and applications for consumer research.[31]

By the early 1930s, however, in part because of its Jewish connections, psychoanalysis was a field that, despite its Viennese roots, was "despised" at the university (in fact, at all universities). Although psychoanalysis was technically banned, Dichter was able to gain a thorough understanding of the field through lectures by Alfred Adler, the founder of individual psychology (the second Viennese School of modern depth psychology), as well as those by Wilhelm Stekel, one of the premier psychoanalysts in Vienna. Dichter was also mentored by August Aichhorn, the founder of psychoanalytic pedagogy, who deepened his knowledge of the officially taboo subject. "Both were psychoanalysts, but of a very practical nature, interested in a more immediate application of analytic principles," Dichter recalled in his autobiography, so "opening up a psychoanalytic practice of a similar nature was therefore a very logical idea for me." Finally, Dichter himself went through Freudian psychoanalysis in Vienna as a learning experience (for free, by teaching his American analyst German), and this no doubt gave him personal familiarity with what the method could reveal about a person's inner feelings and desires.[32]

With a Ph.D. in psychology from the University of Vienna in hand (after

a brief stint at the Sorbonne in Paris, where he studied literature), Dichter
began his own psychoanalytic practice in 1934 (in rooms across the street
from those of the now elderly Sigmund Freud, whom Dichter never met).[33]
Dichter's forte was as a career counselor, helping young men (many of them
referred by Stekel) figure out what to do with their lives. Dichter's work fun-
neled back into Lazarsfeld's Psycho-Economic Institute, which used Dichter's
"data" in its sociological and market studies. Times were hard for Dichter, but
fortunately his wife, Hedy, was a concert pianist, and she was able to support
the household through her recitals. A few years later, Dichter got a job at
the city's Psychoanalytic Institute, which gave him more training in Freudian
and Adlerian theory. It was during these years, through his exploration of
people's motives, that he recognized a link between his academic training in
psychoanalysis and his fascination with consumer behavior. While in Vienna,
"Ernest had already discovered his talent for the application of psychotherapy
to the commercial arena, to marketing and advertising—in short, what he
later established as motivational research," Hedy remembered more than half
a century later.[34]

After the Nazi takeover of Austria (and especially his month-long detain-
ment for his association with the decidedly leftist Psychoanalytic Institute),
the thirty-year-old Jewish man recognized that his life was in danger. Unlike
many of his classmates (and two younger brothers), Dichter was actually not
a Marxist, but he heeded the advice of one of his professors (a Nazi, in fact) to
leave Austria.[35] The first stop was Paris, where Dichter worked as a salesman
for a year, which gave him firsthand understanding of the power of a brand's
"image." Dichter sold fake labels from expensive clothes, to be sewn into
cheaper garments to make them appear to be the real thing. Although it was a
shady business, Dichter could not have received a better education in how the
perceived value of a product was more important than its quality—an idea he,
perhaps more than anyone else, would bring to American business.[36]

With the Nazis on his tail, Dichter, like other Austrian and German Jews
(including Otto Preminger, Billy Wilder, Peter Drucker, and Bruno Bettel-
heim), decided to flee to the United States. When asked at the American
consulate in Paris how he planned to make a living, Dichter replied he intended to "change the methods of marketing"; this made such an impact on
the French official that he personally interceded to ensure that Dichter and
his wife received their visa without paying the usual $5,000 per person fee.[37]
He and Hedy were fortunate indeed to have been granted a visa (some of
Dichter's extended family in Austria were killed in the Holocaust). They ar-

rived in New York in September 1938 with a total of $100 in their pockets. One of the first things Dichter did was to ask his secretary's brother-in-law, Henry Lee Smith, a Columbia University professor of phonetics (who had a radio program called "Where Do You Come From?"), help him develop "an all-American accent," so that people "would not be suspicious of my foreign background." Unlike many other immigrants (including Lazarsfeld, who would never lose his heavy Austrian accent), Dichter's English soon became nearly perfect, which helped him navigate the world of WASPish corporations and Madison Avenue.[38]

In New York, Dichter soon found work doing conventional market research studies for various firms and ad agencies, hating every minute of it. Finding what he was doing simply unbearable, Dichter one day bought some letterhead paper and wrote letters to about a dozen companies, making them a hard-to-resist offer: to tell them why consumers did or didn't buy their products. "I am a young psychologist from Vienna and I have some interesting new ideas which can help you be more successful, effective, sell more and communicate better with your potential clients," the letter read, convincing enough to generate four replies. From this modest direct-mail campaign, he landed his first real consulting job, advising *Esquire* to focus its advertising on the nude pictures included in the magazine at the time, something that had not occurred to the publisher. Although today the idea of applying the principles of European-based psychology to marketing and advertising seems perfectly obvious, clients were—not surprisingly—initially taken aback by Dichter's literally foreign ideas ("His way of thinking was not American," as Sheer explained it).[39] Knowing that Lazarsfeld had already established himself as a rising star in the field, Dichter also called his ex-professor, who had fled to the United States five years earlier, hoping he could help him break into the small but growing area of "depth research." Interestingly, Lazarsfeld suggested that Dichter think twice about his career plans, telling him that American businessmen were obsessed with numbers and statistics and had precious little interest in using psychology to decode consumers' wants and needs.[40]

Dichter was, of course, undeterred. Lazarsfeld recommended Dichter to Compton Advertising, the agency for Ivory soap, and Dichter was soon telling executives at the agency that bathing was both an erotic experience ("one of the few occasions when the puritanical American was allowed to caress himself or herself," he said) and a purification ritual, observations that were not the kind of thing that businessmen in 1939 were used to hearing. Dichter also talked about Ivory's "image," the first time that the term was used in marketing or advertising. ("I stole it," Dichter later admitted, explaining that the source of the term was the Latin *imago*, which in Gestalt psychology means the overall impression of a person.)[41] For the Ivory project (and a fee of $2 per interview), Dichter spoke to a hundred people about bathing and soap, one of his key findings being that the Saturday night bath was considered very special among women going out on a date, in case romance happened to come their way. "So he saw that soap was more than soap, and a bath was more than a bath," his wife Hedy remembered almost sixty years later. Dichter even came up with an advertising slogan for the brand: "Be smart, get a fresh start with Ivory soap"—"because," he explained decades later, "bathing, in its old, ritualistic, anthropological sense, is getting rid of all your bad feelings, your sins, your immorality, and cleansing yourself, baptism, etc." Finally, Dichter explained that the personality of a brand should match that of the consumer, a notion almost as shocking as his sexual interpretation of bathing, in what was the first motivation research study in the United States.[42]

If his projects for *Esquire* and Ivory were groundbreaking, his work for his next client, Chrysler, was positively radical. Dichter had been asked to help Chrysler and its ad agency figure out how to market Plymouth models, and he came up with the idea that an automobile was perceived by American men as either a kind of wife or a kind of mistress. Dichter also told Chrysler to put sexual double entendre in its advertising ("It fits me like a glove" and "You just slip it in" were two lines he suggested), certainly not something the car company had heard before. Based on his research, Chrysler decided to run ads in women's magazines, the first time in automobile history such a thing was done. As coup de grâce, Dichter advised Chrysler that it could sell more Plymouth sedans by advertising more convertibles, this kind of logic only adding to the man's reputation for unconventional thinking.[43]

Dichter's work for Chrysler made him nationally famous, his nontraditional views reported first in the trades and then in *Time* magazine.[44] During the war years, with few consumer products for people to sell or buy, Dichter worked alongside Lazarsfeld at CBS under Frank Stanton, then the director of research. As a program psychologist for CBS, Dichter analyzed radio programs, especially soap operas, trying to match shows with particular personality types. "Not being particularly fond of Germany," as he later put it, he also volunteered to analyze Hitler's speeches and develop counter-propaganda, doing his bit for the war effort. As soon as America was back in business, Dichter founded the Institute for Research for Mass Motivation, a company he would run for more than four decades (renamed a number of times).[45]

Unlike his mentor, Paul Lazarsfeld, Dichter was convinced that psychology was exactly what American business needed after the war, making his case to an increasingly receptive audience intent on jump-starting the postwar economy. Consumption was falling "behind" production, and the prewar ways of selling were now outmoded and inefficient, he explained in a 1947 *Harvard Business Review* article. In order to evolve from a "medicine man" approach, marketers had to address consumers' emotions, irrational behavior, and unconscious drives, which were much more basic and powerful than logic. Dichter extended his thinking in his first book, *The Psychology of Everyday Living*, arguing that the things around us mean much more than appearances would suggest.[46]

Although Lazarsfeld and Dichter didn't agree on the long-term viability of psychology in the business world, Lazarsfeld's 1935 article "The Art of Asking Why" had a profound influence on Dichter (and many others), helping him make the connections between psychoanalytic theory and qualitative market research. Through his depth interviews, Dichter listened with what Theodor Reik had called "a third ear," encouraging subjects to tell stories, recall memories, and free associate to get beyond rational thought. Role-playing through "psychodramas," in which subjects pretended they were objects, companies, or other people was one of Dichter's favorite techniques. Many other techniques that Dichter clearly borrowed from psychoanalysis—the Thematic Apperception Test (TAT), transactional analysis, phrase completion, association tests, caricatures, animal comparisons, and the Rorschach test—soon became the standard tools of motivation research. Dichter's written reports were as nonlinear as his interviews, filled with verbatim quotes from subjects, stories, and off-the-cuff impressions, a long way from other researchers' statistical tables and charts.[47] Dichter "sifted out the essentials [of Freudian psychology]," noted Patrick Schierholz, who considered Dichter more than any other psychotherapist in history "especially concerned with the practical application."[48]

Perhaps more important than anything else, the psychoanalytic foundation of motivation research shifted the dynamic between marketer and consumer from an "us versus them" relationship to much more of a partnership. Dichter frequently recommended that the client "reorient" consumers by encouraging them to try new things and by advertising products in emotional terms rather than through facts (Esso's "tiger in your tank" versus "high octane rating" is probably the most famous example). Dichter was also fond of telling clients to give consumers what they wanted, something which of course makes a lot of sense but was (and is) frequently not done. Many Americans in the early 1950s wanted to borrow money but didn't want to take out loans, for example, so Dichter told the bank he was working for to provide what would become known as overdraft protection, the first time this was done.[49] Dichter also came up with the idea of the car clock, telling automobile manufacturers that drivers wanted to know how fast they were going in real time rather than just according to the speedometer's miles per hour. Thinking moms did not like to be considered bad mothers, so Dichter told his supermarket client to place candy at the cash registers to make it more of an impulse item rather than regular food, just one of many ideas he had regarding how grocery store layout should be changed.[50] Throughout his career, Dichter consistently maintained that the role of women in the family's purchase decisions was greater than popularly believed, which alone was a major contribution to marketing thought.[51]

While he drew from the Platonic (and Aristotelian) tradition of problem solving through discussion, Dichter challenged Plato by arguing it was emotion, not reason, that ruled human behavior. Dichter took an "existentialist approach to human self-realization through action," wrote Cudlik and Steiner, maintaining that self-understanding could be achieved only through internal means rather by external religious or philosophical systems and beliefs. God was inside, he insisted, and the institutions of faith actually hindered true self-fulfillment and happiness. In Dichter's perfect world, the human being was his or her own God, disinclined to delegate his or her freedom to a "higher" power. The Edenic paradise of the popular imagination was one of ignorance and static tranquility, an illusion compared to the very real (and more demanding) paradise consisting of intellectual growth and creative challenges. Dichter thus fully embraced Kant's idea of "liberation from self-inflicted dependency," that one was free only if one had faith in oneself. Rather than spend time and energy dreaming of a perfect paradise perhaps waiting in the future, it was the journey of this life, not its destination, that really mattered (contentedness, he believed, was equivalent with death). Dichter defined his own primary motivation as "creative discontent," even subtitling his autobiography in the original German version "The Autobiography of a Creatively Discontent Person." "Getting there is all the fun" was Dichter's motto, the process not just half of the joy to be had in life but every bit of it.[52]

The Research Bug Is Spreading

Mostly due to Dichter's work for a growing number of curious clients, motivation research was by the early fifties beginning to be taken very seriously in formal advertising and marketing circles. It was regarded as having stolen the show at the American Marketing Association's 1952 annual convention in Chicago, for one thing, and the social sciences were featured in the *Chicago Tribune*'s prestigious Distribution and Advertising Forum that year. In addition, the lead article in the fall issue of the *Journal of Marketing* was devoted to the role that psychology could play in the business world, as clear a sign of official recognition as any.[53]

As it became a genuine, recognizable entity, motivation research was considered a key turning point not just in market research but also in American business, offering managers something they had never possessed before—the "why" driving consumer behavior. "When it comes to explaining the things that spur people to buy or act, the researchers usually have to bow out," wrote *Business Week* in 1953, this not knowing what prompts people being "a fact that has long galled advertising men." But now, finally, there was something that could penetrate consumers' thick skulls, a technique grounded in that mysterious, somewhat dangerous realm, psychology. "Madison Avenue is preparing a concerted onslaught on the consumer to find out what makes him tick," the magazine reported, "this effort to pry off the top of the consumer's head . . . a long time in the making." Motivation research wasn't just a new technique, however, it was quite possibly the key to the new way of business in the postwar years. The century-old age of "economic man," in which consumers acted predictably according to their income level and how much products cost, was over; a new age of "psychological man" had begun. Understanding this new man—unpredictable, complex, independent—required a new, more sophisticated set of tools, and motivation research was, by all appearances, the handiest one in the kit.[54]

Given the range of things motivation research could supposedly do, it's not surprising how excited marketers were when it became water cooler talk. Motivation research could serve as a predictive tool, many thought, tipping off marketers to consumers' behavior before they acted. Knowing how consumers decided to spend their discretionary money was a gold mine, and motivation research was said to be able to expose the factors leading someone to choose to buy new furniture, for example, versus a new car. Insight into the dynamics of brand selection was another huge deliverable of motivation research, went the thinking at the time, as the technique was able to pinpoint why a consumer purchased Brand X versus Brand Y. Marketers operating in categories in which there was little real differentiation—beer or cigarettes, for example—were especially thrilled at this possibility, viewing motivation research as the magic bullet to make their brands the desired Brand X.[55]

The definitive indication that motivation research had reached the big time in 1953 was the publication of *An Introductory Bibliography of Motivation Research*, which listed almost five hundred books and articles related to the subject. What made the book significant was that it was published by the Advertising Research Foundation (ARF), the joint research organization of the American Association of Advertising Agencies (AAAA) and the Association of National Advertisers (ANA). With this book, the ARF was essentially canonizing motivation research, giving its blessing to the technique as a legitimate research tool that marketers and agencies could and should use. ARF's appointing a Committee on Motivation Research the previous year would in fact mark the beginning of a deep commitment to motivation research over the next decade or so. The following year, ARF published a glossary of more than five hundred motivation-research-related terms that advertisers should be familiar with, educating advertisers about this still relatively new technique. Just a couple of definitions included in the *E* section of the glossary suggested that motivation research really was like a foreign language requiring its own dictionary, with psychology-challenged marketers learning such terms as:

> EGOISM (Psychiatry): the classification and evaluation of things only
> in terms of one's personal standards and values.
> EIDETIC IMAGERY (Psychology): remembering by being able to call
> up and "see" in the *mind* a vivid, almost real, picture of a previously seen *object* or situation.[56]

As one might imagine, the ARF's arming its members with a psychology-oriented bibliography and glossary was hardly an easy task. Besides the sheer volume of material contained in Psychology 101, there were of course different schools of thought in the field whose members often saw the sky in very different colors. Negotiating the distance between the Freudians and the Adlerians, say, or between the behaviorists and the Gestalt people, was a tricky business, leading the ARF to try to stay somewhere in the middle of the enormous field. Interestingly, one word used (a lot) in motivation research that the ARF opted not to even attempt to define in its glossary was "motivation," the consultants it hired to do the job advising that it just meant too many different things to different psychologists. Many of the terms the ARF was tossing out to its members were certainly esoteric, but advertisers were often quite familiar with their meanings as used in their trade. "Voyeurism" and "narcissism" may have been new words to some, for example, but businesspeople immediately recognized their meaning upon reading their definitions, well versed in appealing to such tried-and-true consumer behavior. After the glossary and bibliography were published, the ARF's next step was to put together a complete listing of organizations that performed motivation research, the psychologists and psychiatrists consulting in the field, and ad agencies with motivation research departments. "Where Madison Avenue will take Freud remains to be seen," *Business Week* wrapped up, but one thing the magazine felt was certain: "The research bug is spreading."[57]

A quick survey of how motivation research was being used and by whom made it clear that the research bug was indeed spreading. A wide range of firms was pursuing a rather startling variety of projects in the early 1950s, with motivation research rapidly becoming the market research technique du jour across the country. Lazarsfeld's Bureau of Applied Social Research at Columbia, with its structured depth interviewing (in which questions were "fixed" or "closed" so the findings could then be quantified), was exploring food mixes, for example, telling its client that it should avoid using the terms "easy" and "last-minute" in advertising copy because many women felt guilt and shame in using convenience foods. Applied Psychology Associates, asked to find out why people who owned television sets continued to see movies in theaters, found through motivation research that people often projected themselves into one or more roles portrayed in films. Role-playing was more real in movie theaters than on tiny, black-and-white sets in one's living room surrounded by relatives, the firm pointed out to its film industry client, information that was no doubt used to make the cinematic experience even more lifelike.[58]

There seemed to be no limit to the kind of insights motivation research could reveal—and the technique was assumed to be able to help resolve any marketing situation or problem. Richard Manville Research, a firm specializing in sensory issues, told its baby oil client that, based on motivation research findings, its product should smell the way a baby is supposed to smell, whatever that is. Nejelski and Company learned that many women bought and kept spices in their kitchens but were afraid to use them, thinking they were only for expert chefs. Weiss and Geller, a Chicago ad agency specializing in motivation research, discovered that many women wore lingerie not for their lovers but for themselves, the sexy underwear functioning as a form of narcissism or self-adoration. In his motivation research work, William A. Yoell ascertained that cat owners felt that their pets got tired of being served the same food everyday, projecting human values onto the animals. Burleigh Gardner at Social Research International (SRI) also was working in pet foods, learning that dog owners didn't like seeing fancy breeds in commercials, thinking they made their own mutts look like, well, mutts. SRI was also using motivation research in the health-care category, coming to the conclusion that users of pain relievers were mostly hypochondriacs and that heavy users of cough drops liked them primarily because they tasted like candy.[59]

Motivation research was shifting the plates of not only market research but also its first cousin, advertising. To some admen of a certain age, motivation research reminded them of when radio invaded their business with a vengeance in the late 1920s and early 1930s and, more recently, when television did the same. And like these two revolutionary media, motivation research was, as one middle-aged gray flannel suiter said in 1953, for the "upward-mobility boys." Much as in the case of another revolutionary idea— the Internet—that would change the rules of business a half-century later, younger agency people were often most receptive to motivation research, seeing an opportunity to jump over their more senior colleagues. Older advertising and marketing executives saw motivation research as a distinct threat, a new-fangled way of thinking that was capable of putting them out to pasture.[60] Indeed, ad agencies like Needham, Louis and Brosby in Chicago were now looking for people with graduate degrees in psychology, economics, statistics, or marketing; the qualifications of advertising past—the right pedigree and a pronounced ability to hold one's liquor—were no longer enough to get or keep a job. Motivation research was also demanding more collaboration among agency employees than before, with a team of a couple of psychologists, an economist, and a statistician typically working together on a project. What happened to the good old days when a winning personality and a big expense account were how to succeed in advertising without really trying?[61]

In addition, some advertising copywriters were struggling with Dichteresque findings, wondering for example what creative tack to take with the idea that teenage girls used soap not to get rid of acne but rather to "wash off the feeling of guilt that comes from newly awakened sexual desire." Smoking, similarly, was really about fulfilling "oral erotic needs," motivation research theory went—hardly ideal fodder for copywriters to pitch cigarettes. Men who didn't like to fly definitely feared their plane crashing, but they suffered from an even greater fear of "sexual relationships with strange women," another motivation research study for American Airlines suggested, which was certainly difficult to work into a magazine ad. This new breed of researchers might be brilliant, some copywriters were thinking, but they sure weren't making their jobs any easier.[62]

Besides upsetting the ad agency apple cart, the rise of motivation research was leading more and more Ph.D.s to become allies of American business, a distressing trend to some. "Seduced by the advertising industry, an increasing number of social scientists are turning into super-hucksters," thought "Ralph Goodman" (a pseudonym), who alleged that these psychologists and sociologists were selling out their expertise in exchange for a fat check. Whether involved in Weiss and Geller's attempt to get coal miners in eastern Pennsylvania to chew more gum (to relieve their frustrations), McCann-Erickson's pursuit to get heavy drinkers to be even heavier drinkers, or SRI's concerted efforts to find a way to tell cigarette smokers that the product was pleasurable and wouldn't kill them, social scientists were now a primary weapon in marketers' arsenal. For better or worse, many if not most of the psychologists and sociologists who were cashing the fat checks were not hacks but bona fide authorities in their field, a world-class collection of current or ex-academics from universities like Columbia, Chicago, Michigan, and Yale. Most disturbing to Goodman was that most of these same types were known for supporting economic reforms to encourage greater social equality, yet here they were eagerly stoking the capitalist machine. "If the social scientist becomes the hireling of advertising and business," he asked, how can he study objectively their social implications?" A reasonable question indeed.[63]

Is the Prune a Witch?

Some outside the industry saw motivation research as a more serious threat than forcing some members of the old boys' club into early retirement, making copywriters work harder, and leading Ph.D.s to become marketers' mercenaries. In his 1953 article "Is the Prune a Witch?" Robert Graham painted a not very pretty picture of how motivation research worked, the first real trickle of criticism that would soon become a torrent: "Advertisements are like tacks placed in the road, and the mind of the American consumer is somewhat like an automobile tire. The outer layers of the tire, made of black, smoke-cured apathy, are resilient and hard to pierce. But a good sharp tack can do it, and a superior tack can go on and puncture the inner tube. When that happens, the consumer comes to a shuddering halt and the man who put the tack in the road, or hired somebody else to do it for him, steps out of the bushes and sells the consumer an icebox."[64] Although there were signs soon after the war that advertisers were placing tacks in the road, Graham thought, it wasn't until the spread of motivation research in the early 1950s that some major blowouts started taking place. Graham called motivation research "the new liturgy" on Madison Avenue ("the Appian Way of the advertising world") and was mightily concerned about the power of this new religion. "If motivational research can in fact supply the right answer, and if the copy writer can translate it into understandable and appealing terms, the adman will have a tack that will penetrate tire, tube, fender, and windshield and stab the consumer right in the gizzard," he fretted.[65]

Graham's problem with motivation research was actually twofold. First, like Goodman, he thought that psychologists were prostituting themselves, applying their knowledge to an area in which they had no business being. And this was no ordinary knowledge, Graham argued, the social scientist being "the inheritor of three thousand years of western man's effort to understand himself." Great minds—Aquinas, Da Vinci, Descartes, Jefferson, and many others—had created the arts and sciences, and now headshrinkers were using this phenomenal body of knowledge to help market detergents and deodorants. Second, Graham claimed, psychologists had what amounted to "insider information" regarding the human mind, he or she whispering sweet nothings of consumers' neuroses into marketers' ears. Equipped with this information, marketers could then not just play upon people's prejudices and anxieties but actually create them, if doing so would help sell their product. "It is possible that an irresponsible social scientist will feed dangerous material to an irresponsible adman," Graham worried, this worst-case scenario capable of causing real harm to individuals.[66]

One social scientist who would be labeled both irresponsible and dangerous was James Vicary. By 1953, Vicary, whom Vance Packard would call a few years later "perhaps the most genial and ingratiating of all the major figures operating independent depth-probing firms," had an impressive roster of clients, including Benton & Bowles, J. Walter Thompson, and BBDO, all blue-chip agencies.[67] Vicary's favorite tool was free word association, in which a word was recited to a respondent, who replied with the first word or phrase that came to mind. This Freudian game of "Password" supposedly revealed people's inner, unfiltered thoughts, but Vicary liked it just as much because it required less time than the hours (and sometimes days) of the depth inter-view and, as important, there was less opportunity for respondents to "cheat." Having to reply every three seconds gave interviewees little time to invent something, in other words, making it much easier to simply tell the truth. Vicary had put himself on the motivation research map with a study for a major brewery, telling executives not to put the word "lagered" into its ads, as they were thinking of doing. Word association had revealed that more than a third of respondents replied with terms not particularly desirable when thinking of beer, specifically "tired," "drunk," "lazy," "linger," and "dizzy."[68]

Vicary's motivation research study for the Chicago-based Commonwealth Edison Company also helped make him the go-to guy for anything word-related in the early 1950s. Again using his pet methodology, Vicary found that of the hundreds of associations given for "Chicago," six were strongest, and he advised his client to not only include them in its ads but also put them in a single sentence in descending order of importance: "Chicago is a *city* in *Illinois*, sometimes referred to as *windy*, is known for its *stockyards, gangsters*, and in the past for the great *fire* which destroyed the town," went the first sentence in the ad, on target from a research perspective, perhaps, but not the stuff of creative genius. (Thankfully, Vicary did not go so far as to recom-mend that the power company try to construct a sentence with other words that respondents frequently associated with "Chicago," including "Sister Car-rie," "jazz bands," "the City of Hogs," and "meat cleavers.") Vicary was so smit-ten with word association that he not only employed it as his top motivation research tool but actually tried to use it to name his children. Expecting a boy, he and his wife decided to name him Simon. "Simon Vicary seemed to us to have a fine sound," he thought, but the name didn't pass muster in a word association test. "When we tried it on our friends," Vicary explained, "we got associations like 'Simon Legree' and 'Simple Simon'," causing the couple to rethink their decision. As it turned out, the Vicarys' conundrum was all for naught. "The child was a girl anyway," he said, and "we named her Anne."[69]

Fortunately for readers of print ads, other motivation researchers were fonder of projective techniques using pictures rather than words, thinking that visual imagery more deeply penetrated the unconscious than did lin-guistics. One such test was "thematic apperception," in which respondents were shown a picture and then asked to construct a story about it. Another test flipped this around, where respondents told a story and were then asked to draw a picture visually representing it. One of the most unusual motivation research tools had to be the Szondi test, in which respondents were shown photographs of human faces and asked, "With which one of these people would you like to go on a long train trip?" or a similar question. The catch was that all the people in the photographs were insane, with respondents presumably likely to pick out the person whose madness most closely resembled his or her own (common psychological thought in the 1950s was that the man or woman on the street was about 5 percent mad). An interesting test, to say the least, but one can only wonder about its value regarding marketers' biggest concern, to move product.[70]

The case of prunes neatly illustrated how motivation research findings could vary a great deal based on the consultant used and his methodology of choice. Vicary and Dichter each deconstructed consumer attitudes toward the dried fruit at about the same time, and the results of the former's word association tests emerged as much different from those produced by the latter's depth interviews. Vicary's research with two hundred men and women indicated that prune marketers should flaunt rather than cloak the prune's *laxative* connotations, as well as remind consumers that the purple things were *plums* and *fruit* (these three italicized words topping his association test.) For prune marketers, this was good news, allaying their fears about their product being best known as a laxative.[71]

Dichter, in contrast, came back to the prune people with less cheerful and far more complicated news. Also interviewing two hundred people, the doctor discovered an array of negative associations with the unpopular fruit, chiefly that it was a symbol of old age, no longer really natural, an unpleasant reminder of parental authority, socially embarrassing to serve to guests, associated with hospitals, the army, and boardinghouses, and, last but not least, primarily eaten by peculiar people. Dichter, however, was just getting going on what he called a "scape-goat food," "Puritan," and something "meager, rough and joyless." "The prune is resented as a freak and an intruder," the psychologist believed, and those who eat them were viewed as equally odd and unwelcome. Dichter also thought the prune was a "witch," the edible equivalent to "a wrinkled, ugly, sterile old spinster," this last observation no doubt making the fruit's marketers downright despondent. The fact that the prune grew year round while most fruits were seasonal was for Dichter a "rebellion against nature," its blackness making it that much more "sinister and dangerous."[72]

Although Dichter's report was far more disturbing than Vicary's, he did see an upside. Among his forty suggestions on how the prune marketers could make the best of their fruit's characteristics, was that they should compare the ugly ducklings with more beautiful products of nature. Prunes could be, Dichter envisioned, "the black diamonds of the fruit family," and such ad copy would persuade housewives to proudly serve them to company, unashamed of their cathartic qualities. Its dignity restored, the prune could be transformed into "the California wonder fruit," Dichter concluded, something the agency of record on the account, Botsford, Constantine and Gardner of San Francisco, took to heart.[73] From this one case study, it's obvious how difficult it was for clients to fully believe Vicary's brand of short and sweet findings and make sense out of Dichter's Homeric ones. The output of motivation research was, as this case study suggested, typically highly unpredictable and often not very user friendly. "In a single lunch hour Dichter will give an adman enough new thoughts to mobilize him upward like a jet plane," observed Robert Graham, but it was then "up to the adman to sort these ideas as an umpire sorts ball and strikes."[74]

They're Selling Your Unconscious

Unable to ignore this new kind of market research taking American business by storm, editors at *Business Week* posed a number of questions they thought "any alert and reasonably skeptical businessman" should be asking himself in 1954. Was this trend sweeping across the landscape of American business a fad, "a novelty that will blow over in a few years?" Was it "a full-fledged technique of human engineering," as reliable as, say, chemistry or electronics? Last, was it so important it could produce "a new way of looking at human nature," that is, be used not just in business but in all kinds of relationships with other people? The magazine was referring to motivation research, and the sort of questions the editors raised clearly showed how central it was becoming to the American businessperson at mid-century. With Americans having more choices than ever in the prosperous postwar years, marketers needed to take motivation research seriously, according to *Business Week*. The magazine suggested that the best way to solve business problems very possibly resided within the enigmatic behavioral sciences of psychology, sociology, and anthropology.[75]

The *Wall Street Journal* too took note of the sea change taking place in American business as motivation research took hold. "The businessman's hunt for sales boosters is leading him into a strange wilderness," Thomas E. McCarthy wrote in the paper in 1954, that wilderness being "the subconscious mind." Fears of "posthumous guilt" and deeply buried memories of childhood spanking had not been particularly foremost in the minds of businessmen, but executives at a host of companies, including Goodyear, GM, General Foods, CBS, and Lever Brothers, were fast becoming conversant in such classic psychological fodder. Corning Glass's discovery that purchasing agents weren't buying the company's pipes owing to the trauma of having broken a glass as a child was particularly profound, and agency people worked hard to figure out a way around the buyers' emotional block. Although some were calling such insights "hocus pocus," eighty firms were now selling motivation research services, with the top firms such as those run by Vicary and Politz having quadrupled their business over the previous few years.[76]

Controversial as motivation research was, those with a sense of history recognized that it was possibly much more than just a new, potentially dangerous tool of marketing. From the long view, motivation research could be said to be the third and most sophisticated level of exchange between a seller and a buyer, quite a claim if true. The first level, which had ruled for thousands of years, was the simple trading of something another person wanted for money (or something else), followed by the creation of markets and demand for things by advertising and other kinds of promotion. By appealing to the subconscious and consumers' hidden motivations, however, motivation research represented something very different, a form of exchange operating on a much deeper and potentially more sinister level.[77]

Whether it was either one of the best things that had ever happened for someone trying to sell something to someone else or a development we would come to regret, there was no doubt that motivation research was here to stay. "The excitement and interest in MR reached a crescendo in 1953 and 1954," Packard wrote a few years later, noting it was during this time that the technique, in current parlance, "tipped."[78] It's not hard to see why and how the business community got so swept up with the behavioral sciences as they became the darling of Madison Avenue. Psychologists, sociologists, and anthropologists were able, or at least appeared to be able, to find out what people wanted, just the kind of information your average businessman was naturally interested in. The growing belief that people weren't always reasonable and often didn't themselves know why they did certain things made the work of behavioral scientists, with their odd but apparently effective arsenal of methods, that much more intriguing. If you could truly understand people, the possibilities were limitless, and this unbounded potential was exactly what was needed to keep the nation's economy moving. Understanding people meant, in short, the ability to manipulate them, a dream so powerful that it was even worth becoming familiar with the ideas of a man who spent most of his career studying middle-class Viennese women decades ago.[79]

The "arrival" of motivation research in the early fifties was all the more remarkable given that it had been around in some shape or form for a couple of decades. American business, caught up in its own travails during the lean Depression years and scarce wartime years, was simply unaware of the strides that had been made in the social sciences over this same period of time, making the emergence of motivation research that much more dramatic. Suddenly, an amazing body of knowledge was there for the taking. Adding to the effect was the mystique that motivation researchers commanded, a breed of egghead unlike any other that had populated the business world. Compared to traditional market researchers, social scientists could somehow tell when consumers were holding back information or not telling the complete truth, it was believed, meaning the surveyors wouldn't fall for any booby traps. And because they were scientifically trained, motivation researchers were considered impartial, analytical, even detached—all things the affable, sales-oriented businessperson was not. At the same time, individuals coming from the social sciences were considered more nimble and flexible than the corporate statistician, able to squeeze themselves into the corners of consumers' minds to find the richest material.[80]

The spectacular rise of motivation research was that much more impressive given that marketers had at their disposal what had been viewed as the definitive reading of "the public pulse." Since 1946, the Federal Reserve Board had been working with the Survey Research Center at the University of Michigan to measure consumers' attitudes, a massive effort to determine Americans' relative "buying mood." Year after year, the center, led by George Katona (another European immigrant) and his colleagues Rensis Likert and Angus Campbell, issued its much-anticipated findings, with consumers' interest in spending money going up and down like a roller coaster. Measuring the "psychological state" of consumers in a quantitative way seemed to be an ideal approach, the perfect blend of large-scale surveys and social science.[81]

With this as the gold standard in market research, Freud's appearance on Madison Avenue was not unlike the arrival of modernism in the art world (or later, perhaps, when Dylan went electric at Newport), a classic example of the shock of the new. Besides learning about what was really going on in consumers' dirty little minds, motivation researchers had the audacity to break pretty much every rule in the book. For one thing, motivation researchers made no real effort to study a representative sample, this in itself a clear violation of basic marketing research practices. The techniques they used to gather information differed dramatically from those of traditional researchers, the former's long and winding questions (and respondents' even longer and more winding answers) considered very bad form by the latter with their cut-and-dried ways. Finally, and most important, the open-ended, even literary ways in which motivation researchers interpreted and presented their findings were the opposite of those favored by mainstream researchers. In a nutshell, motivation researchers believed that less could very well be more, and their rejection of the postwar consensus mantra that bigger was better was as radical an idea as Mies van der Rohe's in architecture.[82]

As it became clearer what motivation researchers were bringing to the marketing and advertising party, the voices of concern among critics like Robert Graham soon became much louder. "Your dreams, your desires, and the rumblings of your subconscious, formerly sacred to you and your analyst, have been charted by advertising psychologists," warned Lydia Strong in 1954; they are "eager to learn how you buy and why you buy, and therefore how they can sell you many, many more products." Even the title of Strong's article for the *Saturday Review*—"They're Selling Your Unconscious"—indicated that something surreptitious and possibly dangerous was afoot, with marketers now apparently able to unlock the secrets of one's mind and thus release the contents of one's wallet. "Motivation research is the hottest trend on Madison Avenue," she correctly observed, and "the fatter the advertising budget, the greater the probability that Freud helped write the copy." Attempts to get inside consumers' heads were hardly new, of course, going at least as far back as Walter Dill Scott's landmark 1903 *The Psychology of Advertising*, and in the 1920s advertisers went positively wild for John B. Watson's psychology-based theory of behaviorism. Marketers' postwar drift toward the Freudian concept that the subconscious was responsible for humans' actions was something new, however; the mingling of business and psychology was considered by critics to be a dangerous collaboration between state and church.[83]

Worse, for skeptics, motivation research was in the process of becoming canonized as it began to be accepted by academics and be taught at business schools. "Motivation research is at present a sort of 'social movement' in advertising," George Horseley Smith, a professor at Rutgers, observed in his 1954 *Motivation Research in Advertising and Marketing*, the first textbook on the subject. Motivation research was still evolving, Smith thought, with techniques and concepts, sample sizes and reporting methods, and relationships between scientists and marketers all in a state of flux, but he felt that it was a long overdue joint venture between business and the social sciences. Smith embraced the idea that consumers were unwilling or unable to tell researchers what they really wanted to know, aligning himself with what Dichter and others were telling their clients. "Under ideal conditions, respondents would tell us briefly and to the point just what they think and feel at a given time," Smith wrote, "but the fact is that most people are severely handicapped in trying to communicate their private experiences."[84]

With his landmark book, Smith helped to spread the gospel of motivation research by arming business school students with the basic theories behind the technique. The professor discussed the motivation research notion that there were three levels of awareness, the first entailing material that could easily be discussed, such as the features or benefits of a product. Even if consumers could articulate why they liked a particular brand and not another— not something that should be assumed—this kind of superficial information just wasn't valuable anymore, Smith explained. The second level of awareness involved material that was rarely discussed, he continued, most of this having to do with identity or social status, that is, how consumers wanted to feel about themselves or be perceived by others. Why people bought a bigger television set or moved into a nicer neighborhood, for example, fitted this category, as did the reasons men drove fast cars or smoked cigars. The last level of awareness involved material that was both unanalyzed and not discussed, Smith instructed marketers-to-be, for this information was not even apparent to individuals themselves because it resided in the deep unconscious. Researchers had to go to this level of awareness to discover the real reasons things people did the things they did (much of it irrational), such as why gamblers gambled (to lose money as a form of self-punishment) or why shoppers hunted for bargains (to outsmart others). Only through psychiatry and what was called at the time "abnormal psychology" could marketers tap such repressed feelings and hidden motivations, Smith concluded, and motivation research was equipped to do just that.[85]

In his textbook published a few years later, Joseph Newman also made the case that motivation research was exactly what the field of market research needed to fulfill its full potential. Newman, a Harvard Business School professor, explained how motivation research was rescuing marketing from its ignorant ways. Before motivation research, marketers' knowledge of consumers' wants had been "woefully inadequate," Newman observed, adding that this "perplexing state of affairs" was one of the major flaws of American business. "We have been wearing conceptual blinders," the professor lamented, and individuals and their wants have been "sadly neglected" due to marketers' obsession with things that could be counted and measured like sales, prices, and market share. Such quantitative information, however, was typically not enough and came after the fact, too little information arriving too late for managers to do any real market planning. The fundamental problem was that marketers had historically viewed the consumer as a mini-company, as he or she methodically used resources to purchase things offering maximum satisfaction. The truth was, however, that consumers did not act with the cold, steely logic of a business enterprise, making this model a poor one when trying to sell them products. The University of Michigan Survey Research Center had learned, for example, that consumers often acted carelessly when shopping by buying things impulsively and not comparing prices, something that would wreck havoc with the best-laid marketing plans. "People often do not consciously know important reasons for their actions or preferences [and] even if they do know, they may rationalize or otherwise cover up the less socially acceptable influences," Newman wrote; consumers' emotions were completely left out of the marketing equation.[86]

It did not help matters, Newman continued, that business schools like his were not preparing students to deal with the real world in which consumers' emotions often ruled. Harvard's case study approach in particular was inadequate, he stated, for the method by which all others were measured ignored consumer motives in its close readings of business situations. "While the marketer often has known that emotional factors are important, he has had no systematic way of thinking about psychological and social meanings," the professor observed. Much more problematic, however, was the fact that Americans were simply not trained to deal with emotions. "Most of us," Newman correctly pointed out, "were brought up in a culture which places high value on logic, reason, economy, and control over feelings," our instincts to deny or overlook the nonrational. Business executives were particularly unequipped to get in touch with people's warmer and fuzzier sides, being much more interested in their products than in whatever might be going on in the mysterious minds of consumers. With motivation research, however, marketers now had a tool to access this huge body of untapped knowledge, its psychological underpinnings opening the window onto "human personality and the social forces that act upon it." With this kind of promise, it was difficult to overestimate how much motivation research could contribute to American business, Newman concluded. "Motivation research promises important conceptual growth and, therefore, appears destined to be a major landmark in marketing's history," he exclaimed, excited to be part of this new movement.[87]

Although their methods differed, motivation researchers generally agreed there were three levels of the mind, each offering marketers useful information. Conscious material was available but not particularly valuable, preconscious material was somewhat difficult to access and relatively valuable, and unconscious material was the most challenging to obtain but loaded with juicy information, as most motivation research practitioners would put it. Dichter's work on M&Ms had already become by the mid-1950s a classic case study of how plumbing the deeper levels of the mind was worth the effort, illustrating how the theory was put in play. Consumers didn't eat the chocolate candies because they tasted good, Dichter's research had shown, but rather as an incentive or reward for doing work they would rather not do. After the company changed the product's slogan from "Everybody likes 'em" to "Make that tough job easier," sales of M&Ms reportedly doubled, the success story prompting other marketers to board the motivation research train.[88]

It was no coincidence that motivation research took off just as the nation's postwar economy kicked into high gear. Dealing just with the conscious may be fine in a subsistence economy, its proponents argued, but not in that of the United States at mid-century with so many discretionary dollars floating around. Likewise, rational thinking was sufficient during the days of Ford's "any color as long as it's black" Tin Lizzie but not in the 1950s when one's car was as much about social status as about transportation. The mere conscious thus no longer revealed consumers' automotive wants and needs, motivation research believers pointed out, leading to such emotion-laden advertising headlines as Buick's "It makes you feel like the man you are." Also driving motivation research was consumers' growing skepticism toward advertising, which related to the sometimes ridiculous claims being made on the new medium of television. Americans were simply more media savvy than they were before the war, motivation researchers explained, making it necessary to break though or go around the defenses they had constructed.[89]

How exactly to penetrate those shields varied a great deal, however, with each motivation researcher going at it somewhat differently. Dichter was partial to his "psycho-panel," which consisted of a group of a few hundred (local Westchester) families sorted by character trait, such as secure versus insecure, escapist versus realist, and so on, with which he would conduct his depth interviews. Psychoanalytic-based depth interviews were in fact the most commonly used tool among motivation researchers, as these hours-long, rambling conversations were believed to ultimately lead to the underlying reasons consumers did what they did and thought what they thought. Word association, another Freudian technique that Vicary specialized in, was also often used to tell researchers what consumers thought of brand names or ad copy on an unfiltered basis. (Such testing occasionally had more practical benefits; after learning that 40 percent of housewives thought the term "concentrated" meant "blessed by the pope," Procter and Gamble dropped the word from its soap advertising.) Sentence completion and picture tests too were employed, but it was lie detector tests that really got people's attention. One Chicago firm, the Ad Detector Research Corporation, specialized in lie detection, flashing advertising copy only after strapping a device onto consumers to see if what they said was truthful. Pulse, breathing rate, and blood pressure were also measured to learn what the subjects felt about the copy regardless of what came out of their mouths.[90]

Such varied motivation research techniques obviously produced a wide range of findings, but certain drives were almost always determined to be the root cause of human and thus consumer behavior. Sexuality, not surprisingly, topped the list, followed closely by issues of security. ("You either offer security or fail," Dichter had said in 1951, no doubt projecting his own sources of insecurity as a youth—his red hair as much as his poverty—onto Americans.)[91] Frustration and hostility too popped up quite often, arguably a function of postwar Americans' pressure to conform to prescribed norms. Like M&Ms, chewing gum wasn't bought for its taste but, in the latter's case, to relieve tension and anxiety, said Weiss and Geller's study, this finding supposedly a bonanza for Wrigley. Edward L. Bernays, the already legendary public relations man who was now dabbling in motivation research, claimed that the most enjoyable thing about breakfast cereals was their crunch, "satisfying an aggressive desire to overcome obstacles." Longing for acceptance and friendship was another common motivation research theme, leading beer marketers to present their product as something that lubricated social situations rather than conveyed sophistication, previously a tried-and-true strategy. Elitism in any situation was deemed off-putting to most consumers, all motivation researchers agreed, dovetailing nicely with postwar America's impetus to fit in. Marketers could learn a lot from the success of Arthur Godfrey, motivation research people mused, the not very good-looking, not especially smart but very popular talk show host making his many viewers feel comfortable and at ease.[92]

As the second half of the fifties beckoned, American businessmen could look forward to much more than figuring out how to infuse some Arthur Godfrey into their products and services. Over the previous quarter century, a new research technique had emerged from a laundry in Vienna to take Madison Avenue by storm, redirecting the trajectory of marketing and advertising. Largely conceived by a Marxist simply looking for a way to fund his leftist agenda, motivation research had become one of the nation's most valuable imports, bringing an intellectual component to American business that was sorely missing. The Nazis' rejection of some of the greatest minds of the day would turn out to be a bonanza for the United States and the American Way of Life, these academics offering U.S. businesses an entirely new way to understand and approach consumers. On the surface strange bedfellows, European philosophy and American pragmatism proved to be a happy coupling, the bridging of social science and business making for a synergistic collaboration. Ernest Dichter's brand of Freudian and Adlerian thought was particularly potent, as the principles of psychoanalysis became permanently ingrained in Americans' cultural consciousness. The early days of motivation research were exciting, but another, much more turbulent era lay ahead.

2

The Sophisticated Sell

This depth approach is the first step toward the chilling
world of George Orwell.
> —Robert R. Kirsch, in his 1957
> *Los Angeles Times* review
> of *The Hidden Persuaders*

Writing for *America* magazine in 1957, John P. Sisk, an English professor at Gonzaga University, posed the idea that motivation research was the devil's handiwork, something that could help advertisers exploit consumers' sinful side. One didn't have to be a theologian to make the case that advertising did indeed zero in on consumers' darker personality traits like greed, lust, selfishness, and narcissism. "One way or another advertisers assume original sin as a highly desirable status quo," Sisk believed, seeing the first "huckster" as the devil himself. The English professor went further with his hellish view of motivation research, locating it in, of all places, Milton's *Paradise Lost*.[1] In book IV of the epic poem, according to Sisk, Satan "uses the methods of the motivation researcher as he whispers in the ear of the sleeping Eve":

Assaying by his Devilish art to reach
The Organs of her Fancy, and with them forge
Illusions as he list, Phantasms and Dreams. . . .
Vain hopes, vain aims, inordinate desires
Blown up with high conceits ingend'ring pride.[2]

In this passage, Satan is softening Eve up for "the sophisticated sell" that occurs in book IX of *Paradise Lost*, Sisk concluded, her experience much like our own as consumers "when what we have been induced to buy fails to give us the satisfaction an advertisement has led us to expect." Like Satan who approached Eve in disguise (specifically a toad), admen using motivation research were concealing the truth through hype and puffery, their products falsely presented as heaven on earth.[3]

Not all attacks leveled at motivation research in the late fifties were as vitriolic (or literary) as Sisk's, but it was clear that the honeymoon the technique had enjoyed for the previous quarter century as it took shape was over. Beginning in the mid-1950s and increasingly through the decade, motivation research would be accused of and blamed for a variety of sins, not the least of which was the leading of consumers down a wayward path. Despite the rising tide of opposition to the technique, the popularity of motivation research would actually grow over these years, benefiting from all the attention it was getting in the media. Whether one was for it or against it, it was now hard to feel indifferent about this thing that had every intention of continuing to whisper into Americans' ears.

A Better Mousetrap

The man whispering (or shouting) the loudest into Americans' ears was of course Ernest Dichter. Dichter's stature was continuing to grow as he replaced marketing's rule book with his own based on Freudian and Adlerian psychoanalytic theory. In a way, Dichter was swapping marketing's essential "four p's"—product, price, promotion, and packaging—with four s's—sustenance, sex, security, and status—thinking it was these basic human drives that determined all consumer behavior. Dichter also challenged traditional marketing thought by rejecting the idea that one had to ask a lot of people (as many as a hundred thousand, some said) to take the national pulse on any particular issue. "Once you establish universal psychological patterns, it's needless repetition and expense to quantify it further," he insisted, his use of about 250 interviews for each study anathema to established research principles. Dichter's use of other unorthodox methods (such as his "shadow box," with which he asked consumers to feel products like soap to get nonvisual reactions) also threw the established marketing research community for quite a loop, the man sometimes acting more like a magician than a businessman.[4]

Dichter's methods may have been unorthodox, even peculiar, but normally staid, risk-averse Big Business was positively fascinated by them. In the mid-1950s, he was a consultant to the two "Generals" of the nation's food business, General Mills and General Foods, advising them on how to more effectively appeal to consumers' unconscious sides. Dichter had told General Mills, for example, that most housewives considered cooking not just another tedious chore but a fulfilling activity that was integral to their personal identity. Based on this juicy morsel, the company started advertising Bisquick as a partner of sorts, the product and housewife engaged in a collaborative and creative effort. And at General Foods, Dichter convinced the brand managers of Sanka to stop attacking regular coffee in its advertising, something that he believed consumers found "insulting" to one of their favorite beverages. Sanka dropped its negative advertising and adopted a new, more positive theme ("Now you can drink all the coffee you want"), another case of how Dichterian psychology was successfully translated into marketing strategy.[5]

It wasn't unusual for Dichter, like other market research consultants, to suggest advertising campaign ideas to clients as part of their services. Dichter told the makers of Ronson lighters that flame was a symbol of sexuality (particularly in "primitive" cultures), for example, and this kernel of wisdom became the foundation for a new ad campaign created by its agency, Norman, Craig and Kummel. (Fire not only had "erotic implications," according to Dichter, it also invoked the Goddess of Light who, in turn, was linked to Eros.) Dichter's finding that women did not like to bake because of "fear of failure" led directly to General Mills's "I Guarantee" campaign featuring easy-to-make cakes produced by its agency, BBDO. To a company that sold grass seed, Dichter explained that "the lawn is an upholstered way of getting a direct feeling, direct contact with Mother Earth"—the origin of this particular insight being a play by a nineteenth-century Austrian dramatist named Franz Grillparzer.[6]

Although even a rather obscure play by a rather obscure playwright was fair game for Dichter to use in interpreting research findings, all roads led back to the consumer and, specifically, his or her unconscious. In addition to answering Dichter's interviewers' questions, subjects were often asked to explain what was going on in pictures, to complete conversation "balloons," and fill in partial sentences, techniques lifted directly from clinical psychiatry. But it was depth interviews, a phrase Dichter coined, however, that served as the heart and soul of his approach to motivation research, another concept borrowed from therapy. Dichter would closely parse the verbatim transcripts (and often videotape recordings) of these two- or three-hour interviews, reading between the lines to discover where the id was lurking. The real reason a consumer bought things was to satisfy deep human urges that he or she did not consciously perceive, Dichter consistently maintained, and only a well-qualified psychologist like himself was able to decode the symbolism of these urges. "The knowledge of basic motivations is necessary, or else you will not see any significance in an important phenomenon," he insisted, for the underlying drives were just as often sociological in nature as psychological. Products "consumed" in public—cars, clothing, even houses—were more about status than anything else, with social standing and aspirations of course playing a huge role in everyday life in postwar America. Dichter in fact kept a group of sociologists on staff to help translate Freudian analysis into sociological terms, this cross-pollination of the behavioral sciences unusual not just in business but in academia as well. Much of Freudian psychology was actually incompatible with if not directly contradictory to the new kinds of sociological thinking gaining traction in the late 1950s (especially David Riesman's theory of the "other-directed" person), but motivation research was uniquely able to accommodate each, all in the name of better understanding (and selling more products to) the American consumer.[7]

Fans of Dichter considered him the equal to arguably the most brilliant thinker in the history of advertising, Claude Hopkins, who virtually ruled the field in the teens and early twenties. Dichter is "widely regarded in the trade as the greatest copy idea man of our times—a veritable Claude Hopkins of the world of repressed symbolism," observed journalist and author Martin Mayer, a sentiment shared by top agency executives like Norman B. Norman of Norman, Craig and Kummel. Dichter "doesn't know where half his ideas come from, but he's right," said Kummel; it was Dichter's sheer intuition that accounted for much of his drawing power in the sea of "sample men." Even if it sometimes seemed as if there wasn't a drop of actual research in his deliverables—because it was difficult to believe that such things could come out of consumers' mouths—Dichter was always thought to be well worth the money. Also, Dichter ("Ernie" to his ad agency friends) spoke not only almost like a native but also largely jargon free, confident enough to not have to use the kind of "researchese" other behavioral scientists (called "whiskers" by those on Madison Avenue) relied on to impress clients.[8]

Dichter differed from his competitors in other, more important ways. Since the late 1930s, when he arrived on the scene and told Procter and Gamble and Chrysler what soap and automobiles were *really* about, Dichter was quite the major thorn in other researchers' sides. Not surprisingly,

Dichter was unaffected by his colleagues' disdain for the kind of research he had brought to the table. "I feel I'm better off building a better mousetrap and antagonizing the conventional mousetrap makers," he said, knowing that many clients preferred his brand of cheese. (Dichter occasionally referred to himself in the third person, a sign perhaps that he was not as insecure as he claimed.) Dichter had little problem recruiting people for his interviews, discussions, and "psycho-drama" sessions (which he was now fond of calling "motivational theater"), for his relative fame drew Westchester locals. (Dichter believed people were people—or at least their ids were ids—meaning a national "sample" wasn't necessary unless the client insisted on one.) Besides the experience of being part of his interesting sociological experiments, interviewees received a "door prize" and were entered in a monthly drawing for an all-expenses-paid evening in Manhattan that included not just train fare, an expensive dinner, and tickets to a Broadway show but also a babysitter.[9]

Of course, there were other fish in the motivation research sea to choose from, most of them also benefiting from the surge of interest in the technique. Although intellectually James Vicary leaned toward the anthropological side of the behavioral sciences, he and his staff of six were still pushing their word association tests, specializing in naming brands and companies. Vicary also did occasional public opinion polling and other standard market research projects to help pay the rent (in his small suite of offices in a converted private mansion just off Fifth Avenue in the East Sixties). He occasionally used depth interviews in his work but admitted that his versions were not very deep. "You might call them *breadth* interviews, if you chose," he stated, as he was interested more in covering a lot of ground than in drilling down into the subterranean strata of consumers' minds.[10]

With his naming business, Vicary had quite a good deal. Clients and their ad agencies would typically forward him the names they were considering— sometimes as many as a thousand or even more—and he and his staff would sort them, choosing the ones they thought best suited the product or company. Vicary and his team would also add a few of their own, and the best of the lot then were circulated to the client's legal department and top management to discard any no-no's (and add any individuals' favorite names, which occurred more often than not). Then it was on to research with consumers to find out which ones were best liked and remembered and most easily pronounced, although sometimes new names sprang out of the interviews. A final pool of eight to ten was then put into a national, quantitative test with about four hundred consumers, out of which emerged the recommended name.[11]

Not just Vicary but all the heavy hitters of motivation research—Dichter, Politz, and Roper—as well as a few smaller research firms were in fact turning the process of naming products—a notoriously subjective enterprise—into more of a science. "There is a noticeable movement away from the incestuous climate where a name is chosen by three or four company executives," said Irving Gilman of Dichter's Institute for Motivational Research, praising those managers who were willing to bring psychology and sociology into the naming mix. Ad agencies too had jumped into the name game via their research departments, as in the case of BBDO dropping fifty-five hundred names on the doorstep of its client Revlon for a new lipstick (the pile included "Red, Willing and Able," "Kissable Ketchup," and "Red-dy for Love"). After six hundred interviews with women, Vicary recommended "Darlan" as a name for a fiber created by B. F. Goodrich (rejecting "Morex" and "Dieuna"), and "direct distance dialing" for AT&T's new long-distance service that did not require an operator.[12]

As usual, however, it was Ernest Dichter who took the cake, with his project for the Farm Bureau Insurance Company of Columbus, Ohio, which wanted to rename itself. True to form, the company had already generated its own abundant list of possibilities, with "Town and Country" at the top of the heap. Dichter, however, had other ideas. Based on his interviews, Dichter came back to his client with the news that "Town and Country" suggested "overpriced insurance that could be afforded by only the wealthy country club set made up of ritzy guys in evening clothes who spend their time skeet shooting and letting ladies out of snobbish station wagons." The much less offensive "Nationwide Insurance" was instead chosen as the new company name.[13]

Other companies experiencing similar difficulties coming up with the perfect name brought in motivation research to save the day. Ford was having a whale of a time trying to name its new "E" line of cars, with the fall 1957 product launch just a year away. Candidates such as "Arrow," "Belmont," and "Saxon" had all been rejected because of their associations (men's shirts, a racetrack, and English muffins, respectively), and "Panther" was currently at the top of the list, even though company executives weren't particularly crazy about it. Some at Ford worried that the company would have to endure a process similar to that of its last major new product launch, when five thousand possibilities were considered before it settled on "Thunderbird." It was better to be safe than sorry when it came to the critical area of names, however. The Socony-Vacuum Oil Company (later Mobil) considered abbreviating its name to "Sovac," but motivation research revealed that the term "had over-tones of Soviet hence Communism," surely a disaster in the making in the middle of the Cold War.[14]

For James Vicary, the relatively easy and very lucrative naming business wasn't quite enough. Despite his low-key style, Vicary was at least as interested in attracting publicity as Dichter, willing in fact to push motivation research as far as it could go if it could get him mentioned in the trades and, ultimately, bring more business. Vicary thus gave considerable thought about different gimmicks that would attract the media's attention and raise his public profile. His first was to hire a group of "trained observers" who could provide "inside information" on what the public was thinking. Besides using these journalists, police officers, and barbers as experts on the American mindset (bartenders were, surprisingly, not included), Vicary announced he would put together a special panel of children who would report what their parents were talking about. Vicary's theory was that children were unequivocally neutral, and therefore best equipped to provide uncensored reports of family opinions.[15]

Although interesting, to say the least, this idea failed to make Vicary a household (or even company conference room) name, so he went to to plan B. On behalf of a women's magazine, Vicary could one day in 1955 be found in a New York supermarket, walking up and down the aisles with a stopwatch in his hand. Vicary was counting shoppers' eyelid blinks, believing he had discovered something very important. Shoppers blinked about fourteen times a minute at the food shelves, but the rate tripled at the checkout counter, Vicary claimed, leading him to believe they were in a "semi-hypnotic trance" while choosing their items. This helped explain why shoppers often bought things they had not intended to, he concluded, although it wasn't quite clear how this information would prove useful to his client. Vicary's eye blink test worked gangbusters from a publicity standpoint, as the press and presumably readers were fascinated by the apparent fact that normally perky housewives entered a trancelike state when they shopped for TV dinners and Tang. After his fifteen minutes of fame were over, however, Vicary would in a couple of years feel the need to go to plan C, which, to his regret, would make him as well known as Herr Doktor Dichter.[16]

Another big fish in the motivation research sea was Social Research, Inc. (SRI), founded by Burleigh Gardner, a Harvard University and University of Chicago social anthropologist. Gardner was heavily inspired by Lloyd Warner's 1948 *Social Class in America*, which instantly became a classic in academic circles. Warner, a colleague of Gardner's at Chicago, made a convincing case that the United States was a six-class society, and his book was discovered a few years later by businesspeople, who found it to be a wonderful resource to segment the marketplace. The *Journal of Marketing*, in fact, considered the sociologist's book "the most important step forward in market research in many years," like Lazarsfeld's "The Art of Asking Why," an (unintentionally created) masterful user's guide to marketing. Gardner invited Warner to become an associate at SRI, one of many social scientists to enlist in the growing army of hucksters with Ph.D.s.[17]

One of the main strengths of SRI was its happy alliance with Pierre Martineau, research director of the *Chicago Tribune*, who was as top-notch a motivation researcher as any of the consultants or admen in the business (certainly the best one on the client side). In 1951, Martineau made a name for himself with a study of beer drinkers in Chicago, followed by important work in cigarettes, detergents, cars, and gasoline. Martineau (who, like Gardner, was a big fan of Warner's work), believed that illogic, not logic, was the key to effective advertising, arguing that getting consumers to fall in love with products was a much better strategy than trying to using reason. Martineau thus saw the marketer's role as a sort of matchmaker, his job to encourage love affairs between products and people. By featuring a product's character or personality in its advertising, consumers with an affinity for those traits would be naturally drawn to it, Martineau thought, viewing the marketplace as not unlike a giant singles mixer.[18]

Among the brainy bunch of motivation researchers, in fact, Martineau was perhaps the brainiest, going back to college as a middle-aged man to gain a better intellectual footing in the field. Soon he was referencing Alfred Korzybski's theories of semantics, Alfred North Whitehead's thoughts on symbolic logic, and Emile Durkheim's views on sociology in his motivation research work for the newspaper and its advertisers, making even Dichter's high-brow observations look less than erudite. By the mid-1950s, Martineau was trying to formulate a metanarrative of modern advertising that, as only he could describe, incorporated "semantics, Cassirer's and Langer's epistemology of symbolic forms [and] the whole psychology of aesthetics," quite a long way from George Washington Hill's ten commandments of advertising (each one "repetition"). Besides being at the head of the motivation research class, Martineau was, along with Dichter, "probably the most enthusiastic missionary for MR in America," according to Vance Packard, "a high apostle of image building."[19]

Edward Weiss, who ran his own advertising firm in Chicago, was another particularly well-read motivation researcher, the library in his agency's office fully stocked with books more likely to be found on an Ivy League campus. Weiss required his employees to regularly check out books from the library, which included such works as Wilhelm Reich's *Character Analysis*, Theodor Reik's *Masochism in Modern Man*, and Ivan Pavlov's *Lectures on Conditional Reflexes*. Also part of the Chicago school of motivation research was Louis Cheskin, whose Color Research Institute focused on package design. Cheskin was particularly adept at making "male" products more feminine, and vice versa, by redesigning a package or its label. By rounding the corners of the Fleischmann's Gin label, for example, sales of the product to women reportedly jumped. Cheskin was also brought in for the regendering of Marlboro, which he gave a big shot of testosterone by designing its now classic red-and-white label, which (along with Leo Burnett's new macho advertising campaign) made Marlboro perhaps the first transsexual cigarette.[20]

The Thriving Little Industry

Such feats of rejuvenation were exactly why motivation research was now the technique of choice for marketers with especially tough challenges on their hands. "If Motivation Research is just a fad, it is a very potent one," thought *Fortune* in 1956, taking note of the "thriving little industry" that had developed in the previous five or so years.[21] Seeing more and more clients express interest in motivation research, all kinds of firms rather quickly labeled themselves experts in the field. Ads offering motivation research services started popping up en masse in the *Wall Street Journal* as research companies and ad agencies jostled for business. "MR is a most modern, up-to-date tool of management," stated one such ad from Creative Market Research, a New York–based company that assured potential clients that the technique made "good, sound business sense."[22] In its own ad, Charles L. Rumrill, a Rochester, New York, ad agency with clients like Corning Glass, Eastman Kodak, and DuPont, explained that every customer had a subconscious "which can be probed fruitfully to find out 'why' he does what he does and what his inner compulsions are."[23]

With more companies offering motivation research services, more people were needed to do the actual work. Job ads (labeled "Positions Available—Male," notably) announcing openings in motivation research appeared regularly in the *Journal* in the mid-fifties as companies across the country sought researchers with backgrounds in the social sciences. In 1957, for example, a

San Francisco firm was on the hunt for an "experienced man with an imaginative approach to consumer packaging problems," the ideal candidate would be able to "relate psychological and sociological factors of consumer preference" via motivation research.[24] Newly minted college graduates interested in careers in motivation research also used the *Journal* to try to find jobs in the hot field. "Beginner, BA—Brooklyn College," began one such ad, the job seeker clearly excited to put his basic skills in "perception, motivation, statistics, & experimental psychology" to good use.[25]

The biggest thing to hit advertising since the introduction of commercial television a decade earlier now in their lap, industry officials rushed to provide additional resources to help more marketers get started with motivation research. Seeing keen interest in the motivation research bibliography and glossary among its members, the Advertising Research Foundation published a 230-page text describing how behavioral science can help solve marketing problems, a directory of 82 research firms fluent in the technique, and a list of 187 psychologists, sociologists, and cultural anthropologists offering their services.[26] Besides wanting to read about motivation research, no doubt to better understand it, mid-century businesspeople were eager to hear experts explain it. Motivation research was a hot topic on the advertising and marketing conference circuit, executives listening patiently to psychologists and sociologists lecture while they picked at their rubber chicken. For example, in July 1955, Wallace H. Wulfeck, chairman of the Advertising Research Foundation's Committee on Motivation Research, gave what he said was his fifty-third talk on motivation research in four and a half years, most recently to the Sales Executive Club of New York, whose members had jammed into a hotel ballroom to pick up a few pointers.[27]

The plethora of information on the subject and its popularity at industry meetings and conferences was all the more impressive given that there was not a single case where it could be proven that motivation research had increased sales of a particular product or brand. "The interest in M.R. continues to mount despite the fact that most advertisers and agencies using it are either unable (or unwilling) to reveal any concrete results that M.R. may have achieved," *Fortune* reported, and even those companies that regularly used the technique kept mum on the subject. There was, however, plenty of anecdotal evidence that motivation research had led to successful product repositionings (including Leo Burnett's "de-sissification" of tea and Marlboro, Dichter's work for American Airlines which eliminated business flyers' "posthumous guilt feelings" about being in a plane crash, SRI's "Everyman" recommendation for beer advertising, and a host of other image overhauls for brands like Ry-Krisp, Pepsodent, Sanka, and Buick). These case histories provided enough positive word of mouth to make other marketers fork out about $20,000 for a soup-to-nuts study.[28]

Although there were dozens of firms and independent consultants clients could choose from, motivation research had by the mid-1950s settled into three basic schools. Dichter, who had completed no fewer than seven hundred studies for clients between 1946 and 1956, was widely and legitimately acknowledged as the poster child for the Freudian school, almost always going to the psychoanalytic well to interpret research findings. Early toilet training, for one thing, was a recurring theme in Dichter's presentation to clients, a concept he relied on as the explanation for adult behavior even more heavily perhaps than Freud himself. (Purchasing toothpaste and giving money to charity, for example, were each somehow linked to one's preliminary encounters with the potty, he held.) Businessmen typically took such interpretations with a large grain of salt but at the same time were dazzled by Dichter, and his ability to peel back the layers of ordinary behavior and make marketing recommendations out of what was left a thing of beauty. A second school of motivation research was more interested in group behavior than classic Freudian theory, viewing consumers as part of the larger cultural organism. SRI, Science Research Associates, and the easy to remember Psychological Corporation in New York were the best-known firms practicing this kind of "psychosocial" version of motivation research, and the fact that quite a few notable academics like Lloyd Warner were active in the field added to the school's reputation.[29]

The third school of motivation research was pursued by McCann-Erickson, led by Herta Herzog since her arrival at the large New York ad agency in 1945. Like Dichter and her husband, Paul Lazarsfeld, Herzog had been blazing the trail of motivation research since the late 1930s, doing radio survey research at Princeton and Columbia. While there, Herzog had the opportunity to work on some interesting projects, her additional asset of having "a woman's perspective" making her an especially valuable member of Lazarsfeld's team. In 1938, for example, Frank Stanton, the research director of CBS, asked Lazarsfeld to find out why listeners had believed that H. G. Wells's *War of the Worlds* broadcast was a report of a real Martian invasion. Lazarsfeld in turn asked Herzog to lead the project, and she produced the widely read article "Why Did People Believe in the 'Invasion from Mars'?" which focused on the many women listeners. Herzog also did path-breaking work in radio soap operas, one of her key findings being that the tremendous popularity of melodramas and love stories were part of a feminine world that seemed to contradict the central mythology of Americans' "rugged individualism." Like her colleagues, Herzog seemed to benefit from being a European immigrant, her outsider's perspective giving her an advantage in the business of studying consumer behavior.[30]

Herzog's Adlerian training pervaded not just her research department at McCann but the entire agency, which was already ahead of the curve in embracing a "total communications" approach rather than one focused just on advertising. McCann's commitment to motivation research was rivaled only by that of Young and Rubicam, which had its own staff of social scientists (continuing the legacy of George Gallup, who, as a young Northwestern University journalism professor, had established the first true research department at an ad agency).[31] Herzog's small department (five people in 1955) was eclectic, employing psychologists of all schools, but it was Adlerian analysis, with its emphasis on "power drives" and the possibilities for individuals to change (a "philosophy of encouragement," Dichter called it), that most influenced the agency's thinking. More so than Dichter, who was decidedly Freudian in his thinking, Herzog followed in Lazarsfeld's Adlerian footsteps (making one wonder what the couple talked about at the dinner table). Working with Marion Harper before he became president of the agency, Herzog advanced Lazarsfeld's research designed to learn what characteristics people who purchased the same brand shared. Using some of the same clinical techniques to diagnose mental illness, such as the Rorschach test, Herzog and her colleagues at McCann soon became adept at matching brand personalities with those of consumers. Matching cigarette brands with their smokers was particularly easy via the Rorschach test, Herzog believed, with aggressive types almost always partial to Lucky Strike and hypochondriacs to Philip Morris.[32]

And while Dichter and even Lazarsfeld believed most of the answers one could hope for could come from individual consumers, Herzog relied heavily on group discussions, the most direct link between motivation research of decades past and today's focus groups. (Dichter is credited for coining the term "focus group," however.)[33] Herzog also stood out in the field, by combining depth interviews and projective tests with more traditional, quantitative research techniques like questionnaires and advertising pretesting. "MR should never be substituted for conventional market research," she said, a strong believer in the approach but convinced that clients should not put all their eggs in one methodological basket.[34] Herzog also headed up the ARF's Motivation Research Committee, her main mission there to try to find a way to validate motivation research results (the ARF awarded grants to those who made a convincing case that they could figure out how). "They'd give a platinum eye tooth to be able to concoct projective techniques that they could prove to have a high correlation with consumer behavior," wrote George Christopoulos, speaking of how motivation researchers were continually being challenged on the validity of their findings.[35]

With the scads of behavioral scientists practicing motivation reasearch in the 1950s having all trained differently and having specialized in different areas of expertise, it wasn't surprising that interpretations of consumers' behavior varied significantly. SRI, especially, with its class-oriented perspective, often zigged when its more Freudian and Adlerian competitors zagged. Burleigh Gardner told his tobacco company client that smoking in America was not a surrogate experience for suckling, for example; rather, puffing on a cigarette was a sign of virility, potency, and vigor in our dog-eat-dog society. For Dichter, however, the partaking of anything indulgent—tobacco, soft drinks, liquor, candy—came with a heavy dollop of guilt, meaning such products had to be presented in advertising as somehow morally acceptable, a well-earned reward. Dichter, as Viennese as a linzer torte, also was partial to looking at financial institutions as father figures, who would best avoid scolding customers for managing their money like children who had broken into their piggy banks. Dichter had won over automakers when he told them to market hardtop cars because they "fooled the id," that is, appeared to be more fun than a sedan but didn't carry the guilt associated with a convertible. Somewhere Freud was smiling, as his theories were not just more well known than ever but successfully applied in the real world by some of the best and brightest minds of the day.[36]

Because motivation research interpretations and recommendations varied so much based on which school of thought the practitioner subscribed to, clients were occasionally known to hire two firms with different views in order to cover their bases. Executives for Dial soap, for example, hired both Dichter and Gardner to tell them if the brand's advertising platform focusing on its deodorizing abilities was on or off target. Dichter came back with a conclusion that, based on his investigation with consumers, the positioning was way off and that this feature in fact "scared them away." People were afraid of losing their distinctive body odor as a marker of identity, he thought, meaning Dial should move away from its deodorant claims. Gardner, in contrast, coming from SRI's more sociological perspective, found that consumers liked the soap for its power to deodorize, and that Dial should thus stress this aspect in its advertising. After listening to the presentations, executives at Dial's ad agency, Foote, Cone and Belding, had reservations about both sets of findings, fairly typical of Madison Avenue's big egos and considerable skepticism for others' ideas. Needing some closure, the Dial executives eventually leaned toward Gardner's "business as usual" recommendation, a not unusual case of expending a major amount of time, money, and energy to arrive at basically the same place.[37]

Not only did interpretations and recommendations differ among motivation research practitioners; once in a while, the same one would contradict himself. Dichter, for example, had said in 1955 that men liked to flex their muscles after getting out of bed in the morning, this simian reflex making them want to eat something crisp and crunchy (apparently ignoring apes' fondness for bananas). A year later, however, Dichter was telling the people at Quaker Oats that their product was in a good place, psychologically speaking. The mushy hot cereal was "emotionally associated in the consumer's mind with a time of sacrifice, virtue and idealism," he now thought, Quaker Oats having "acquired a virtuous character among morning cereals." What a difference a year makes, those keeping track of Dichter's musings might have concluded.[38]

Some of Dichter's thinking might have been occasionally inconsistent and often wacky, but it was clear that the man was crazy like a fox. His view of the postwar American consumer ("an entirely new type," he believed) was particularly insightful and, looking back half a century, way ahead of its time. Consumers wanted to be treated as individuals, to take part in the marketing process, and to be creative, he said, all things that are today considered progressive thinking. In March 1956, Dichter started publishing *Motivations*, a newsletter providing yet another outlet for his outpouring of opinions on what he described as "the changing American taste." Dichter's company was bringing in just $750,000 a year from his thirty or so clients, charging $250 for a half-day session, but it appeared he was about to make his move, having recently landed a $60,000 study for a major automaker.[39] By hiring Dichter, advertisers also had to deal somehow with concepts like food being gendered (rice, tea, and cake were feminine and potatoes, coffee, and cake were masculine, while some foods, notably roast chicken and oranges, were bisexual). Other, brand-specific motivation research findings, such as Bufferin users having more "hostility towards life and living" than Anacin users, were interesting but difficult to incorporate into advertising, some agency people complained, contributing to the bigger argument that Freud had a place in psychology but not on Madison Avenue.[40]

Some of those religiously inclined definitely didn't think Freud belonged on Madison Avenue, convinced as they were that motivation research was theologically questionable at best. "For what purposes are you studying human nature?" asked *Christian Century* in 1957, suspicious about the motives behind motivation research. "'Scientific curiosity' can mean game-playing [or] Peeping Tom-ism," the magazine felt, worried that delving deep into the recesses of peoples' minds could "serve unworthy or selfish aims." Between the lines was that more committed Christians perhaps saw motivation research as a potential threat to religion's own inquiry into human nature, and that this secular version might produce answers leading some away from the flock.[41] As motivation research gained momentum in American business, *Fortune* could see there might be major danger ahead because of its controversial ways. "MR is undoubtedly an invasion of the consumer's privacy, but the real trouble . . . is that it often seems to recommend . . . that U.S. business nourish . . . weaknesses and pander to them," according to the magazine, with only time to tell if the technique would be recognized as "a legitimate exploitation of healthy human desires."[42]

Alice in Wonderland

Even within market research there were those who wished motivation research would just go away. And just because they wore bow ties and had advanced degrees, researchers with differing opinions about how best to gather and interpret information were not above mixing it up once in a while. A battle royal of sorts occurred in 1955, for example, when two factions in the field had it out at a symposium hosted by the University of Illinois. Motivation research supporters, known in the trade as the "small-sample" people, took issue with the way that their archrivals, the "large-sample" people, were going about their business, and vice versa, the two sects verbally duking it out like the Hatfields and McCoys. "It isn't science, it isn't research, and the rules are made up to suit the occasion," stated Darrell B. Lucas, professor of marketing at New York University, firing an opening salvo at his small-sample foes, who preferred in-depth interviews over quantity. "The use of conventional market research techniques may be unscientific and misleading," countered Irving

Gilman of Dichter's IMR, taking some wind out of the numbers-oriented large-samplers on the other side of the room.[43]

More than ideological supremacy was at stake in this marketing research showdown, of course, as the victor would be able to snag more clients and command higher fees in the increasingly competitive field. The two groups had been enemies since the very beginnings of motivation research but had enjoyed an uneasy truce, recently broken at a conference when large-sample king Elmo Roper, who had been studying public preferences since his days as a jeweler in Iowa in the 1920s, threw the gauntlet down at the feet of some small-sample soldiers. The hostilities escalated at a couple of other conferences leading up to the University of Illinois symposium where all-out war was declared by both sides. Just when it looked as though the opposing schools of thought would engage in a do or die battle, small-sample general Gilman produced an olive branch by suggesting that different research problems called for different research solutions. Calmer heads prevailing, large-sample general Lucas conceded that the Advertising Research Council, of which he was technical director, was already "addressing itself to the validation of all methods used in motivations research," enough of a peace offering for the two sides to, for the moment, simply agree to disagree.[44]

Although they were increasingly in the minority, anti–motivational researchers made some very good points. The idea that conscious factors, such as need, usage, and price, were less relevant than subconscious ones, such as fear, insecurity, and sexual frustration, was simply ridiculous, critics sensibly argued, especially as consumers were, James Vicary's claims notwithstanding, seemingly conscious when they shopped. Albert J. Wood, who had long run his own research firm and even employed motivation research techniques back in its early days, felt the need to place a full-page ad in the *Wall Street Journal* to warn businesspeople of what he in 1957 considered an "Alice in Wonderland" approach. If consumers weren't buying your product, Wood told readers, it was because it was inferior in some way to a competitor's, not because "it reminds them of the time their mother beat the old man over the head with the frying pan."[45]

Not helping motivation researchers' cause was the fact that some in the field did not hesitate to make recommendations to their clients based on sometimes questionable research. One psychologist, for example, told an airline that it should use only middle-aged stewardesses because, depth interviews had led him to believe, this would ease passenger's fears by tapping into their "mother complex."[46] Motivation researchers' penchant to use any tool in the clinical psychologist's kit also sometimes backfired. One ad agency, Ruthrauff and Ryan, used hypnosis to probe consumer attitudes, which was almost universally considered ethically out of bounds. Those induced into such a state apparently did make some interesting revelations, but the firm quickly backed away from the technique, very aware of the criticism it would no doubt continue to draw (and this before Packard's book was published).[47]

More effective in preventing motivation research from completely dominating market research was the pure genius of one man, Alfred Politz. Elmo Roper's innovative questionnaires for business in the 1930s and for the army during World War II blazed the trail for Politz to take this kind of market research to a whole new level in the 1950s. Politz believed that consumers' purchasing behavior was too complicated for any single research methodology to provide all the answers, but he had faith in their ability to answer direct questions honestly, with no particular need to view their responses as simply the tip of a psychological, bottom-heavy iceberg. Besides any deep, underlying motives and wide range of possible social purposes that buying something served, Politz and his supporters held, there were the simpler, less glamorous issues of price and convenience to consider (not to mention the actual benefit of consuming the product). And whereas Dichter would talk his head off to anyone and everyone with a marketing problem and a spare $500, Politz worked just for a handful of Fortune 500 clients like Coca-Cola, Chrysler, DuPont, U.S. Steel, Bristol Myers, and Kimberly Clark. (In exchange for a long-term contract with one of these blue-chip companies—and at least $200,000 in annual fees—Politz agreed not to work with a competitor.) In 1956, Politz's firm brought in a tidy $2.5 million from its small portfolio of clients, far more than archrival Dichter was making. Politz was considered so important by his select clients that they would not think of approving a new ad campaign until he blessed it, a sign of confidence that few outside consultants were awarded.[48]

Even when he was just a child in Berlin, it was clear that Alfred Politz was an extraordinary person who would very likely achieve great things. A protégé of the famed nuclear physicist Max Planck, Politz wrote his first scientific paper when he was fifteen (the title alone—"The Deduction of Gravity from the Concept of Mass"—indicates its sophistication). Politz earned his Ph.D. in theoretical physics when he was twenty, but he chose not to be a physicist, knowing the Nazis would want to use his knowledge for military applications. Although he wasn't Jewish, it was no secret that Politz was part of a resistance movement in Germany, and he decided to flee to Sweden along with his fiancée. (Fearing they would be discovered and taken back to Germany, Politz and his fiancée changed hotels almost daily.) While marketing a popular German headache remedy in Sweden, he "fell in love with advertising," as he later put it, this romance only intensifying when he arrived in America in 1937 and read Claude Hopkins's 1923 textbook *Scientific Advertising*. (Politz even had the book republished in 1952, believing it was as relevant as ever.)[49] Politz initially felt his English was not good enough to work in the field, however, and planned to market the headache remedy in America. The FDA didn't approve the pill, however, making Politz wonder what he should do with his life. "Which profession makes the money with the least intelligence?" he asked himself, and the answer was, of course, advertising.[50]

Referred by pen magnate Kenneth Parker, with whom he had become friendly while in Europe, Politz began working for the legendary Elmo Roper. Despite his boss's unquestionable research skills, Politz was astounded by how unprofessional and illogical the field in general was, and, much like Dichter, he was determined to reinvent it. After a few years with Roper, Politz joined Compton Advertising but took issue with the kind of research the agency's biggest client, Procter and Gamble, was doing. In 1943, Politz, whom Martin Mayer considered to be a "complete empiricist" and "didactic by temperament," opened his own research company, with the mission to purge the "illogical" from the field via his buttoned-up questionnaire design and reliable sampling methods. With his wife as secretary and receptionist (his fiancée had come to America in 1939, and they soon married) and Jane Klein, his assistant at Roper (who had majored in math at Bryn Mawr), Politz's firm quickly became what Mayer called "the most respected and incorruptible research organization in the business." Colleagues on both the client side and the agency side were more likely to believe the results of his studies than those of any other outside consultant—perhaps the ultimate compliment in the business. Politz's company became the hot research shop of the 1950s with a staff climbing to 220, his self-imposed noncompete condition of one client per industry making it sort of a status symbol to work with him.[51]

What made Politz a virtual overnight success was mostly his unsurpassed technical chops, particularly the random sampling technique he introduced in 1944, followed a few years later by what was the first national probability sample used in commercial research. Early clients included *Life* magazine and DuPont, the research managers at these companies considering him far ahead of everyone else in his ability to accurately test advertising and media effectiveness. Politz's scientific background was apparently paying off, his skill in knowing what questions to ask, how to interpret answers, and what conclusions to make putting him in a league all his own. Also not hurting his career was his boundless energy, something that we would probably label today as "hyperactivity." Politz typically ran to work from his apartment in Manhattan, including the eight floors of stairs leading up to his office. He also occasionally ran to client meetings, during which he was known to do handstands. Before speeches or presentations, Politz would often walk on his hands, this stunt another way to burn off nervous energy and squeeze in a quick workout. Some considered him the Bill Bernbach of market research but, given his athleticism, postwar fitness king Jack LaLanne may be more like it.[52]

Looking back, it was particularly interesting that one of the biggest battles in American business at mid-century was being waged between Politz, an ex-German physicist, and Dichter, an ex-Austrian psychologist. Politz used motivation research as the perfect foil to make his brand of research seem that much more credible, while Dichter, hardly a shrinking violet, sniped at Politz and his methodology. "But, Alfred, ten thousand times nothing is still nothing," Dichter reportedly once said to Politz after being criticized for using small samples of respondents, claiming that his kind of qualitative research went far deeper than more numbers could ever do. For Dichter and others, qualitative research was literally "qualitative," meaning it offered users quality (versus quantity). A strict adherent to the Hopkins school of "reason-why" copy, Politz was not particularly impressed with the new kid on the advertising block, however, believing that mass psychology was a contradiction in terms and motivation research mostly smoke, little fire. "Qualitative statements are just quantitative statements made at a sloppy level of approximation," he once said, a direct attack on Dichter and his school of market research. If Dichter and Vicary promoted motivation research in the media to get business, Politz got plenty of publicity by attacking it. Motivation research was fine as one research tool, but it was hardly the panacea its proponents claimed it to be, Politz said over and over in speeches and articles, and it certainly wasn't a provable technique. Dichter, meanwhile, always insisted his findings were as "provable" as anyone's, maybe not numerically but substantively as a result of his interdisciplinary approach to the social sciences.[53]

In many ways, however, the two men were much more alike than one might have thought. The much publicized ideological divide between them was smaller than appearances suggested, much of their tongue wagging no doubt a way to each get mentioned in the trades and, increasingly, the mainstream media. The truth was that Politz often included Dichterian un-structured interviewing in his process, not seeing any inconsistency with his otherwise straight-as-an-arrow approach. In fact, Politz had eighteen psy-chologists on staff in 1956, his firm routinely using motivation research to ex-plore consumer attitudes and shape questionnaires.[54] And like Dichter, who with his psychological mumbo-jumbo maddened more traditional business-people, Politz didn't make too many friends with his vitriolic criticism of the field. (He once suggested that the Advertising Research Foundation be dis-solved, creating a firestorm of controversy.) As with Dichter, interpretation of research findings was where the magic resided with Politz, and his clients hung onto his every word even while knowing they'd probably be criticized for the way they were running their businesses. Something else the two re-search giants shared were hidden flaws that deeply affected their personal lives. Dichter was, according to his son Thomas, not a very good father and an absolute cheapskate, never having fully recovered from his childhood pov-erty despite his later financial success. Politz, meanwhile, was an alcoholic, which was a big factor in the downfall of his firm in the 1960s.[55]

The Engineering of Consent

Someone else, meanwhile, was determined to put anyone who used moti-vation research immediately out of business. With his book *The Hidden Persuaders*, which was published on April 29, 1957, Vance Packard was on a mission to send Freud and his intellectual descendants right back to Vienna. The book clearly reflected the views of a Methodist farm boy who grew up during the Depression, when business was blamed for America's economic woes and FDR's social reforms were popularly viewed as the nation's salva-tion. After graduating from Columbia University's School of Journalism, Packard wrote for the *Boston Herald*, Associated Press, and the Crowell-Col-lier group of magazines, his beat the never dull foibles of human behavior. As biographer Daniel Horowitz explained, *The Hidden Persuaders* grew out of an article Packard wrote for *Reader's Digest* that was never published. Edi-tors at the magazine had read a 1953 article in the *Reporter* about advertisers' increasing use of psychology and asked Packard to write about "the increased use of 'motivational research' by merchandisers." Soon after Packard submit-ted his article, however, *Reader's Digest* decided to begin accepting advertis-ing and the piece was shelved, as the magazine worried that some companies or agencies would be less than happy about it. (Packard still got paid.) Not long after that, fortuitously, an editor at the David McKay Company, a publisher, asked Packard if he had any book ideas, and he sent her the squashed article. The editor, Eleanor Rawson, liked what she read, and encouraged him to expand the piece into a book. While keeping his day job as a staff writer at *American Magazine*, Packard did research for the book and then wrote the whole thing in less than two months. (As part of his research in 1956, Packard spent a few days with Ernest Dichter at his castle, an investment of time that would prove fruitful for both men.) Packard sent off the manuscript for *The Hidden Persuaders* just as he lost his job at the magazine when it folded, a perfect example of one door opening as another closes.[56]

The door that opened for Packard with the publication of *The Hidden Persuaders* would turn out to be a very big one. Although in hindsight a book critical of advertising and its effects might be considered a sure-fire success, this was hardly the case in 1957. A popular book attacking advertising hadn't been published in more than twenty years, a clear sign that challenges to the postwar American Way of Life were not particularly welcomed by the publishing business. A number of movies had, however, presented admen as an especially sebaceous bunch, and advertising itself (especially television commercials like Anacin's "drumbeat" spot) had primed Americans for a harsh critique of the industry. By the late 1950s, the huckster had become the urban version of the guy in the black hat, his intentions suspect at best. With motivation research, Packard had the perfect device to announce that something was really rotten in the state of advertising, capitalizing on Americans' fear of outside forces of all kinds.[57]

Advertisers' powers deriving from motivation research were truly amazing, almost unearthly, according to *The Hidden Persuaders*. Advertisers knew things no one else had the ability and perhaps right to know: why Americans loved big cars, why we were afraid of banks, and why housewives went into a peculiar mental state as soon as they walked into a supermarket—knowledge that was certainly beyond the limitations of familiar market research tools like surveys and questionnaires. Even more alarming, consumers themselves didn't know the answers to such questions, the book implied, only advertisers apparently possessing this kind of knowledge because of their secret weapon. Why men really smoked cigars or how women chose shoes could be determined exclusively through shrinks' bag of tricks, Packard suggested, the bottom line being that businesspeople knew Americans better than the population knew itself. Given such a premise, should it have been at all surprising that *The Hidden Persuaders* shot up the best-seller list?[58]

To his credit, Packard acknowledged the legitimate reasons why marketers were originally attracted to motivation research, because the technique filled a gaping hole in market research. Motivation research grew out of marketers' frustration with being misled by consumers when they asked them what they wanted, according to Packard, which was a fair assessment of the situation. A classic case was, at least the story goes, when an automaker in the early 1950s learned from surveys that consumers wanted a "sensible" car, meaning something that was easy to park, made tight turns, and had no unnecessary frills. Knowing the customer is always right, the automaker produced such a car, but, surprisingly, few people bought it. Instead, huge, Technicolor, tail-finned models were flying off dealer lots, making executives seriously question the kind of market research they were doing. "Errors of this sort convinced manufacturers and advertisers that they must explain the subconscious areas of the consumer's mind," Packard wrote in an article for *Harper's Bazaar* coinciding with the release of his book, in order to "discover his hidden quirks and yearnings, and guide their campaigns of persuasion accordingly."[59]

Somewhat paradoxically, Packard challenged much of the validity of motivation research but also believed that its techniques were "subject to scrutiny on the ground of morality" and that the approach "raise[d] ethical questions of the most disturbing nature." Specifically, motivation research enabled marketers to exploit consumers' weaknesses, encouraged irrational behavior, and, perhaps worst of all, was "reshap[ing] our national character in the direction of self-indulgent materialism." Advertisers "buil[t] into products the same traits that we recognize in ourselves," Packard wrote, viewing the marketplace, more than ever, as a prime opportunity to carve out one's unique identity. "Studies of narcissism indicated that nothing appeals more to people than themselves," Packard continued, "so why not help people buy a projection of themselves?" Packard aligned himself with the theologian Reinhold Niebuhr, who believed that the cycle of production and consumption was a vicious one, and that the American Way of Life was more about enslavement than freedom. Despite his setting up shop on both sides of the fence—motivation research didn't work as well as its users claimed and yet it worked too well— *The Hidden Persuaders* became a phenomenon, striking a very loud chord with the American public.[60]

The Hidden Persuaders became a number-one best seller, staying on the *New York Times* top nonfiction list for a year. (Packard's next two books, *The Status Seekers* and *The Waste Makers*, did the same, this run of three best sellers in a row something that few if any other nonfiction authors achieved.)

People from all walks of life read *The Hidden Persuaders*, a hit not just in the United States but around the world (especially in Germany, another country with a reputation for fearing outside forces of all kinds). Harry S Truman was a fan, as was the Soviet writer Boris Pasternak, illustrating the book's broad appeal. Professors assigned the book in college, knowing that young people would eagerly read it to find out how they were being brainwashed. (Todd Gitlin, a cofounder of the Students for a Democratic Society who would go on to become a noted media critic and author, remembered the book as especially popular among more "curious" students like himself.) A police officer, learning that Packard was in the back seat of a car he had pulled over, did not issue a ticket to the driver. *The Hidden Persuaders* would earn Packard $350,000 over the course of his life (about half of that in the first year after its publication), which was not bad for an unemployed magazine writer.[61]

It would be an underestimation to say that Packard's 1957 book (its cover featuring an apple with a fishhook in it) caused quite a sensation. Packard went directly after marketers' attempts to sell commodities and candidates through motivation research, their techniques consistent with what Edward Bernays had called in the title of a 1947 essay "the engineering of consent." (Not only was Bernays, the "father of public relations," a Viennese Jew like Lazarsfeld, Herzog, and Dichter; he was also Freud's nephew, his views heavily steeped in psychoanalytic theory.) Packard offered a laundry list of examples of how motivation researchers were using the secrets they had uncovered to make Americans buy things they didn't want or need. "Tenderness" was all the rage in cosmetics advertising to counter the rise of career women and their alleged loss of femininity; cigar smoking was simply an adult version of thumb sucking and all of its oral implications; fountain pens were phallic symbols, hence the popularity of larger ones; deep freezers offered comforting assurance against Depression and wartime shortages; and convertibles were surrogate mistresses, offering men youth, romance, and adventure while not risking their marriages (well, maybe a little).[62]

Simply put, Packard's book (which cost $4) went off like a bombshell, shocking even many in the media with the news that psychology was being used on Americans without their knowledge. "Depth psychology now probably has more influence on the U.S. at large through business and advertising than through clinics or mental-health programs," *Time* reported soon after the book was published, describing motivation research as "a solidly entrenched and complex specialty." Through "mass psychoanalysis," the magazine informed readers if they already didn't know, motivation research was being used to "condition" consumers, much as Pavlov's dogs were trained to salivate at the sound of a bell. The goal of advertisers was to have Americans "drool at the sight or sound of a selling gimmick with a symbolism that appeals to the subconscious," as *Time* rather clunkily saw it, quite a scary scenario if Packard knew what he was talking about.[63] As media-friendly a book as can be imagined, *The Hidden Persuaders* was soon a true cultural phenomenon. The name of the book quickly entered the lexicon of consumer culture, even occasionally appearing in ads, ironically enough. "All-weather linings are the hidden persuaders in these toppers that wear well on the campus," ran an ad for coats in the *Chicago Daily Tribune* in 1958, the copy perhaps designed to attract the attention of college students intrigued by the best seller.[64]

While his exposé of advertising and diatribe against motivation research was a tour de force of investigative journalism, Packard told the story in an entertaining way, making the book very readable. Two-thirds of the biggest ad agencies were already using motivation research, Packard informed his readers, their messages "trained to meet the needs of the id."[65] In addition to all the ad agencies practicing motivation research, the few dozen firms specializing in the technique were taking unfair advantage of Americans too, Packard claimed. Marketers were thus exploiting basic human needs like security, self-worth, and love, he explained, needs identified through motivation research techniques and then turned into advertising fodder. Even Liberace was sold to the American public based on motivation research, Packard claimed, as the then young but ever fabulous showman was targeted to older women using Oedipal symbolism. "Because it deals with the unconscious, MR is probably more influential than Gallup polling, and potentially more sinister," *Time* concluded, warning Americans to be on the lookout for hidden persuasion.[66] Seeing this kind of response, Packard's publisher took full advantage of the pandemonium the book created. "Are You Being Brainwashed?" asked the headline for the "3rd Big Printing" of the book in June, telling readers of the *Wall Street Journal*, "If you are in advertising, publicity, marketing, selling, manufacturing, finance or are a consumer, this book is for you or, perhaps about you!"[67]

Although his strategy would backfire, Packard singled out one man in particular for the problems motivation research was causing: it was Ernest Dichter, working his black magic from his imposing twenty-six-room fieldstone mansion perched 536 feet above the Hudson River, who presented the largest threat to the nation's collective subconscious. ("The castle is the perfect setting for a mad scientist—one half expects to find Bela Lugosi working over a corpse in the library," said one visitor.)[68] It was true that Dichter was partial to watching children watch television in his mountaintop lair, secretly observing and taping them like a technology-equipped ogre in a Grimm fairytale. His "psycho-panel" too had evil intent, according to Packard, the anxieties and hostilities of hundreds of guinea pigs exposed and exploited. Whether it was manipulating children, playing upon our hidden weaknesses, appealing to our illogical or irrational sides, prying into our sexuality, or, perhaps worst of all, using "subthreshold effects to slip messages past our conscious guard," motivation research, especially that carried out by its king, Ernest Dichter, was bad news for the American public.[69]

Of course, Dichter felt that Packard missed the point of motivation research, that it was about fulfilling individual's wants and needs rather than fueling the nation's economic growth. Was it that enemies of motivation research feared change or independence, Dichter wondered, or were they threatened by an alternative to the Edenic paradise that awaited them in another life?[70] Either way, rather than make marketers realize the error of their ways—that turning Americans into more avid consumers through motivation research was a bad thing to do—*The Hidden Persuaders* made the public and the media that much more interested in the links between business and psychology. The book was especially helpful for the person most responsible for hidden persuasion. "Ironically, Packard's attack was more successful in bringing Dichter notoriety and business than it was in catapulting him into the ranks of widely read social critics," Daniel Horowitz wrote. The exposé was more effective than any public relations campaign the researcher himself could have orchestrated. Dichter had been relatively well known, but now he was a celebrity, his office flooded with requests for media interviews and invitations for speaking appearances around the world. (Dichter actually wrote Packard a letter in January 1958 thanking him for making "the whole world motivation research conscious," and specifically for all the work he was getting because of the book.)[71] Rather stocky now, his once bright red hair more coppery-blond, the fifty-year-old Dichter was clearly enjoying the power he wielded as the world's most famous (and infamous) motivation researcher. Like a god, "he hurls down thunderbolts in the form of reports aimed at influencing a nation's spending patterns," observed an article in the *Los Angeles Times* six months after Packard's book was published, Dichter's parsing of depth interviews ("analysis in the best Freudian tradition," the newspaper's reporter stated) the thing that separated him from the rest of the motivation research pack.[72]

Caveat Emptor

The reviews of *The Hidden Persuaders*, not surprisingly, came fast and furious. A. C. Spectorsky of the *New York Times* called it a "fascinating book . . . frightening, entertaining and thought-stimulating to-boot."[73] The word "frightening," in fact, seemed to pop up in many reviews. "It is this research which is providing the accurate psychological information undergirding current advertising campaigns and which accounts for the frightening effectiveness of many of them," wrote the *Library Journal* in its review, with the *Los Angeles Times* calling it "easily the most frightening book of the year."[74] Some reviewers considered the book much more than "frightening." "This description of the role of psychologists and sociologists in the planning of subtle mass campaigns to manipulate the responses of consumers and voters is a hair-raising progress report on the march of time toward 1984," wrote Jerome Spingarn in the *Washington Post*, wondering if the need to keep our GNP growing was worth the price of dabbling in the "black art of motivational research."[75] Many reviewers recognized Packard's ability to send an alarm while somehow keeping a sense of humor, however. "Hucksterism has entered a new era, in which its oracle is the psychologist," the *Atlantic Monthly* wrote in its review of Packard's book, finding it to be not only "often appalling" but also "often very funny, and continuously fascinating."[76]

At the very least, *The Hidden Persuaders* seemed to serve as a loud wake-up call for many. The *Christian Science Monitor* felt that, if nothing else, the book opened "to fuller public view an important area in American life which deserves closer scrutiny than it has been getting," a fair observation.[77] "There seems to be some reason to keep a pretty close watch on the motivations of the motivation researchers," agreed the *Springfield Republican*, its wait-and-see attitude another voice of reason.[78] Others felt that given what Packard had uncovered, reason was not called for. "It isn't later than you think—but it's late enough," Gilbert Seldes fretted in his piece for the *Saturday Review*, hoping the exposé would be a resource for smarter Americans to resist falling for such hidden persuasion.[79]

Those aligned with the interests of business were naturally a lot less impressed with Packard's book. "How can the reader judge how much of the findings should be taken literally and how much should be discounted as unsubstantiated, or just plain wrong?" asked Leo Bogart of the *Management Review*, a complaint many businesspeople made.[80] (With his journalistic style, Packard provided no footnotes in the book, making it difficult to track where he got his information.) With Pierre Martineau, one of the top motivation researchers in the country and one of the strongest advocates for the technique ensconced at the *Chicago Tribune*, the paper not surprisingly thought hidden persuasion was little to worry about. "Our libidos may get a pushing around as this thing gains momentum, but, with everyone pushing in a different direction, it is doubtful that we will be shoved off balance," thought Henry Greene of the paper, giving his readers the sensible advice, "caveat emptor."[81]

Besides arguing that Packard offered no real evidence that anything he wrote in his book was true, critics of *The Hidden Persuaders* were also quick to point out that he didn't mention any of motivation research's (many) failures or, for that matter, explain how and why motivation research was so successful when psychoanalysis itself often was not. Packard also seemed to ignore the obvious fact that he was, for goodness sake, writing about advertising people—those who were in the very business of making exaggerated and sometimes suspect claims. No advertising person worth his or her salt would admit they had wasted clients' good money, after all, making pretty much everything in *The Hidden Persuaders* subject to a certain level of skepticism. Also largely omitted from Packard's book was the fact that advertisers had long exploited socially defined needs rather than focus exclusively on rational features and benefits; any number of things—beer, perfume, cars, soap, cigarettes—had been sold this way for decades. Some went so far as to say that the success of the best seller proved Packard's point more convincingly than its contents—that the wild popularity of the book was a direct result of its appealing to consumers' unconscious fears of being unwittingly manipulated. "It would be interesting to see the results of a word association test done on the book's title," Henry Greene contemplated in his review, raising a question that was on a number of people's minds: Was *The Hidden Persuaders* the quintessential example of hidden persuasion?[82]

Those on the other side of the market research fence were just amazed at how much attention the book was getting, especially among the intelligentsia. Elmo Roper was surprised at how many smart people were concerned about so-called experts' ability "to diagnose the mass mind with . . . diabolical cunning," doing his best to show that there was really little to fear. Roper thought motivation research to be "two parts research, three parts high I.Q., and in some instances five parts chicanery" and Packard's book "straight out of Orwell," each pure fiction intended to shock. And rather than being "hidden," motivation researchers wanted as much publicity as they could get, Roper argued, their "success" stories mostly fabricated in order to get more business. Last, motivation research wasn't even that similar to psychoanalysis, he pointed out, as the latter was never manipulative, incapable of being directed to the "masses" and always taking a lot of time and costing a lot of money. "The techniques are not that good, nor is the public as naïve as [Packard] fears," Roper concluded, urging Chicken Littles to rest assured that the sky wasn't falling.[83]

Like market researchers, advertising executives were naturally not pleased with how Packard portrayed their industry. (Having a copy of the book in one's office was tantamount to displaying a copy of *The Communist Manifesto*.) Besides being just plain malicious, *The Hidden Persuaders* had grossly exaggerated admen's powers, those in the industry were quick to point out, for nobody was able to do what Packard claimed. At least advertising was acknowledged as propaganda, some said, while Packard's book alleged to be pure truth. One writer suggested that Packard himself may indeed actually have used motivation research to write the book, and that the fears he raised were designed to penetrate the reader's subconscious. Even worse, perhaps, Packard was considered by some conservatives to be a Marxist, his book intended to undermine the capitalist system.[84]

Even if it was a paper lion, *The Hidden Persuaders* appeared, at least superficially, to have an immediate effect. Soon after the book was published, the country slipped into a recession, making Packard wonder if Americans were indeed fighting back marketers' best efforts to turn us all into consume-at-any-cost robots. (Dichter viewed the recession more as a psychological phenomenon than an economic one, with those who "are frightened by continued prosperity" most to blame. Some consumers, in other words, felt sinful about the postwar boom and their good fortune, and stopped spending money in order to relieve themselves of their guilt.)[85] But in October 1957, the USSR launched its Sputnik satellite, another sign that we might be spending too much time gorging on the horn of plenty and that we might want to reexamine our priorities as the Cold War heated up. The nation's love affair with one of the primary symbols of postwar material abundance—the big-as-a-battleship, chrome-encrusted automobile—also seemed to be over, making Packard believe that the hidden persuaders may have been exposed.

For Packard, however, motivation research was just a symptom of a disease, the real issue being "the growing power of admen," as he called an article he wrote for the *Atlantic Monthly* in September 1957. As "masters of our economic destiny" and the "major wielders of social control in America in this second half of the twentieth century," the advertising industry was doing anything and everything it could to keep consumers buying. As Tocqueville and Emerson had each famously observed, consumption was without a doubt in Americans' blood, but the nation's current ability to produce things faster than people could use them up was a huge problem for marketers. In order to keep the economic train running (and their own power intact), advertisers' knowledge of the American consumer had to become increasingly deeper, which demanded new, ever more ambitious efforts. "Straining to become more persuasive," America's thirty-three hundred ad agencies were indeed spending millions of dollars in research, BBDO's "National Panel of Consumer Opinion" a good example of how far they were willing to go. The thousands of housewives included on the panel were ready, willing, and able to tell the agency pretty much anything it wanted to know about their lives and consumer habits, a window into the American female. Gallup's "Mirror of America" was another resource for marketers to get intimately familiar with consumers, a bank of people designed specifically to reveal what factors most influenced their buying decisions.[86]

These methods were sociological small potatoes compared to motivation research, however, with Packard seeing the use of psychiatry to "get inside the consumers' subconscious" as an abuse of advertisers' tremendous power. Most of the larger ad agencies had psychologists, psychiatrists, or both on their staffs, some of them spending millions of dollars on a single motivation research study (McCann-Erickson had recently forked out $3 million for one such megastudy). Another Chicago-based agency had not long before put no fewer than eight leading social scientists (two psychoanalysts, a cultural anthropologist, a social psychologist, two sociologists, and two professors of social science) together in a hotel room and had them watch television for twelve hours straight, this Sartrean experience intended to generate brilliant insights otherwise unobtainable. "When our motives are fathomed the experts then shape and bait psychological hooks which will bring us flapping into their corporate boats," Packard wrote in the article, which extended the argument of the book, the cognitive expeditions of motivation researchers like catching fish in a barrel.[87]

A few months later, agency man Fairfax Cone felt the need to reply to Packard, also using the *Atlantic Monthly* as a public forum for his views. Cone admitted that while nobody really needed a washing machine, electric shaver, or five shades of lipstick, no one was forcing Americans to buy such things, and agencies were hardly the omnipotent monsters Packard believed them to be. "Advertising is not a plot," he made clear, and agency men were just salespeople doing their jobs by trying to understand their customers as best they could. The tools of motivation research—depth interviews, projective picture and word association tests, and even the galvanometer (lie detector)—were used in many fields outside advertising, Cone explained, and were employed by agencies in order "to know more about people and how they think and what they want and why." Simply making advertising better was the real purpose of motivation research, he insisted, something that was good for everyone in America.[88] As soon as he saw Cone's reply to his article, however, Packard dashed off a note to the editor of the *Atlantic*, his rejoinder published in the very next issue. Packard took exception to Cone's use of the word "plot" and distanced himself from such an allegation. "I never used the word, nor suggested that a plot existed," he wrote from his home in New Canaan, Connecticut, but there was little doubt that his wildly popular book had created the idea among the public that some kind of sinister doings were afoot within the hallowed halls of American business."[89]

With a hot property on his hands, Packard hit the road to deliver speeches based on his best seller, taking the opportunity to also rebuff counterarguments by Cone, Dichter, and others. Preaching to the choir, so to speak, Packard gave a talk to the Religious Education Association in Chicago in November 1957, his beef with Madison Avenue not surprisingly playing very well with this particular audience. Packard was sure to make it clear at the luncheon that motivation research was a product not of the lunatic fringe of business but rather of big corporations, two-thirds of them having already used it in their marketing plans. More alarming was an industry report predicting that psychologists would be consulted on all major ad campaigns by 1965, this news no doubt making some of the pious choke on their weak coffee. Packard continued to single out his arch-nemesis, Ernest Dichter, for leading the motivation research parade, the man most responsible for "creat[ing] a mood in America that will assure a larger market for . . . product[s]." Dichter's running theme of "moral consumption" was in direct opposition to Packard's thesis that the nation was becoming "more self-indulgent, more pleasure-minded, more materialistic, more passive, more conforming," all of this "more" a sure sign of the decline of American civilization.[90]

Coming back to the overarching theme in his book, marketers' invasion of the privacy of our minds through psychology and their encouragement of irrational behavior were certainly concerning, but it was the change in American character that worried Packard most. The pressure for consumers to become bigger and better ones—arguably the guiding philosophy of the

American Way of Life, at least in the postwar years—reminded Packard of French geese that were force-fed grain to make them (and specifically their livers) fat, as the need to keep up with our increasing production capacity made us "overstuffed with material goods." Leading economists like Sumner Slichter of Harvard had solidly endorsed the idea that continued growth relied on increased consumer spending, such a policy making "overeating" an official act of patriotism. Were our own livers ready to burst? Packard wondered.[91]

The Science That Spills the Beans About You

Those doing the feeding, meanwhile, had other things on their minds. At ARF's first annual convention following the publication of Packard's book, admen were understandably nervous about the attention their industry was getting. Advertising, ground central for the huckster, had always been viewed with suspicion if not outright distrust, but *The Hidden Persuaders* had opened up an entirely different can of worms. "The general public is beginning to stir uneasily," reported *Business Week* in its coverage of ARF's 1957 meeting, noting that ad agencies had recently taken special measures to move their motivation research operations to the "back room" in a somewhat ironic effort not to be labeled "hidden persuaders."[92]

The champions of motivation research were quick to defend advertising and marketing from the bold, perhaps irresponsible claims Packard had made in his book. In his *Motivation in Advertising*, published in the fall of 1957, Pierre Martineau considered the idea that advertising was nefarious "bunk," the well-read research director of the *Chicago Tribune* making it clear that it was simply a means of communication.[93] Louis Cheskin's *How to Predict What People Will Buy*, also published that fall, backed up the central motivation research premise that consumers' behavior was often emotional and nonrational, the director of the Color Research Institute showing how the sometimes inexplicable purchase decisions of shoppers spoke for themselves.[94]

Packard wasn't the only one capitalizing on American paranoia in the late fifties and making the public stir uneasily when it came to advertising, however. Perhaps inspired by Dichter's interpretation of the prune (and Packard's windfall), Ernest van der Haag, coauthor of the 1957 book *The Fabric of Society*, considered motivation research "Madison Avenue witchcraft," seeing it as part of Americans' perfectly justified fears of being brainwashed by both politicians and advertisers. "This specter looms large in the recent publicity [of] the success of Communist governments in brainwashing some captive Americans as well as their own citizens," van der Haag wrote in a 1957 article in *Commonweal*, the fact that other mindbenders like lobotomies and tranquilizers were in the news only adding to people's jitters. For van der Haag, however, motivation research "top[ped] it all," outdoing these other methods of head shrinking because it was openly used. "The attempt of advertisers to exploit and manipulate the *unconscious* desires and fears of their prospects the better to sell them frightens everybody frightened by his unconscious desires," he wrote, which meant nearly everyone had cause for alarm.[95]

Although undeniably schlocky, van der Haag's book had a certain populist appeal and, more important, helped turn Packard's anti–motivation research platform into more of a social movement. Also, van der Haag gave what had to be the most interesting definition of motivation research: a "drama in which the public plays Gretchen to a business Faust inspired by a Madison Avenue Mephistopheles." However, van der Haag thought that by focusing on motivation research Packard was missing the larger issue. It wasn't hidden persuasion that was the real problem when it came to advertising, he thought, but rather that it was often useless, wasteful, and, worst of all, annoying. "It raises false ambitions, it fosters de-individualization and it tends to destroy culturally important values by homogenizing tastes," he alleged, these harms being much greater than some silly kind of research. Yet another book published in 1957, William Sargent's *Battle for the Mind*, also argued that mind control was a real threat, nearly all of us vulnerable to the power of suggestion if the conditions were right (more accurately, wrong). Induced fatigue or anxiety could make one confess crimes one didn't do, convert to others' ideologies, or believe "planted" messages, Sargent explained; even psychoanalysis was something that could and occasionally did replace reason with fantasies. Equally sensational and pulpish as van der Haag's book if not more so, Sargent's added fuel to the fire that all kinds of hidden persuasion were afoot.[96]

With advertisers, and their potentially wicked ways, now in the spotlight, editors at publications who would otherwise have little interest in the workings of market research soon joined the attack against motivation research. Usually content to explain how things work, *Popular Science* got caught up in motivation research mania after the publication of *The Hidden Persuaders* and these other books, illustrating how concerns about consumer manipulation were running amok. In the magazine's November 1957 issue, an article entitled "The Hidden Reasons Why You Buy a Car" by Gary Shipler, Jr., described "the science that spills the beans about you" and specifically how "De-troit is using the knowledge to influence your choice among the new models." In the post-needs marketplace of the late 1950s, carmakers had to dig deeper to get consumers in new wheels, Shipler explained, discovering that when it came to automobiles, transportation had taken a back seat to social and mate-rial status. Through motivation research, carmakers had reportedly learned that most Americans would be prouder owning a new automobile than if they were elected president, such research gems showing how high emotions ran when it came to what they were seen driving. "For the average guy, the modern servo-mechanism is a substitute for the palace servant who comes at the crook of a royal finger," one motivation researcher pontificated, according to Shipler, just the kind of stuff the Big Three automakers wanted to hear to remind them that their product was the single most powerful expression of social status in America.[97]

Regardless of all the public scrutiny, it was full steam ahead for motiva-tion research on Madison Avenue, the attacks leveled against the technique and its practitioners only making more businesspeople intrigued about what it could possibly do for their brands. Their services in more demand than ever, motivation researchers were now determined to refine their methods and find ways to apply their kind of findings to new and different business problems. "For most companies the question is no longer 'Shall we use motivation re-search?' but 'How can we best use motivation research?'" said one motivation researcher at the 1957 ARF meeting, implying that along with the greater op-portunities came greater expectations for the technique to work its magic.[98]

Despite the dustup that Packard's book and its knockoffs created, research-ers had good reason to be confident about the future of motivation research. Although it was difficult to get precise numbers on how many motivation research suppliers and users there were in 1957, one study showed that in the past three years both had doubled. More encouraging, motivation research was continuing to spread beyond its bread and butter, consumer goods, with clients in all kinds of industries increasingly signing up for studies. Motiva-tion researchers were earning a particular reputation for being able to iden-tify negative associations held by consumers toward a product or service and then offer a more opportunistic positioning. GE, for example, was putting young models in its ads for electric blankets after finding out through mo-tivation research that many consumers thought its product was just for old and sick people (as well as downplaying its electrification, which some found scary). New Mexico's Travel Bureau discovered via motivation research that many Americans viewed its state as hot, desolate, and boring, leading tourism officials to present it in advertising as green, bustling, and fun.[99] Also, the Book-of-the-Month Club had decided to downplay rather than emphasize how many books members received each year after motivation research revealed many felt "a sense of inferiority" about their growing pile of unread tomes.[100] With news of such remarkable turnarounds making the trades, it's not surprising that more clients were hoping that motivation research could mend their own ailing product or service. Another, much more powerful kind of hidden persuasion was about to be revealed to the public, however, one so frightening that it made ordinary motivation research seem perfectly innocent.

3

The Secret Pitch

Unless we are much mistaken, the next phrase that
is going to be on everyone's tongue is "subliminal
advertising."

— *Nation*, October 5, 1957

I n June 1958, a short story called "The Communicators" appeared in a popular pulp of the day, the *Magazine of Fantasy and Science Fiction*. In the story, a group called "the Communicators" (note linguistic resemblance to "the Communists") had developed a way to insert invisible messages into television programs, a propaganda device as powerful as any that could be imagined.[1] During one program, "the Communicators" flashed this message, as the story went, "at the speed of microseconds, so fast that the conscious eye and mind could not perceive" it:

CITIZENS OF TEXAS
The Communicators
Are Your Friends!
Obey the Austerity Program!
BE STRONG!
BE DISCIPLINED!
WORK AND OBEY!

Edward S. Aarons, the writer of the story, described the horror of this kind of particularly insidious hidden persuasion: "The viewer knew nothing of this

steady, monotonous invasion of his subconscious senses. . . . The Communicators had learned how . . . to keep the people enslaved. . . . It was hideous,
cruel, vicious. It made a mockery of man. It fashioned puppets out of the
millions who lived and worked and obeyed in reply to the tug of invisible
strings."[2]

Not coincidentally, an intense, very real fear was pervading the American
landscape precisely when this magazine was on newsstands, a fear that was a
response to a new form of advertising that bore an uncanny resemblance to
that of "the Communicators." It was called subliminal advertising—a major
portion of a psychological phenomenon known as subliminal perception.
Subliminal perception was motivation research on steroids, taking Freud's
theories of the power of the unconscious to a terrifying extreme. And like
motivation research, subliminal perception was possibly a device that could
spin the wheels of capitalism as fast as possible, a weapon in the Cold War
that was at its chilliest point. The subliminal perception craze didn't last very
long—just about a year, in fact—but represented a seminal moment in postwar American history, both reflecting and shaping the hyperparanoia of the
times.

A Question of Science

Before Freud gave it some respectability, the concept of subliminal perception had quite the dubious history, made most famous by one F. W. H. Myer,
a nineteenth-century seer. For Myer, subliminal perception entailed methods such as automatic writing, table rapping, and the ouija board in order to
communicate with the dead, forever imprinting the idea with a sense of both
mysticism and surrealism.[3] Scientific experiments in subconscious perception also dated back to the nineteenth century, with studies first appearing
in academic journals around 1900. As with motivation research, however, it
would be Sigmund Freud who would put subliminal perception on the psychological map through his focus on the human subconscious. One of Freud's
theories was that subconscious "observations" often appeared in dreams, this
idea tested in 1917 by an Austrian neurologist, Otto Poetzl. In his experiment, Poetzl flashed slides of landscapes for one-hundredth of a second to
a group of subjects, the images hardly registering in their consciousnesses.
Asked what their dreams were the next day, however, the subjects reported
details found in the landscape scenes, confirming Freud's theory.[4] The seeds
of subliminal perception had been planted, no one suspecting that one day

millions of people around the world would be keenly interested in and concerned about the results of similar, rather esoteric tests.[5]

It would take a different continent, a different field, and four decades for these seeds of subliminal perception to fully bloom. Subliminal possibilities for advertising were first raised in 1913, but there could not have been a more fertile time and place for them than psychology-obsessed, watch-your-back postwar America. A year or so before subliminal advertising exploded on the scene, Edward (E. B.) Weiss had been prescient about its rise, writing a column about something very similar for *Ad Age* in May 1956. After hearing about some experimental research that involved electrical stimulation of the brain, Weiss immediately understood the possibilities of manipulating people's behavior, specifically the role that advertising might play in that: "It is entirely probable that some day at least some of the brain's functions may be controlled by *external* electrical penetration. (I get frightened as I write this!) . . . Will advertising, some day, consist of broadcast electrical discharges beamed to penetrate specific brain areas for the purpose of shaping specific buying behavior patterns?"[5]

Just a little more than a year later, many of Weiss's fears were realized, as a technology-based form of external brain control swept through the advertising industry and American society like a tornado. News of subliminal advertising first leaked out sometime in late 1956, when few people were really sure what it was or if it even existed. "For a year or so tantalizing rumors have been drifting around the fringes of Madison Avenue," reported *Business Week* in September 1957, "rumors about a startling kind of 'invisible' advertising that sells products while leaving buyers unaware they are getting a sales pitch." With a press conference held by a never-heard-from-before company named Subliminal Projection, Inc., in mid-September, however, the cat was fully out of the bag, the story all the more interesting given that motivaton researcher James Vicary was behind it. Not just the business press but also mainstream media jumped on the story, although some reporters did have to look up "subliminal" in a dictionary, as they were not familiar with the word or how to use it in a sentence. Many readers too no doubt consulted their handy Webster's to learn that the word meant "below the threshold of consciousness or beyond the reach of personal awareness," which did not ease their concerns in the least.[6]

Subliminal Projection's big news was that it had conducted a test of subliminal advertising in an undisclosed New Jersey movie theater over a period of six weeks. A "strange mechanism" had been fitted onto the film projector, as reported on the front page of the *Wall Street Journal*, and, over the next month and a half, 45,699 movie patrons were "subjected to 'invisible advertising' that by-passed their conscious and assertedly struck deep into their subconscious."[7] Once every five seconds, a message was flashed throughout a film for 1/3,000th of a second—too fast to be seen by the human eye but supposedly long enough to be registered in the subconscious of the unsuspecting movie-goers. After "COCA-COLA" and "EAT POPCORN" were invisibly blinked on the screen, sales of each reportedly jumped (18 percent and 58 percent, respectively), these results quickly becoming the talk of not just Madison Avenue but also Main Street.[8]

After a century or so of lurking in the dark netherworlds of science and psychology, subliminal perception had been suddenly thrust into the light of day. A media sensation on their hands, Vicary and his two partners, industrial film producers Francis C. Thayer and Rene Bras, quickly hired a marketing consultant, Richard E. Forrest, as well as a patent attorney, Floyd Crews of Darby and Darby of New York. For the forty-two-year-old, well-respected Vicary, subliminal perception could be not just his gravy train but a way to make history. "If we get a patent," he said in September, "it will represent the first time one has been issued on what is essentially a social invention." Indeed, some likening the situation to Freud receiving a patent on psychoanalysis, the implications for humankind just as significant.[9] Subliminal Projection was moving quickly to find a movie chain willing to screen subliminal messages and to find advertisers interested in showing "invisible commercials" in theaters or on television, determined to strike while the iron was red-hot. Flashing an image at a three-thousandth of a second wasn't yet possible on television, but experts believed some kind of subliminal perception equipment could be developed for the medium (which would be able to slip subconscious messages past current monitoring methods).[10] Subliminal Projection was testing the use of pictures of brands in place of slogans or messages as televisual stimuli, the company licking its chops at the prospect of flashing as many as ten thousand impressions during a fifteen-hour broadcast day (one every five seconds).[11]

To his credit, Vicary never imagined subliminal advertising being used without viewers' knowledge. Broadcasters would announce that subliminal advertising was about to be shown, he envisioned, with the messages then embedded in the entertainment portion of the show. Television would thus consist purely of entertainment, with no need for commercial breaks. Advertisers and network executives were intrigued but cautious about such an amazing possibility. "This business is so mysterious I would not judge whether we would use it until I was exposed to it myself," said William Dye,

advertising manager of Rheingold beer. Stockton Helffich, manager of conti-
nuity at NBC, was "very interested," as long as Subliminal Projection fulfilled
the Communications Act of 1934 requirement to identify the product and
advertiser on all shows. Ad agency people were the most delighted about a
world in which commercials were effective but never seen or heard, and on-
staff psychologists at Madison Avenue shops were sent off to study whether
such a thing could really work and, if so, how.[12]

James Vicary was an unlikely candidate to be the principal firer of what
the press would soon call "the advertising shot heard round the world." Vicary
grew up during the Depression, the son of an often unemployed opera singer.
At fifteen, he took a summer job at the *Detroit Free Press* and, with no one
else around to do it, was told to poll voters for the upcoming mayoral election. The teenager's survey came within six-tenths of a percent of the actual
results—an amazing feat, even by today's standards—and a market researcher
was born. Vicary continued his polling work at the University of Michigan
(sharing an early IBM computer with Jonas Salk) and then held various research jobs with the likes of the J. L. Hudson department store and the Gallup
Organization. In 1945, he started his own company, unaware of course that
a dozen years later he would be, for a little while at least, the most famous
market researcher in the world and at the epicenter of a fierce battle involving
business, politics, science, and even religion.[13]

Vicary's company was not the only group wading in the subliminal perception waters, however. A team of New York University psychologists, led by
Sheldon Bach and George S. Klein of the Research Center for Mental Health,
had recently conducted experiments in subliminal perception that supposedly
proved the effectiveness of what was perhaps the ultimate form of hidden persuasion. These tests involved showing a drawing of a man's face with a neutral expression to two different groups of subjects, one group exposed to the
face with the word "happy" flashed underneath it and the other with the word
"angry." True to form, the first group considered the face it had seen to be a
happy one and the second an angry one, this manipulation of judgment serving
as additional "proof" of the power of subliminal perception.[14] Auditory tests too
had shown that some high-frequency sounds could not be heard by the human
ear but still registered in the consciousness, additional evidence for the validity
of subliminal perception. Furthermore, there was little doubt among scientists
that sight was selective, that we all choose from an astounding array of visual
impressions to determine what we see, with the "discards" from our field of vision probably still rattling around somewhere in the recesses of the brain.[15]

News of Vicary's movie theater test and the New York University experiment prompted others to disclose that they too were investigating subliminal perception. On June 22, 1956, the BBC revealed that it had conducted what was likely the first large-scale subliminal perception experiment when it flashed a four-word message, "Pirie Breaks World Record," to five million viewers at one twenty-fifth of a second during a television program. After the show (*A Question of Science*, featuring a ballet), the scientist in charge of the test told viewers that a news item had been shown during the program and asked anyone who had seen anything to write in. Of the 430 replies the BBC received, 130 had the message (about English middle-distance runner Gordon Pirie) almost right, and twenty had it exactly right, strong evidence that there was something to subliminal perception. Other anecdotes stemming from this test—one lady repeatedly waking up with the word "break" on her mind, and another who reported she inexplicably kept thinking about the runner and his record—also suggested that there was something to this mysterious psychological phenomenon.[16] Many Americans agreed, although they were much more concerned with how such an apparently powerful tool could be used and misused by those with evil intent. If subliminal perception could possibly be employed to alter viewers' opinions about advertisers on television shows like *The Restless Gun* or *December Bride*, why couldn't it be used to make citizens more amenable to socialism, say, or for that matter homosexuality?

Another company, New Orleans–based Experimental Films, was also blazing the subliminal perception trail, marketing a device to be placed on retail counters that flashed subliminal messages at the point of sale. This company claimed that it had filed patents for the process a year before Subliminal Projection and, in fact, that it began investigating subliminal perception as early as 1950, way before its competitor had thought of the idea. Headed by Hal Becker, an assistant professor of neurology at Tulane University, and Robert E. Corrigan, a psychologist at Douglas Aircraft, Experimental Films had developed a piece of equipment originally designed to help educate challenged students but, with Vicary's machine making headlines, was now apparently suitable to teach consumers a thing or two.[17] In addition, a Hollywood company called Westin-Rush Productions announced in late 1957 that it was inserting subliminal scenes into a sci-fi film to, as *Business Week* described it, "heighten the dramatic effects."[18] Until there was proof to the contrary, why not take advantage of the tantalizing possibility that the invisible was more compelling than the visible?

Welcome to 1984

"Welcome to 1984," wrote Norman Cousins, editor of the *Saturday Review*, as soon as he got word of the goings-on in subliminal perception. Cousins was just one of many among the intelligentsia to take subliminal perception extremely seriously, even though there was no real evidence that Vicary's machine actually worked or that the other tests were scientifically valid. Vicary had applied for a patent for his invention but didn't disclose any information about its process, making it impossible for even other experts to tell whether he could achieve what he said he did. Still, the thought of invisible commercials was terrifying to many, especially to those of the belief that American culture had already become overcommercialized because of television. Cousins worried that not being able to see such commercials meant the inability to filter out any and all undesirable messages, the implications of this raising all kinds of red flags. Subliminal perception was the worst case of "breaking and entering" that could be imagined or, even worse, the psychological equivalent to radioactive fallout, he thought. "If the device is successful for putting over popcorn, why not politicians or anything else?" he asked readers, the disguising of people's real character the most frightening aspect of subliminal perception.[19]

An editor for another magazine for brainy types, the *Nation*, was similarly distressed upon hearing the news of Vicary's allegedly successful test. This writer considered subliminal advertising to be a "hybrid spawn of psychology, Yankee know-how and economic enterprise (greed)," a concoction that was bound to have a powerful kick. Even if subliminal perception couldn't make one partial to things one didn't already like, as Vicary made clear at the press conference, there were plenty of things around that most people did like but had the better sense not to buy. "How do we know someone can't persuade us to mortgage our insurance and buy a sports car with the ill-gotten cash?" the editor worried, such out of control consumerism bad for individuals and the country as a whole. Even more alarming was how subliminal perception could be used beyond advertising, specifically with regard to already tense international relations. "If an ad agency can massage our subconscious into thinking that another nice, cool glass of beer is just what we want," the *Nation* continued, "still another kind of agency might tickle our egos into thinking that it would be fun to annex Mexico or show the Russians who's boss." During this especially icy period of the Cold War, "subliminal advertising is the most alarming and outrageous discovery since Mr. Gatling invented his gun," the magazine concluded, much more than a clever device to sell more popcorn and Coca-Cola in movie theaters.[20]

Other intellectuals chirped in on what was, for those with any kind of libertarian streak, a sitting duck of an issue. Gerald W. Johnson of the *New Republic* considered the advent of subliminal perception to be "immense," rivaling and perhaps surpassing in scope what he believed to be the pinnacle of American advertising up to that point, Senator Richard Nixon's 1952 "Checkers speech" (which made the public quickly forget about the Republican vice president candidate's acceptance of $18,000 in illegal campaign contributions from certain oil and real estate interests).[21] The misuse of subliminal methods could be said to be a "rape of the mind," as Marya Mannes of the *Reporter* suggested after attending Subliminal Projection's press conference, one of the journalists in the room who went after Vicary and his partners "like terriers."[22] Expectedly, Vance Packard, the man who had recently exposed the underbelly of Madison Avenue to the world through his best seller *The Hidden Persuaders*, continued his diatribe against motivation research and offshoots like subliminal perception. Rather than "subliminal," Packard thought the new development should be called "surreptitious," "sneaky," or "*sub-rosa*" advertising, these terms more accurately capturing the covertness of it all.[23]

Left-leaning members of the intelligentsia were not the only ones of the Fourth Estate to attack subliminal perception and its promoters more like a pack of wolves than a roomful of terriers. Editors of newspapers representing a cross-section of political bents added to the feeding frenzy surrounding subliminal perception, bringing the issue into local communities across the country. "Our first reaction is skepticism . . . but our second reaction is one of bitter resentment," wrote the editor for the *Milwaukee Journal*, the captive audiences of subliminal advertising perhaps to become "victim[s] of brainwashing such as even the Communists haven't conceived."[24] Writers at major newspapers seemed thrown for a loop, not sure what to make of this thing that came completely out of the blue. "There's a new scheme afoot to capture the minds of men and stimulate them into action," announced the *Chicago Tribune*, confessing that "the whole thing worries us."[25]

One reporter who attended Subliminal Projection's demonstration of its "new monster of motivational research" was Phyllis Battelle of the *Washington Post*, who concluded that Vicary and his partners had "no business meddling in my id." "This may well be the most appalling assault upon the human brain and nerve system yet concocted by civilized man," she wrote, very much bothered by what she had seen and heard (or not seen, one might say).[26] Bat-

telle presented a scary scenario of the near future should advertisers decide
to use the device: "Visualize the parlor in 1960. A housewife is sitting plac-
idly beside her husband, watching a Western-Mars movie on their 62-inch
screen, when suddenly she darts to the bathroom and begins shampooing her
hair. The reasons for this sudden suds-conscious urge, of course, is that every
five seconds during the movie, the name of a dandruff-remover shampoo
has been flashed into the dark depths of her mind. Without logic—possibly
without dandruff—she has obeyed this Svengali impulse."[27]

With brainwashing on Americans' minds, so to speak, during these hypersensitive days of the Cold War, journalists not surprisingly saw subliminal perception through a reddish lens. The Russians were far ahead of us
in mind control techniques (just as they were in the space race with their
recent launch of Sputnik), most would agree, but subliminal advertising suggested we were catching up fast in the former. "America has come up with a
new propaganda 'weapon' with the most sinister thought-control potentials
of anything ever devised," declared Donald Craig of the *Los Angeles Times*,
extremely alarmed at "this amazing device [that] fires images electronically
into the subconscious mind." Because reason was beyond the ability of the
subconscious, viewers could only accept and carry out what they had been instructed, Craig believed ("subliminal is merely a fancy word for hypnotism,"
he thought). Should viewers not execute their command, "mental strife (neu-
rosis) results," the amateur shrink told his many readers, a recipe for disaster
if there ever was one. "What will happen to us average Americans if enough
comrades . . . get their hot little Red hands on enough subliminal projec-
tions?" Craig asked Los Angelenos.[28]

Many readers no doubt felt likewise, some taking the time to let newspaper editors and fellow Americans know what they thought about subliminal perception. One man wrote to the editor of his local newspaper that
Vicary should be "shot out of a cannon," something that not even the harsh-
est media critics had suggested. (Getting wind of this particular news item,
Vicary promptly got an unlisted phone number, fearing he might indeed become cannon fodder or suffer an equally unpleasant fate.)[29] Some readers responded with outrage after learning about subliminal advertising, surprised
that citizens hadn't yet risen up en masse to destroy this new thing before it
destroyed us. "Our religions cannot stand up to a technique which can fix
our consciences without our knowledge or slightest awareness," wrote James
Staver of Chicago in his letter to the editor of the *Washington Post*, and "our
republican institutions and our democracy" too would go out the window

should subliminal advertising come to pass. America would become "a god-less slave society beside which sovietism [*sic*] would be freedom," Staver posited, trying to rally others to drop the bomb on this "clearly subversive and immoral" threat.[30]

Although the media and more alarmist readers were expectedly critical of subliminal perception ("the intellectuals will land hard on the idea," Vicary correctly predicted right after Subliminal Projection's announcement), the Christian community were unrelenting in their criticism. Religious leaders seemed most concerned that subliminal perception would be used to make Americans binge on alcohol and sleeping pills just as easily as on popcorn and Coke, their guard let down for who knows what.[31] The *Christian Century* considered Vicary's unwitting moviegoers "guinea pigs," his invention a "demon" that represented "another giant step toward the robotization of man." The editor of the magazine called for "massive retaliation" because of the significant possibilities of brainwashing, telling readers not to go to the movies, to turn off their televisions, and to avoid buying brands that were sold subliminally, should the "invisible monster" go beyond the experimental stage. How could Americans be sure, for that matter, that subliminal commercials weren't already on the airwaves, a disreputable advertiser or two sneaking invisible messages into shows they produced? The *Christian Century* had one more bit of advice should what it considered a "nearly ultimate weapon" be activated: "Plan a down payment on some sort of Walden Pond," the magazine suggested, the little blinking machine to be feared almost as much as an atomic bomb.[32]

Rather than react with the usual pulling of hair and gnashing of teeth, however, some journalists chose a lighter approach to tell readers about subliminal perception. "Last week (*Drink!*) we attended a private demonstration of subliminal advertising, about which (*Coca-Cola!*) there has been so much talk of late, and we are happy to report that the dangers of this new variety of hucksterism have been greatly (*Drink!*) exaggerated," wrote an editor for the *New Republic* in early 1958. The editor thought the whole thing so ridiculous that it didn't deserve to be treated seriously, and he couldn't understand why so many of his colleagues were so upset by it. "Others can say what they please, but as for ourselves, we sat through the entire demonstration and have not observed the slightest alteration in our accustomed mode of life, except for a trifling matter of a constant and insatiable thirst for (*Coca-Cola!*)."[33] Other critics found the story neither terrifying nor absurd, thinking that if subliminal perception could really be limited to advertising, there was no harm done, since viewers were exposed to commercials anyway. Still others pointed out that anything "subliminal" could be said to be at the core "sublime," which made advertising of that persuasion awe inspiring and morally pure, linguistically speaking at least.[34] Such placid voices were in the minority, however, a tiny murmur in the sonic boom that James Vicary had set off in telling the world about his startling discovery.

A New Band in Human Perception

Everyone was interested, of course, in what those who would use and benefit most from subliminal perception thought about it. The initial response by Madison Avenuers was more of skepticism than of wild enthusiasm or anger, the general consensus being that the thing probably didn't work and, even if it did, was not very practical. Before even getting into the ethics of it, agency people had serious technical concerns about subliminal perception—mainly, if and how it would work on television. The scanning process used in broadcasting would limit how fast messages could be flashed, for one thing, and the brightness of television screens could make the messages invisible to some. Individuals' receptivity to subliminal perception (like hypnosis) seemed to vary greatly, making it at best a highly inefficient advertising technique in a time obsessed with reaching a mass, homogeneous audience. Viewers' different perception levels was yet another wild card that cast major doubts on the viability of subliminal television commercials, all of this unpredictability making advertisers not take them very seriously. And if subliminal perception could work only as a "reminder," as Vicary and the New York University team had each said, new products would have no place in it, immediately disqualifying it as a primary tool of advertising.[35] Most important, however, subliminal advertising was totally opposite from the tried-and-true technique of delivering the simplest and least ambiguous message as many times as possible, the thought of burying key selling points considered anathema if not downright ridiculous. Perhaps subliminal perception could somehow even make consumers steer away from their clients' products rather than attract them likes bees to honey, a nightmarish scenario that by itself was virtually enough to nix the idea.

Besides the rational reasons to take subliminal perception with a very large grain of salt, some agency people agreed it raised serious ethical issues, especially if it was used in political campaigns. What if the Russkies used it to get a Red elected president, both advertising professionals and laypeople worried, a prime example of how any kind of "rogue" psychology was considered a potential weapon during the Cold War. At least one agency executive, Frank Ewing, head of Fensholt Advertising in Chicago, felt obliged to personally write to Federal Communications Commission chair John C. Doerfer, wanting not only to do his patriotic duty but also to shield his industry from further public scorn. "I strongly believe that subliminal advertising is distinctly un-American," Ewing told Doerfer, "that its perpetrator belongs in the same class as the Russian brainwasher and the Japanese thought police or the office snoop." *Advertising Age*, the leading industry publication, agreed, its official stance in opposition to subliminal perception (contrary to motivation research, which it had no quarrel with whatsoever).[36]

Despite their public pooh-poohing of Vicary's experiments, Madison Avenuers decided to investigate "subconscious" television commercials on their own, with experiments in subliminal advertising "going on all over town," as one researcher had put it in late 1957. At least so far, however, agency researchers were finding "the secret pitch" to be an unequivocal bust. "The results of tests are tending in a negative direction," understated Virginia Miles, motivation research director for McCann-Erickson, in assessing her agency's experience with subliminal commercials. "Our experiments don't excite us," echoed Peter Langhoff, director of research at Young and Rubicam, also of the opinion that ads should remain directed to viewers' consciousness.[37]

That subliminal advertising was not only further damaging admen's reputation—something almost impossible to do—but, even more frustrating, also proving to be useless was doubly bad news for an industry already under attack. "If there are more furrowed brows than usual these days along Madison Avenue," wrote an editor for the *New York Times* as 1958 began, "the reason is probably to be found in two words that have only recently become current: 'subliminal advertising.'"[38] It was clear that Americans' fears of being brainwashed to buy products they didn't want or to elect another Stalin or Lenin president was far more intense than admen's interest in or intent of doing so, but this did little to make people relax. "With some of the public already grumbling over the increasing torrid love affair between psychology and advertising," as *Business Week* put it, invisible commercials were felt to pose too tempting a possibility for a business already distrusted and disliked.[39]

In addition to wanting to know admen's position, many were also especially interested in where the founding father of motivation research, Ernest Dichter, stood. Would Dichter bless this new limb growing off his tree or did he want it chopped off as soon as possible? Seeing the media flock to one of his main competitors, Dichter responded to the news of Vicary's magical device almost as quickly as it flashed, issuing a press release blasting what he considered a "gimmick." Dichter was actually a firm believer in the science of subliminal perception but worried that Vicary's stunt would "give the whole field of motivation research a bad name" (and, almost as bad, that he might lose his spot as the top dog of motivation research). Embedding a subliminal component in normal advertising was one thing, Dichter thought, but secretly embedding messages directed to unsuspecting viewers was just bad form. "The American consumer [will] resent and resist any form of subliminal manipulation," he made clear in his statement, distancing himself from such amateurish parlor tricks, which could bring down the whole motivation research house.[40]

Not about to let Dichter or anyone else ruin his big day in the sun, however, Vicary quickly responded to the tsunami of criticism leveled at him and to the esteemed doctor in particular. Dichter's public response to the experiment was "grossly inept," Vicary told reporters, simply sour grapes that he hadn't come up with the idea first. In addition, the notion of subliminal perception being ideological dynamite was just ridiculous, he counterpunched; it was no more sinister than your run-of-the-mill commercial. "It's like saying a whiff of a Martini is worse than a swallow," Vicary explained, subliminal perception being "simply a new band in human perception, like FM."[41] Vicary also astutely argued that subliminal perception was a form of free speech and thus protected by the Constitution. "We have a freedom to communicate," he said, ready to go all the way to the Supreme Court if his right to do so in his particular way was threatened.[42]

Knowing there would be at least some negative reaction to their stunning announcement that subliminal perception could cause people to act in a certain, desired way, Vicary and his partners also cleverly acknowledged that their machine could possibly be used for nefarious purposes. Viewers should be informed when they were being subjected to subliminal perception and/or have the government regulate it in some way, Vicary openly suggested, trying to avoid the inevitable associations with "mind control." By admitting some controls and regulations would be in order regarding subliminal perception, he was not only deflecting some of the mountain of criticism leveled at him but also adding to the credibility and perceived power of his invention. If the thing didn't work or work very well, why bother to suggest putting in place measures to limit its capabilities? For Cousins of the *Saturday Review* and others, however, this wasn't nearly enough. "There is only one kind of regula-tion or ruling that could possibly make any sense in this case," he proposed, "and that would be to take this invention and everything connected to it and attach it to the center of the next nuclear explosive scheduled for testing."[43]

Not everyone felt that Vicary's gizmo (and perhaps Vicary himself) should be blown to kingdom come as soon as possible, however. One psychologist employed by a large New York ad agency felt that subliminal advertising would actually be more honest than the soft-sell school that currently reigned in the industry, which used much more subtle tactics (often grounded in motivation research) to persuade consumers to buy particular brands. Furthermore, not many commentators had a problem with there being fewer commercials on television, ever-increasing "clutter" making the programs themselves seem almost incidental. "There is much to be said for any technique that could make TV commercials invisible," a *New York Times* editor thought, "and the more invisible the better."[44]

For Vicary, this was precisely the point, thinking that television com-mercials that didn't intrude on viewers' consciousness were a far better thing than the constant interruption of shows with annoying ones. Vicary in fact claimed that he had invented his machine because he thought that commer-cials were well on the way to taking over the shows, subliminal perception being the logical way to quell advertisers' clamor for more and more on-air time.[45] Interestingly, no one seemed to be asking viewers what they thought of subliminal advertising, specifically whether some people would prefer a secret pitch over repeated (and repeated) commercial interruptions, just as Vicary argued. If there had to be advertising to make television "free," a rea-sonable argument could go, why not have it be invisible?[46]

One of the few academics to support subliminal perception was Ross Wil-helm, a marketing instructor at the University of Michigan. Wilhelm believed that we were actually already being exposed to subliminal perception on a daily basis; each time we drove by a billboard too fast to read it, quickly flipped through a magazine or newspaper, or rapidly changed television channels, a blip was registered by our unconscious. "And yet, have we to date seen any of the dire effects which the critics have feared?" Wilhelm asked, thinking that both the fears and the expectations of subliminal perception were very much exaggerated.[47]

Other supporters of subliminal perception were simply interested in mak-ing a fast buck off it should it turn out to be a flash in the pan. Hal Roach, Jr., the Hollywood producer of movies and television shows, for example, announced he was going to make a feature film called *ESP* using subliminal perception, even hiring a UCLA psychologist to help the screenwriter figure out what kind of "dramatic and emotional" images to insert into the script. What was perhaps an even more solid endorsement of subliminal perception came from *Vogue*, of all places, which featured a new "subliminal dress" in an issue in late 1957. The black silk crepe dress "tapp[ed] out its message to the subconscious," according to its maker—if true, quite a bargain even at its $160 price tag.[48]

Further developments in the process also kept the subliminal perception fires burning even as they was being doused by the press. In Scotland, for instance, a researcher named Peter Randall said he had made subliminal perception "new and improved" through something he called, shades of a B-movie, "Strombonic Psycho-Injection." Three-fourths of an audience would receive subconscious messages if his method was used, Randall claimed, making subliminal perception much more effective than via Vicary's clunky process.[49] Consumers certainly weren't clamoring for subliminal perception, but a fair number of people were determined to bring it to the marketplace anyway. "Seldom has a bandwagon been leaped upon with so little question or reason as has the 'subliminal' bandwagon," thought R. M. Kidd of Nowels Advertising in Tucson, Vicary's dream machine sparking not just an intense industry debate but a true cultural phenomenon.[50]

The Best-Kept Secret of 1957

Somehow, the subliminal perception craze was about to get even crazier. Getting quite the scoop, *Motion Picture Daily* learned that Vicary's experiment did indeed take place in a New Jersey movie theater (the Fort Lee Theater in Fort Lee, revealing what McCann-Erickson executive and Northwestern University professor Steuart Britt called "the best kept secret of 1957"). The manager of the theater reported there was no increase in sales of either popcorn or Coca-Cola, however, directly contradicting what Vicary and his partners had claimed in their announcement. His findings publicly refuted in the trade newspaper, Vicary met with Charles Moss, head of the group that operated the theater, allegedly to share his "test data." Moss seemed satisfied with what he saw (or perhaps pocketed), issuing a neither-here-nor-there statement that "this type of subconscious advertising could help increase sales" but needed "additional testing." Vicary had asked *Motion Picture Daily* to run a retraction of its story alongside Moss's statement, but the newspaper refused, sticking to its guns that the test hadn't generated an additional mouthful of corn or sip of pop. Covering his bases, Vicary made it extra clear that the New Jersey test was done just to file its patent application and urged advertisers and networks to do their own testing before using it commercially.[51]

Despite the very real possibility that the most notable test to date on subliminal perception was, as one writer put it, a "chimera," the debate surrounding it intensified. Gay Talese weighed in on subliminal perception for the *New York Times* in early 1958, coming up with what had to be the best euphemisms for it: the "phantom plug" and "psychic hucksterism." Talese was one of the reporters present when Subliminal Projection announced its coup and screened a short film to demonstrate the process. During the mini-movie of underwater life (*Secrets of the Reef*), 159 messages of "COCA-COLA" flashed amid the fishes on the screen, although no one could see them. Feeling no particular desire to consume carbonated beverages of any sort, Talese went beyond the call of duty by returning a few days later to the company's offices for another dose of subliminal perception. This time he was subjected to even more (230) blinks of "COCA-COLA" but still felt positively pop-free. Talese was, in his own words, "not consciously aware afterwards of any urge to drink Coke nor did [I] consciously experience any visions, dreams, drives, images, trances, inclinations, or hangovers that were not directly attributable to conscious guzzling of something else than Coke the night before."[52]

A Subliminal Projection spokesperson was quick to explain why Talese did not become the least bit fizzy. "You don't like Coke," he told Talese, making it clear that subliminal messages worked only in a "reminder" capacity and were thus unable to change people's existing preferences. "They might move you to do something you like doing," the spokesman added, "but they'll never make a Democrat out of a solid Republican and they'll never make a Scotch drinker out of a teetotaler." Members of the New York University team agreed with this assessment, one of them describing the effects of subliminal perception along similar lines. "Subliminal messages do not put something new into the mind," the NYU professor explained, but rather "activate what is already there." Critics' fears of subliminal perception being an agent of brainwashing—specifically that many flag-waving Americans would instantly be flying the hammer and sickle over their houses after being blinked a couple of hundred times by a Communist in capitalist's clothing—were apparently unwarranted, according to those most familiar with it.[53] Talese's colleague at the *Times*, Jack Gould, expressed this same idea with a bit more wit. "The system might nudge a woman in the direction of buying a form-fitting accessory," he winked and nodded, "but if the distaff viewer is well equipped she won't hunger for the unnecessary."[54]

Despite his levity, Gould, the newspaper's television critic, was actually a lot less amused than Talese about subliminal advertising creeping onto the airwaves and into Americans' minds. "The idea of secretly tickling a viewer's subconscious so that he will be hypnotically impelled to cozying up to Big Brother or, even better, buy the king-sized package, threatens to supplant toll video as the season's most engaging controversy," Gould wrote in late 1957, referring to the (twenty-years-too-early) rumor that pay television was on the way. For Gould and others, the threat of subliminal perception being used for political propaganda was the real issue, far more dangerous than someone unintentionally buying a sports car instead of a sedan. "If the villainous chaps along Madison Avenue" were successful, Gould thought, "designing politicians presumably would go on to [flashing] something such as 'STALIN,'" this latter possibility making subliminal advertising essentially dead in the water before it even had a chance to swim. "Most of the lively assaults on subliminal perception have come from those deeply concerned over the specter of remote control of national thought," the television critic believed, these parties' worst fear being that "it will be no time before the electorate goes goose-stepping to the polls."[55] One of Gould's bosses agreed that the cost of such "free" advertising would be too great, believing that an ultrasoft sell was an "eerie development" that raised "alarming possibilities." "Certainly any form of message-delivery that sneaks up on the subject without his consciously seeing, hearing, tasting, smelling or feeling it is an invasion of privacy such as George Orwell hardly dreamed of," an editor for the newspaper suggested to his readers.[56]

Cooler heads prevailed, however, among those more familiar with the science of subliminal perception. Richard Barthol, an associate professor of psychology at UCLA, thought flashing "COCA-COLA" could very well make viewers not want to consume the soda but rather do things that linguistically resembled the brand of soda. Because "specificity" was typically lost in subliminal perception and messages often got distorted, in other words, people might have a desire to drink Pepsi-Cola or, according to Barthol, "take cocaine," "eat coconuts," or visit their friend "Colonel Corcoran." Due to such breaks in the subliminal perception chain of communication, the professor was confident that both consumerism and politics would remain brainwash-free. "The advertiser—or potential political dictator—cannot present complex thoughts, and can never be sure that even a single thought will be received and interpreted in the way he wants," he assured Nervous Nellies like those from the Stanford Research Institute who called subliminal advertising "a virtual social H-bomb."[57] Besides the unpredictability of subliminal perception, pure common sense suggested that there were easier ways for admen to skin the consumer cat. "Why bother to sneak around to the back door when the front door is open?" Jack Gould sensibly asked.[58]

Keep Watching

Fearing that some marketers or politicians would still like to squeeze through the back door, even if it was open just a tiny crack, those controlling the airwaves were determined to slam it shut for good. By late 1957, the three networks and the National Association of Radio and Television Broadcasters (NARTB) had banned stations from using subliminal advertising, seeing little upside on the issue and a ton of downside. "There may well be grave concern over the idea of advertising which affects people below their level of conscious awareness, so that they are not able to exercise conscious control over their acceptance or rejection of the messages," the NARTB wrote to the networks and its roughly three hundred member stations.[59] The networks needed little persuasion, so to speak, to make subliminal advertising off-limits, with orders sent down through the chain of command from the very top. The general himself, Robert Sarnoff, made NBC's position on the matter crystal clear in a December 1957 intra-office memorandum, with his counterpart at CBS, Merle Jones, also sending around a memo to ensure there would be no "psychic hucksterism" or "phantom plugs" on their watch.[60] Subliminal Projection's public relations machine, however, didn't skip a beat. "We're delighted they banned us," said Vicary upon hearing about the networks' decision; his spin on what was actually disastrous news was that "it should keep all our imitators away" and that "the less competition the better."[61]

Although it actually had no power to censor programs, the FCC was also considering nailing the subliminal door shut at the urging of Senator Charles Potter (R-Michigan) and Representative William A. Dawson (R-Utah).[62] The new technique had "worrisome, if not frightening aspects," Dawson told FCC chair Doerfer, something "made to order for the establishment and maintenance of a totalitarian government."[63] Dawson liked to think of subliminal perception not as "subliminal projection" but as a "secret pitch," along the same lines as a pitcher trying to throw a baseball past an unsuspecting batter. Dawson's pet fear was that teenagers who happened to see beer or liquor television commercials (the latter still legal, of course) might suddenly have an uncontrollable urge to take a swig (this scenario providing an entirely different answer to another one of the big Cold War issues of the day, "Why Johnny can't read"). "Contemplate, if you will, the effect of an invisible but effective appeal to 'drink more beer' being poured into the subconscious of teenage television viewers," Dawson wrote in a statement submitted to the House of Representatives, urging the FCC to ensure the bar would not be open for underage drinkers.[64]

Initially silent on the issue, Doerfer seemed to be getting religion about subliminal advertising, dashing off a letter to a group of congressmen when he heard that a secret pitch might have leaked onto the airwaves. "There is some indication that this technique may have been used in television," he wrote, the news of this possibility causing considerable alarm, despite the three networks and Vicary denying any involvement in the matter.[65] Whether the invisible commercial had aired or not, it appeared to be a no-win situation for subliminal advertising: if it didn't work, there was no real reason the FCC should approve it, and if did work, the agency was almost certain to make it illegal.

While the FCC pondered the matter, individual states moved to nip subliminal perception in their own backyards. In January 1958, New York State Assemblyman Bentley Kassel introduced a bill to make movie theater operators tell viewers "consciously and visibly" when they would be exposed to subliminal ads, wanting no repeat performance of the "Eat popcorn, Drink Coca-Cola" double bill that played in the neighboring state.[66] The bill was passed by the state senate without discussion in March but had to go to the assembly for action, a considerable amount of taxpayer money going toward an issue that so far was mostly smoke with very little fire. Meanwhile in Texas, Representative James Wright, Jr., proposed a bill to fine any subliminal advertiser as much as $5,000 or put him or her in the clink for up to thirty days, thinking such a measure would spoil the best-laid plans of many an unethical marketer. "Try to imagine what would happen to the old bank account if during your wife's favorite television program some advertiser started sneaking in flashes to 'buy a mink stole today,'" Wright explained, his position being that women and children in particular needed protection from predators like sellers of expensive furs.[67]

The California state senate went even further than New York or Texas, voting unanimously to ask Congress to completely ban subliminal advertising from television, to wipe it out with one fell swoop.[68] With Los Angeles television station KTLA aggressively pursuing subliminal advertising, a bill to ban it in California was soon in the works. Consumers wouldn't know they were "being sold a bill of goods until somebody ends up at a drugstore ordering a brand of toothpaste he never heard of and doesn't want," said Senator Richard Richards in introducing the bill to the California legislature.[69] As with Hollywood's blacklist, a witch hunt against subliminal perception was in full swing as fears that it had special powers ran amok in postwar America.

Before government and network officials could completely burn subliminal perception at the stake, however, a few cinders were able to flare up on a local New York City station. During a thirty-minute program on Channel 9 called, appropriately enough, *Ad World*, an advertising trade group flashed an image of the familiar Red Cross symbol along with an indistinguishable message. Jack Gould of the *Times* found this feeble attempt at subliminal advertising not spellbinding but rather "merely annoying and intrusive," neither the semivisible commercials nor the program reason enough for viewers to abandon their favorite shows in the same time slot, *Alfred Hitchcock Presents* and *The Dinah Shore Chevy Show*.[70]

Although they too didn't know whether "id ads" could make people buy products they couldn't afford, had no use for, or were unhealthy or dangerous, the British also made moves to stop subliminal advertising in its tracks before it was too late. In early 1958, the Institute of Practitioners in Advertising (IPA)—the British equivalent of the AAAA—organized a committee to look into it, not wanting its industry to be as publicly scorned as that across the pond. "Any medium of communication in unscrupulous hands is something to be guarded against," said Douglas M. Saunders, chairman of the British office of J. Walter Thompson, the institute determined to both "safeguard the public" and "preserve its own reputation." The BBC too had recently decided to investigate subliminal advertising, setting up a committee in its "Science Review" program made up of psychologists from London universities. Each organization was responding to rumors that the makers of a popular brand of toffee, Sharps, was planning to test subliminal perception in local cinemas, the fear perhaps that the United Kingdom would become a nation of out-of-control candy eaters.[71]

After six months of "exhaustive" study, the IPA banned subliminal communication in any form, deeming it "professionally unacceptable" and advising its 243 member agencies to avoid using it in both advertising and sales promotion. The IPA did its homework, not just reviewing the available information but doing its own experiments and even publishing a booklet on the subject.[72] Despite this firmer than firm mandate by the British, subliminal advertising or something like it did rear its allegedly ugly head a few months later, much as the Red Cross symbol had appeared on television in New York. The row began when the *Daily Herald* accused Television Wales and West (TWW) of airing an image of a winking eye with the message "Keep Watching" at one-twenty-fifth of a second, an Orwellian scenario if there ever was one. TWW readily admitted it was running the mini-spot but said that it lasted a full two to three seconds, disqualifying it as a subliminal ad. "There is nothing sinister about it, and it is in no way subliminal suggestion," a spokesperson for TWW said. With the real Big Brother—the BBC—looking over its shoulder, however, the company agreed to take its Orwellian eye off the air, ending Britain's brief fling with subliminal perception.[73]

Rather fittingly, a Briton who had given much thought to the horrors of a future totalitarian state, Aldous Huxley, piped in while the subliminal advertising fur flew in the United Kingdom and United States. Huxley, the social critic and author of *Brave New World*, offered his view in May 1958 on *The Mike Wallace Interview*, a show aired on WABC-TV in New York, shortly after his new book, *Brave New World Revisited*, was published. Best sellers by William Whyte, C. Wright Mills, and Vance Packard had only reinforced some of the ideas he laid out in his 1932 book, with Big Business wielding the sort of power he feared a quarter century earlier. Huxley fretted about the recent attempts to penetrate individuals' subconscious, thinking nothing less than democracy itself was at stake. Although he hadn't mentioned subliminal advertising in his classic novel, Huxley saw clear parallels with it and the kinds of mind control he imagined (such as "sleep teaching"). Like others, Huxley was especially concerned that subliminal advertising could be used in political campaigns, a "rather alarming danger" that could make "nonsense of the whole democratic procedure which is based on conscious choice on rational ground." Hidden persuasion was a little too close for comfort for Huxley, with advances like Vicary's machine smacking of the brave new world that both he and Orwell had envisioned should technology succeed in subverting human free will.[74]

Playing with Fire

More entrepreneurial types seemed undeterred by such the-sky-is-falling warnings, however, taking advantage of what would turn out to be subliminal perception's brief fame. In early 1958, what was believed to be "the first subliminal letter" was mailed to radio program directors in New York and New Jersey by VA Information Services, a seller of scripts to be used on air. "Use VA scripts" was placed in very small type between the other regular-size words in the letter, with the intention of persuading recipients to follow the simple directions, subconsciously of course. If it worked in movie theaters, some were beginning to think, why not through the U.S. Mail?[75]

James Vicary and his ambitious partners were meanwhile moving ahead with much bigger plans. Working around the FCC's and networks' objections, Subliminal Projection was able to test its process in January on a Bangor, Maine, television station, WTWO, asking viewers to "write WTWO." No additional mail was received by the station, however, making the Maine test a total dud.[76] The Canadian Broadcasting Corporation (CBC) also agreed to let Subliminal Projection do a trial over two programs after getting approval from its board of governors and the Department of Transport, the first national tests of the process. On the first, an announcer told viewers that a message was being broadcast on the popular Sunday night program *Close-Up* and to look out for "anything unusual." Nobody noticed anything unusual, however, consciously or otherwise, although many viewers did report they learned how to pronounce the word "subliminal." One CBC executive admitted the test had at best ambiguous results, particularly among members of his own family. "I felt like a beer, my wife had an urge for some cheese and the dog wanted to go outside in the middle of the program," he reported. Bob Blackburn, television critic of the *Ottawa Citizen*, too was less than overwhelmed. "If the message was 'Go to sleep,' I got it," he wrote in his column; "there was something about the program that made me feel like it."[77]

This first test only made Subliminal Projection want to shift its flashing machine into a higher gear for a second test about a week later, however. This time the message, "Telephone Now," was flashed 325 times during the program, after which viewers were asked to send letters reporting what they had seen. Half of the five hundred viewers who replied did indeed feel compelled to "do something," but only one was motivated to "telephone now" (others had the urge to "eat something," "remove their shoes," "drive safely," and, a little oddly, "buy an electric frying pan").[78] Subliminal Projection described the results of these tests as "inconclusive," but the CBC was less generous, the program's announcer considering them "a dismal failure." Those who followed the tests with a vested interest were even less kind. "The Canadian Broadcasting Corp.'s experiment in subliminal projection fell through with a thud that was very perceptible across the nation," quipped *Ad Age*.[79]

Independent radio stations in the United States too were dabbling with subliminal perception, despite the tidal wave of opposition to it. Already having lost much of their advertising business to television, radio broadcasters were eager to get a piece of the subliminal perception action should it develop into the next big thing. WAAF in Chicago and WCCO in Minneapolis, for example, were testing subliminal perception commercials to find out if they increased product sales before offering advertisers the service.[80] WCCO was using three public service messages ("Slippery Roads," "Mail Cards Now," and "Ike Tonight") to test what it called "phantom spots," while WAAF was whispering "Drink 7-Up" and "Buy Oklahoma Oil" into its listeners' ears.[81] On KKOL, a Seattle station, subliminal messages were delivered at three different sound levels in a test to see if volume was a factor in listener response. During the song "Yellow Dog Blues," an announcer asked, "How about a cup of coffee?" at a volume level that most people could easily hear, not truly subliminal but close enough. Another message ("Answer the phone") was inserted at a lower volume over a record of "Twenty-Six Miles," and the third message ("Someone's at the door") was also read softly. The station received about a hundred phone calls from listeners, most of them not surprisingly reporting they had heard the loudest message, suggesting a cup of joe.[82]

The point of the test being to drum up interest among advertisers, KKOL found what it believed to be very interesting findings. Two women said they made coffee immediately after hearing the message, one of whom didn't drink the stuff herself but kept some around for her husband, who wasn't home ("Non-Coffee-Using Housewife Made Fresh Coffee After Hint in Subliminal Radio Test," went the rather sensational title of a news story about the test). Even more amazing, to the subliminal faithful, several listeners picked up their phones although they had not rung, and one woman actually looked up from her work to see if someone was at the door, startling stuff given that these other two messages were only whispered. One advertiser, impressed with these results, asked KKOL to run its own subliminal ad, but the station manager ultimately declined, saying it all was just "an interesting experiment."[83]

Others in early 1958 tried to establish, one way or another, whether subliminal perception was legit to determine its fate as a potential advertising technique. Three hundred television and radio broadcasters attending a conference in San Francisco in March volunteered to be subliminal perception guinea pigs, viewing a film chock-full of invisible ads for Coca-Cola (which apparently had become the official soft drink of subliminal perception).

Asked later to write about what they had seen, if anything, most thought they had viewed ads for Chrysler or Wrigley's gum. The broadcasters were also asked to describe their emotions while watching the film, with thirty-five saying they felt "nervous," twenty-nine "lethargic," twenty-three "tired," and seven "sexy." Finally, the group was asked if the film made them feel like doing something, with forty-two saying they wanted to smoke, twenty-six drink, twenty-one eat, and ten chew. As with past subliminal perception tests, the orchestrator of this one, Robert Haber of Stanford University, was reluctant to admit it was a bomb, simply describing the results as "nothing much."[84]

All these tests were merely appetizers preceding the main course, however. Despite (or because of) its fiascos in Maine and Canada, Subliminal Projection got another chance to prove that subliminal perception both worked and was harmless, this time in Washington, D.C., before a much tougher audience—members of Congress, the FCC, and the Federal Trade Commission. In front of a standing-room-only crowd at local station WTOP (which included a few foreign observers as well), Vicary demonstrated his invention via a closed circuit broadcast (of the film *The Grey Ghost*). In this first public display of his mysterious machine, he, Francis Thayer, and Rene Bras were eager to show those on Capitol Hill that subliminal was not, as the *New York Times* nicely put it, a "bugaboo," and therefore should be approved for commercial use.[85] If they obtained the FCC's blessing, the partners stood to make a fortune by leasing the company's equipment and the use of their proprietary process to local stations and the networks. It was high noon in Washington as the three men with big dreams faced off against Uncle Sam.

David would not win the day over Goliath, however. After "EAT POPCORN" was flashed in a program on a television screen and the viewers were asked if they felt any different, one Congressman said he wanted a hot dog, another said he was thirsty. Popcorn not doing the trick, Subliminal Projection played a different film, laced with "FIGHT POLIO," thinking perhaps that a public service message might be more likely to register in the subconscious of those in public service. Alas, this too went completely over (through?) the heads of the Washingtonians, one Congressman guessing, "Contribute to the Red Cross?"[86] "I don't think it will work," concluded Robert E. Lee, the FCC commissioner, not at all worried that his airwaves would be taken over by rogue propagandists with malicious intent.[87]

The media, only a few months earlier in near shock regarding subliminal perception, was beginning to be a lot more relaxed about it as it became clearer that it wasn't the end of the world as they knew it. "If anybody can find a use for it, it ought to be this administration," joked an editor for the *Chicago Tribune*, thinking subliminal advertising would be just the thing to help President Eisenhower get his proposed $74 billion budget for 1958 through Congress.[88] The *Wall Street Journal* too began to laugh off its recent panic attack. "Quite frankly, we were rather skittish at first about subliminal advertising," admitted an editor of the *Journal* in March 1958 (who had called it the "ultimate weapon of the Grey Flannel Suiters" just six months earlier), the recent findings allaying his fears that somebody could be persuaded to do something he or she didn't want to do.[89] With a *New Yorker* cartoon satirizing subliminal advertising, it could be said that the craze was at least unofficially over, turned into pop culture fodder. In the cartoon, a rather macho-looking man in an undershirt is sitting in front of a television set, his hair in curlers and a box of Toni nearby on the floor, says to his wife entering the room, "I don't know what came over me. I was just sitting here watching television."

By the summer of 1958, the evidence that subliminal advertising was a canard was mounting. After reviewing forty-nine studies on the subject, two Purdue University psychologists announced that not only did subliminal perception not work, it didn't really exist. If a message was invisible, said the two professors, so were the results, with any change in people's behavior simply a matter of "partial recognition." Subliminal advertising, less than a year before taken very seriously, was rapidly turning into a not particularly funny joke both within the field and among the public.[90]

There was, in fact, a whole body of scientific literature addressing subliminal perception, much of it summarized in an article that had appeared, very conveniently, in the September 1957 issue of the *Bulletin of the American Psychological Association*. Despite the assurances from Subliminal Projection that subliminal perception was for real, those who took the time to read the jargon-filled article learned that experimental studies to date indicated it was slightly more real than a three-dollar bill. It was true that subliminal perception could influence behavior in certain situations, but nobody testing it had ever been able to produce consistent results—the benchmark of scientific validity. "There is no experimental evidence available that shows subliminal projection can influence product sales on television or in the movies," summed up Arthur Koponen, a psychologist at J. Walter Thompson, a voice of reason in the media din.[91] Psychologists were admittedly very interested in finding commercial applications for their work, as they were doing in motivation research, but drew the line at subliminal advertising. The growing field of perception research, for example, was considered a perfectly legitimate way shrinks could go beyond the classroom or the couch, and pick up a few extra bucks in the process. Hawking subliminal perception, on the other hand, was viewed by most colleagues as slumming it, if not grounds to be kicked out of the club.[92]

A new study by three psychologists from the University of Michigan reported in *American Psychologist* offered more evidence that Vicary's movie theater test was a bunch of boloney. The academics were highly skeptical of his findings, asking the good question, "Did members of the audience rise like automatons during the course of the movie . . . to satisfy a craving for popcorn?" The authors of the article didn't mention Vicary by name but attacked his findings like a school of piranhas, stating that any number of problems—"unwarranted assumptions," "invalid applications," "unjustified conclusions," "serious methodological and technical defects," "paucity of data"—made them of no use to anyone. Much worse, the members of the Michigan team were concerned that Vicary's research violated psychologists' code of ethics forbidding anything done for "devious purposes," and they worried that the firestorm surrounding subliminal advertising could damage their own field.[93] "Anyone who wishes to utilize subliminal stimulation for commercial or other purposes can be likened to a stranger entering into a misty, confused countryside where there are but few landmarks," the three wise men warned.[94]

Amazingly, Vicary was perfectly nonplussed by the criticism leveled at him by the academics, saying he was actually "delighted" by the *American Psychologist* article. In fact, Vicary said he was disappointed that he wasn't mentioned by name, wanting full credit for bringing the field of subliminal advertising into the open. And rather than say his work deserved a better grade than the big fat F given by the professors, Vicary saw the article as "perfectly legitimate" and "very good," something that would "alert potential users to the hazards." Vicary admitted, however, that he thought his equipment and process would have been widely used by advertisers by now, but that he was hopeful that any publicity, even the kind that he was getting, would eventually be good for business.[95] Vicary would be proved wrong.

A Third Communication

With subliminal perception on the ropes, comers from near and far moved in for the knockout. Loyd Ring Coleman, the managing director of J. Walter Thompson in Sydney, Australia, took the time to do the math behind subliminal advertising, pointing out that something smelled rotten in the state of subliminal perception. If the brain could really process two words like "eat popcorn" flashed at one two-hundredth of a second (fifteen times *slower* than Vicary's movie theater blinks, giving him a big benefit of the doubt), it could handle four hundred words a second or twenty-four thousand words a minute. Using these figures, someone could read a novel of average length (seventy-two thousand words) in three minutes, something clearly impossible even for a graduate of Evelyn Wood's speed reading course. Likewise, Coleman figured, at this same rate a semester's worth of lectures could be recorded, sped up, delivered, and understood in just an hour or so, shaving a heck of a lot of time off a university education. Most amazing of all, these feats could be accomplished while the reader or student watched television or took in a movie, letting the unconscious do the heavy lifting. "The technique of the subliminal stimulus in advertising is manifestly a scientific absurdity," Coleman concluded, all of us far smarter than the fastest Univac in the world if Vicary's findings had any validity at all.[96]

The advertising community was not quite ready to put subliminal perception out to pasture, however. The "unconscious sell" was the number-one issue at the 1958 Advertising Conference held at the University of Michigan in April, not surprisingly, with no fewer than four speakers—two psychologists and two admen—giving talks on the topic. (Man of the hour Vance Packard also was there, urging advertisers to refrain from tapping consumers' subconscious if other, less invasive tools could be used.) The two admen—a copy director and an art director from Detroit agency Campbell-Ewald—saw subliminal advertising as "a third communication," which went "over and beyond" their own domains of words and pictures. "We believe it's there—even though the advertiser may not know it's there, or may not want it to be there," the creative team explained, not really able to say what "it" was but nevertheless convinced "it" was powerful stuff.[97] This idea was similar to that posed by other subliminalists, that subliminal perception operated outside the five "traditional" senses, that is, was a form of extrasensory perception. Backers of subliminal perception, especially those trying to make a buck off it, also often argued that it was beyond the realm of our current intellectual powers, something that only people in the future would be able to fully understand and appreciate.

The two shrinks, each from the university hosting the conference, were much less taken with subliminal advertising or any other kind of "third communication," thinking that much more research had to be done before saying subliminal perception was or wasn't effective. There was another technique, still in its infancy, however, that posed a much bigger opportunity and threat than subliminal advertising, the professors told attendees, who no doubt leaned forward in their seats. One day marketers would be able to push a button to advertise their products to housewives as they rolled their carts down supermarket aisles, once psychologists could figure out how to electrically and remotely stimulate the brain—just as E. B. Weiss had feared a couple of years earlier. Subliminal advertising could thus just be a stepping-stone to much bigger things in the area of hidden persuasion, the professors warned, the manipulation of minds through blinking messages mere child's play compared to the possibilities that lay in the future (and now just starting to be realized).[98]

In the 1950s, however, budding mind controllers would have to rely on more primitive methods. Interest in subliminal perception had shifted west in 1958, directly due to the efforts of the New Orleans company that had quickly jumped into the game after Vicary's announcement. Experimental Films had changed its name to the much less scary Precon TV, with ambitious plans to see if its subliminal perception process worked on air. Precon (from "preconscious") spent eight years on lab research to develop its process, the company claimed, racing against Vicary to get a patent granted to own the rights to the basic technology.[99] Rather than try to go head to head with officials in D.C. as Subliminal Projection had done, Precon headed to Hollywood to try to align itself with the exploding television industry that was rapidly stealing New York's thunder. Company officials made their pitch to the Los Angeles Advertising Club, after which they were quizzed by a panel of journalists and agency execs. Precon (which Vicary called an "imitator") must have made a convincing case, because soon after the January meeting the independent television station KTLA announced it would test subliminal public service messages ("Drive Safely," "Support Your Community Chest," and "Don't Be a Litterbug") on televised programs within ninety days. If successful, the station planned to air subliminal commercials, assuming there were any advertisers willing to be among the first to use the "secret pitch."[100] The station manager, Lewis Arnold, imagined, for example, "subliminally overlay[ing] a beautiful invisible ham cooking in the background" for an advertiser, not seeing any inconsistency at all that something could be simultaneously "beautiful" and "invisible."[101]

As in the case of Vicary's company, however, things would not go as planned. Letters, petitions, and telephone calls poured into the television station ("adverse public reaction," KTLA termed it) as Los Angelenos reacted with the kind of anger that James Staver believed was called for.[102] So many people complained about the planned test on KTLA that it was "postponed," as there were too many legal and ethical issues surrounding subliminal perception to find out if it even worked. The station and Precon blamed "a lack of a clear position by the FCC on the subject of through-the-air transmission of subliminal messages" for the cancellation, but there was little doubt that the public outcry had forced them to change their minds.[103] (The *New York Times* felt similarly, thinking that KTLA was "playing with fire.") "We have ample proof that it works," insisted Corrigan, but he wouldn't get his day on the airwaves to make Los Angelenos better citizens.[104]

For Precon, however, this was just a bump in what it believed would be a long road with subliminal perception, based on some exciting findings. The company claimed that when a corporate trademark was subliminally inserted into a film, audience members transferred the pleasure they felt from being entertained to the symbol, thereby establishing instant goodwill toward the advertiser. (It was not clear how watching popular movies currently playing in theaters like *The Cosmic Monsters* or *The Crawling Eye* would affect the unfortunate viewers' sentiments toward the flasher.) In addition, Precon had designs on using subliminal material to make movies and television shows more intense experiences, something it was confident the entertainment industry would gobble up in order to drive up ticket sales and ratings. A few carefully placed invisible but provocative images, sexual or violent, no doubt, and presto!—a hit was almost a sure thing.[105] Even already popular films could be improved through subliminal perception, the Precon people thought. Corrigan envisioned a subliminally enhanced *High Noon*, for instance, in which Gary Cooper's (invisible) six-shooter increased in size and flashed at a faster and faster rate in the climactic duel scene, something that would have movie lovers wanting to see the film over and over again.[106]

Precon made the rounds in Southern California in the spring of 1958, convinced that "the industry" would take to subliminal perception like a fish to water. Working with Precon, a chain of local movie theaters decided to test subliminal perception to see if it could increase sales of its own popcorn, swayed by the apparent success story back East. Also at Precon's urging, Twentieth Century–Fox was considering piping in subliminal messages over its internal loudspeaker (softspeaker?) system, presumably to create a happier or more productive work environment. This *1984*-esque scenario was a clear admission that at least one of the two leading proponents of subliminal perception had every intent to use its process well beyond advertising, seeing the workplace as ground worth mining. Precon believed that what would later be called "content" represented the biggest opportunity for subliminal perception, however, partly because it was outside the realm of the FCC, the networks, and local broadcasters. Furthermore, entertainment was illusion, after all, and it was the job of makers of films and television shows to heighten illusion, perhaps making subliminal effects—a psychological equivalent to technological special effects—a natural fit.[107] "Such evidence shows that early keen interest in subliminal advertising has not been seriously blunted by negative reports," wrote Jack Patterson for *Commonweal* in April 1958, its promoters determined to turn it into a commercial success.[108]

Indeed, if what Precon was telling the media was true, things were looking quite rosy for subliminal perception. Jack Sinclair, Precon's sales manager, claimed that Seagram, the liquor company, was thinking of using subliminal point of sale advertising and, even more impressive, that the U.S. Army's Human Factors Research Division at Fort Belvoir, Virginia, was looking into the possibility of "subconscious education" (secretly, of course). Precon was also trying to get funding to determine if its technology could be used to "painlessly" teach kids multiplication tables and other things learned by rote, seeing a big fat contract from the Department of Education if such a thing worked.[109] Rumors were that a national sponsor wanted to run subliminal ads, and that only the hefty price—$100,000—was preventing it from actually happening, keeping hopes for subliminal perception alive.[110]

Up the California coast, a San Francisco ad agency, Guild, Bascom and Bonfigli, also believed that the report of subliminal perception's death was premature. Perhaps picking up on the smattering of evidence that inaudible sounds could still register in the subconscious, the agency claimed subliminal perception as its official turf, aggressively offering to produce subliminal radio commercials for its clients. For Nucoa margarine, for example, Guild, Bascom and Bonfigli created a jingle with a soft-spoken message woven into the music, and the commercial played on radio stations across the country (a television commercial with the same subliminal-perception-infused jingle had also aired). The Nucoa ad was conceived by Glen Hurlburt, the agency's thirty-year-old music director, who happened to be blind. Hurlburt wouldn't reveal what the message was, as that "would rob the commercials of their subliminal value," but admitted that they worked in a "contrapuntal fashion," like music that contains two or more voices heard simultaneously. Hurlburt also saw subliminal advertising much like a magic trick, a "technique of diversion" that "posses[es] a command which the conscious ear will not recognize." While the conscious was being diverted by the obvious, in other words, advertisers had the chance to trick consumers' subconscious, subliminal perception thus not much more than a simple act of prestidigitation.[111]

I'm a Researcher

The flurry of interest in subliminal perception on the West Coast in 1958 quickly faded, however, with many by the fall convinced it was a not-so-clever magic act. "Subliminal advertising, introduced publicly a year ago this week, seems to be going nowhere fast," reported *Ad Age* in its September 15, 1958, issue, with clear signs that now the writing was on the wall for subliminal perception. Outlawed in Britain and Australia, banned from the American airwaves, and deemed the devil's handiwork by religious leaders, subliminal advertising was having a pretty rotten one-year birthday party. Even ad agency executives and psychologists—some of the very people who had the most to gain from subliminal perception—had distanced themselves from it, not wanting to be associated with such a controversial and, it seemed more and more, ineffective technique. Even James Vicary, the once beaming father, had recently changed his tune, now wanting to have nothing to do with his baby. The researcher refused to make any more comments to the press on the subject, his dreams for what he thought would be his proudest achievement shattered. Vicary had undertaken a new challenge, however, which he was excited about: leading a class in motivation research at Fairleigh Dickinson University. "I'm much more interested in teaching the kids than the practitioners," he said, his experience suggesting that those who can't do really do teach.[112]

Experiments done by a couple of professors at Indiana University in early 1959 effectively sealed the deal, concluding that subliminal perception had absolutely no persuasive powers. Subliminal commercials run on Indianapolis television station WTTV did not increase sales of a product or raise ratings of a program, the professors found, in as definitive a study as was ever done. "Subliminal phenomena are apparently little more than interesting effects which can be produced under laboratory conditions or in classroom demonstrations," they concluded, providing one more nail in subliminal perception's coffin.[113] As if there were any doubts by 1961, Raymond A. Bauer, a social psychologist at Harvard, made it clear that mass brainwashing by subliminal advertising was nothing to worry about. "I am skeptical about the extreme pictures of hidden persuasion that have been drawn for either the present or future of business or politics," Bauer told a group of hospital administrators, thinking that it was highly unlikely a whole society could be controlled psychologically. While late to the party to squash subliminal advertising paranoia, Bauer did have a good read on why it had started in the first place. Fears of omnipotent powers-that-be resulted from "our primitive anxiety over manipulation" and, more specifically, that "we have lost control over our own destiny," a nice interpretation of postwar Americans' state of mind that had allowed subliminal advertising to grab the nation's attention.[114]

The autopsy of subliminal advertising continued in the early 1960s as many wondered how such a thing could have arrived as such a sensation so fast, captured America's attention for a year, and then quickly disappeared almost as if it had never happened. "Did it die because it couldn't do what it claimed, or was it killed because it was too far ahead of its time?" Fred Farrar wondered in 1962, offering one more possibility: "Is it still with us and we just don't know it?"[115] The subliminal advertising phenomenon now seemed almost like a bad dream, enough time having gone by to fully appreciate the bizarreness of it all. "Five years ago today subliminal advertising burst on Madison Avenue," *Ad Age* wrote that same year, remembering that, "the development brought quick, nearly universal condemnation." The man most responsible for the most hidden of hidden persuasions had weathered the storm, now the survey research director for Dun and Bradstreet and able to reflect on the tinderbox he had lit. "I never regarded myself as a wheeler-dealer," Vicary wistfully recalled, "but the people who were putting up the money thought I should stir things up." The now forty-seven-year-old Vicary explained that he and his wheeler-dealers hadn't wanted news about their movie theater test in Fort Lee to get out until approval of their patent, but it did, forcing them to go public before they were really ready.[116]

News of Subliminal Projection's test appearing in *Motion Picture Daily* before the company had all its ducks in a row wasn't the only problem, Vicary explained. Packard's book being on the best-seller list at the time didn't help matters one bit, the public's sensitivity to any and all forms of hidden persuasion at an all-time high. The launch of Sputnik in October 1957—just a few weeks after their announcement—only furthered Americans' Cold War paranoia, another in the series of unfortunate events that helped sabotage the team's big plans. Also complicating things was the fact that the entrepreneurs had done no research beyond what was necessary to file the patent (that being the fraudulent New Jersey movie theater "test"), something that professional psychologists could and did spot a mile away. "All I accomplished, I guess, was to put a new word into common usage," Vicary now thought, an O. Henry–like twist for a man who had made a successful living advising big corporations on what words they should use in their advertising. Although Vicary had met every requirement, his application for a New York psychologist license had recently been turned down by the state, a rejection he attributed directly to his being known as "Mr. Subliminal." "I should have had my head examined for using the word 'subliminal,'" he admitted in his last words on the subject; "I'm a researcher, not a salesman."[117]

The end of the subliminal perception in 1958 hardly meant the end for its bigger, older Freudian brother, motivation research. Subliminal perception had clearly pushed the boundaries of psychology too far for Americans' comfort; the fear that consumers would buy things they didn't need or, especially, elect politicians with a concealed Soviet agenda was simply too great for it to last very long. Figuring out what consumers wanted remained a priority for Big Business, however, with their subconscious still perfectly fair game for those ready, willing, and able to explore it. Just as one man, James Vicary, was able to redirect the trajectory of advertising and, in a larger sense, American society with a provocative idea and not much else, so would other individuals step up to the plate in the late 1950s to master the art of hidden persuasion.

4

The Fertile Moment

If you give somebody enough rope, he will hang
himself on his own.
—Popular saying often quoted by Ernest Dichter

In 1956, having trouble coming up with a good name on its own, Ford Motor Company asked its ad agency, Foote, Cone and Belding, to come up with some possibilities for its new, very special project. Code-named "E-Car" ("E" for "Experimental"), this project wasn't just another automobile for Ford. It was in fact the first car to be introduced by the company since 1938 when the Mercury made its debut, and this twenty-year stretch was more than enough time for engineers and designers to think about how to build the perfect automobile for the American consumer of the 1950s. Also, the E-Car would be not just a single model but four different series comprising a total of eighteen cars—essentially a new, entire automobile company. For many Americans, what came to be called the Edsel would be the first really new car they had a chance to buy after the war, its introduction an important event in the history of automobiles.[1]

FC&B, which had just been awarded the large account, not surprisingly went all out for its new assignment, including asking employees in its Chicago, New York, and London offices to come up with possible names for the automobile. The employee who came up with the winning name would win an E-Car, such a prize no doubt explaining the volume of entries the agency received. No fewer than eighteen thousand names poured in, six thousand of which were presented to Ford for consideration in alphabetical order in beautifully bound books, complete with each name's word associations. Not knowing what to do with such a large list, Ford's market research director, David Wallace, asked a research company in Ann Arbor to find out which ones the public liked best, and to add any others that seemed to resonate with consumers. Four names—Corsair, Citation, Pacer, and Ranger—topped the list, but Wallace and a colleague working on the project, Bob Young, were unsatisfied. Nothing less than a special name for the special car would be acceptable.[2]

The logical path not having worked out, Wallace and Young decided to ask someone who was skilled with words but not familiar with the auto industry to come up with something better. As it turned out, Young's wife happened to know a very good poet who she felt would be happy to help out. Marianne Moore, whose *Collected Poems* of 1951 had won the Pulitzer Prize, the National Book Award, and the Bollingen Prize, was indeed delighted to apply her imagination to the project, coming up with such unquestionably imaginative names as Utopian Turtletop, Andante Con Moto, Mongoose Civique, Pastelogram, Intelligent Bullet, and Bullet Cloisonne. "Name after name was submitted from the florid pen of Miss Moore, each reaching undreamed of heights of poetic fancy," wrote Thomas E. Bonsall in his definitive autopsy of the Edsel, "none of them even remotely suitable for the E-Car."[3]

With the product launch rapidly approaching, and names like Utopian Turtletop clearly not going to fly, Wallace and Young presented the four top research-tested names at an executive committee meeting headed by Ernest Breech, a vice president at the company. "I don't like any of them," Breech growled, "let's take another look at some of the others." Among the rejects considered by Breech and the other top dogs at Ford were Drof ("Ford" spelled backwards), Benson (one of Henry Ford II's sons), and Edsel (the name of Henry Ford's son who had died at the age of forty-nine in 1943). "Let's call it that," said Breech of the Edsel, the name reluctantly accepted by Henry Ford and Edsel Ford's widow. The ill-fated decision, just one of many surrounding the new car, would have poor Edsel rolling in his grave for eternity, his name forever linked to what Bonsall called, and used as the title of his book, "disaster in Dearborn."[4]

Market Research Is a Mess

The Edsel was proof positive that, despite its unarguable progress, market research still had a long way to go. Speaking before a group at a June 1957

meeting of the American Marketing Association, the sales planning manager
of Edsel had been bullish on Ford's new car that was to be introduced in September of that year. "We have reasons to believe that the mood for consumer
buying will be good at the time of our introduction," he told his colleagues,
thinking that the company's goal of selling at least two hundred thousand Ed-
sels in the first year was easily achievable. Much of the speaker's confidence
had to do with the huge amount of market research that Ford had invested
in, more in fact than had ever before been put behind any new product. For
the past ten years, the company put had Edsel through its research paces, exploring every conceivable factor—economic, psychological, stylistic, and so
on—that would affect how well the car would play with consumers. No fewer
than four thousand separate decisions, it was said, had been made by Ford in
designing and building the car, with the company spending a whopping $250
million to make the Edsel a reality.[5]

Six months after the Edsel's introduction, however, much of the wind had
been taken out of Ford's sales when it came to its pet project. Sales were dismal, and it looked very unlikely that Ford would hit even half of its minimum
first-year goal. Advertising campaigns for the new car seemed to be changing
monthly, and the company was awarding its dealers an extra $300 for every
Edsel they were able to move off their crowded lots. The Edsel was turning out
to be the biggest bomb since Fat Man and Little Boy, its name well on the way
to becoming synonymous with a marketing blunder of epic proportions.[6]

Where did Ford go wrong with the Edsel? Which of the four thousand
decisions that managers and designers had supposedly made were, in retrospect, bad ones? Critics were quick to provide some answers, blaming one
thing in particular for Ford's woes—faulty market research. "An aborigine in
darkest Australia couldn't have made a more incorrect economic-marketing
projection," said one of the most vocal critics, Ed (E.B.) Weiss, now director
of merchandising at Doyle Dane Bernbach, in March 1958, taking issue with a
host of Ford's research-based assumptions. Research had led Ford astray with
the Edsel, Weiss thought, noting that the founder of the company had done
pretty well with his Model T without doing a single market study. Marketers
like Ford clearly had to do a better job of "turning surveys into sales," as *Nation's Business* had put it, Weiss and others believed, and not simply pursue
research for research's sake.[7]

With so much blame to go around, especially with regard to market research, it wasn't surprising that motivation research was assigned a starring
role in the Dearborn disaster. "The Edsel's subsequent failure would set the

cause of motivational research back twenty years in Detroit," wrote Bonsall. Wallace brought in both Pierre Martineau's research department at the *Chicago Tribune* and Lazarsfeld's team at the Bureau of Applied Social Research at Columbia, the latter doing sixteen hundred depth interviews with car buyers in Peoria, Illinois, and San Bernardino, California.[8] What Wallace was looking for were gaps in the marketplace from an image standpoint; he wanted to determine which makes of cars afforded what kind of status and if there were any big holes that the E-car could fill. "It was almost pure sociology," Wallace remembered, and these motivation-research-based competitive analyses were considered essential to help decide how Edsel should be positioned and advertised.[9]

The result of all this research? "The Edsel is the car for the young executive on his way up," Wallace reported, the car's elegance and classiness the reason why junior gray flannel suiters would choose it over Pontiacs and Dodges (too working class), Chevrolet (too boring), or other Fords (too brash). The Edsel would, however, go directly up against the Oldsmobile, which the research had shown to be the current automobile of choice for the adventurous man in early middle age. "Our research staff thought this was the best research they had ever seen," said Fairfax Cone, head of FC&B; the sheer volume of information gleaned from consumers was extremely impressive. Cone couldn't resist making one crucial and very significant change to what he called "Wallace's prescription," however, switching the target audience from the "young executive" to the "middle-class family" in hopes of driving huge sales for his client. This change would in retrospect turn out to be one of many that would make most consumers wonder whom the car was really for and why they should buy it, the Edsel's all-things-to-all-people positioning actually narrowing its appeal considerably. By essentially just adding up what people said they wanted in the "ideal" car and giving it to them, Ford painfully discovered that more could indeed be less.[10] The Edsel would never recover from its wishy-washy, neither-here-nor-there brand image, a classic case in which good research leads to bad decision making.

Although it was by far the worst example of good research gone bad, the Edsel was part of an even bigger problem. Lots of people were coming out of the woodwork to criticize market research in the late 1950s, most of them saying that vision and intuition were more valuable when it came to making business decisions. "Market research is a mess," Joseph J. Seldin had observed in the *American Mercury* in 1957, believing that businesspeople were throwing away millions for "nothing more than hunch, surmise, and opinion, buttressed by pages of statistics" that were presented and taken as gospel. Seldin was hardly the only one thinking that market research was a bunch of hooey, the field increasingly attacked by leading academics. Research was "vastly overrated," opined John E. Jueck, dean of the University of Chicago business school, who considered it not much more than "a compound of cookbook statistics." Much as those in the business world believed or wished market research to be a science, it was not and never could be, Jueck felt; it was at best a distant cousin to a field whose methods could be proven.[11]

The causes for the mess in market research were many, critics pointed out. Bad practices, such as changing respondents' age or gender in order to fill sample quotas, were commonplace, as was interviewers' occasional habit of completing good chunks of surveys themselves (feeling they had a good sense of what the actual answers would be, saving everyone a lot of time and trouble). Researchers' going to the same well too often was another complaint by critics of market research. "A great many of this nation's surveys are based on results from an enormously overworked and inbred sample of inactive American women," alleged Paul Gerhold, research director of FC&B, and he was in a position to know. Audience measurements, whether by telephone interviews, viewer or listener diaries, house-to-house canvassing, or electronic monitoring, too were openly criticized as being flawed in some way.[12]

Ed Weiss, who seemed to be relishing the Edsel's crashing and burning because so much research had gone into it, firmly believed intuition was superior to the "pseudo-scientific mumbo jumbo" most marketers were so attached to.[13] "I don't think marketing research is worth a damn," echoed Benedict Gimbel, Jr., president of WIP-FM, a Philadelphia radio station, his take being that businessmen had convinced themselves they were operating in a scientific field when this just wasn't so. The credit that market researchers had received for helping turn Marlboro into a popular brand by emasculating it particularly bothered Gimbel. "All you needed to do was go into a few restaurants and you could have seen that more women were smoking them than men," Gimbel claimed, with no need for a research study to tell corporate executives that Marlboro was, in his words, a "sissy" cigarette. (Many men switched to filtered brands after it was revealed that cigarettes caused cancer, and this had a lot to do with the decision to regender the Marlboro brand.) Researchers' recommendation that Leo Burnett, the agency of record, give the brand a macho image by featuring a tattooed man in its ads had already become advertising lore, however, something that made Gimbel fume. Rather than pursue such supposedly scientific studies, Gimbel felt the key to

marketing success was "a sense of what will sell" along with "a sense of when
to sell it," with "no research or set of principles [able] to replace these two
paramount assets." "Play your hunches, trust your instincts," he advised marketers, and "don't be afraid to rely on the greatest computer of them all—the
human brain."[14]

Less vitriolic but as passionate were the words spoken by Donald R. Longman, director of research for J. Walter Thompson, at an AAAA meeting in
1958. Longman suggested that intense competition for clients on Madison
Avenue was leading to "scientific evidence that does not exist," a bold accusa-
tion that no doubt caused attendees in the room to exchange nervous glances.
"Showy, saleable work" that looked like real research but was flawed or weak
was corrupting the field, Longman thought, a disturbing and dangerous trend
for all parties concerned. "It is time to make a reappraisal to recall research
fundamentals," he told his colleagues, justifiably concerned that research was
rapidly losing much of its credibility.[15] Meanwhile, Andrew Heiskell, publisher of *Life*, scolded management for their "gross misunderstanding and
misuse of market research," believing that it was they who were principally at
fault. Whether it was their "wish to evade responsibility in making decisions"
or simply "sheer laziness," Heiskell felt, management should be blamed for
the mess that was market research. Could the mess be cleaned up?[16]

Sex, Symbolism, and Sensationalism

Cleaning up market research would mean tidying up the most unkempt part
of the field, motivation research. With the Edsel fiasco and the subliminal
advertising scare making motivation research more controversial than ever,
those working in or around it recognized the need to take a fresh, objective-
as-possible look at this thing that was causing so much trouble. *Advertising
Agency Magazine*, the weaker sibling to the official magazine of the trade,
Ad Age, did exactly that in its first issue of 1958, attempting to set the record
straight once and for all in an article entitled "You Can't Escape MR." "Despite
the mysteries of the occult and 'manipulations' of minds which many 'money'
writers and sensationalists would have the public believe shroud motivation,
this type of study is being used for more and more accounts by more and more
leading advertising agencies, both with and without their clients' request or
even knowledge," the article began; the magazine had learned through an "intensive investigation" that motivation research was as common on Madison
Avenue as a bow tie. "Sex, symbolism and sensationalism," said the article,

were certainly making the headlines when it came to motivation research, but the plain truth was that the technique was a sound and even logical way to guide market planning and inspire creative people. Admittedly, "pseudo-technical" terminology was getting in the way of motivation research's realizing its full potential, the magazine also found by talking to some advertising folks; the misperception that it could be a panacea for all marketing problems was another thing hurting more than helping it. (Some agencies even shunned the label "motivation research," believing that the term "motivation" instantly aroused suspicion; FC&B, for example, preferred "attitude-use" studies.) Motivation research is "nothing more or less than research devoted to getting the best possible answers to the question: 'Why do people behave as they do?'" proposed Lyndon Brown, head of media, marketing, and research at Dancer Fitzgerald Sample, as good a definition of motivation research as one could come up with.[17]

Also realizing that the motivation research controversy was coming to a head in 1958, two University of Illinois professors who no doubt had attended the 1955 symposium at the university, Robert Ferber and Hugh G. Wales, gathered a collection of essays by top practitioners in the field and published them in a book, *Motivation and Market Behavior*. The book's uniqueness was that it included essays by both those who supported motivation research—including Dichter, Martineau, and James Vicary, a little belatedly—and those who did not, notably Alfred Politz and L. Edward Scriven of A. J. Wood and Company. The book served, and continues to serve, as a nice time capsule of sentiment toward motivation research in its heyday, capturing the passion those in market research felt about the subject, one way or another.[18]

Those straddling the motivation research fence were also invited to contribute to the book, as voices of reason in the still heated debate. Charles Cantrell, the well-known psychologist now working at George Katona's University of Michigan's Survey Research Center, for example, cleared the air by reminding readers that motivation had long been an area of interest in a wide variety of fields, with marketing and advertising only relatively recently discovering the concept or, perhaps, simply the term. Psychologists, whether sociopsychologists like Kurt Lewin, clinicians, or those working in labs, were especially convinced that all human behavior occurs for a reason, making motivation foremost in their thinking. It was inevitable that marketers would look to psychology to try to explain the reasons consumers behaved the way they did, Cantrell thought. He was a firm believer in motivation research as long as businesspeople understood the theories behind the techniques (something that should definitely not be assumed).[19]

In his essay, Wroe Alderson, a partner in Alderson and Sessions, made the much needed point that while Watsonesque behaviorism had been perfectly fine advertising theory a generation ago, the idea that consumers were blank slates demanding massive, endless repetition was now unduly simplistic and inadequate as a strategic platform. As with wine and cheese, perhaps, it would be Europe that Americans with more discerning tastes would look to for more interesting and complex varieties of psychology to use in their advertising and marketing plans. Alderson also did everyone a big favor by tracing motivation research back to the two principal schools he believed it sprang from, Gestalt psychology and psychoanalysis, showing how these bodies of thought had found a hospitable home in the United States, especially within the business world. Whether leaning toward Gestalt's emphasis on the conscious mind, rational decision making, and goal-directed behavior or toward the instinctive drives and dominant role of the unconscious in psychoanalysis, European psychology was a far richer pool for marketers to wade in than the shallow waters of American behaviorism.[20]

Of course, no one in the world would agree with that more than Ernest Dichter, who also contributed an essay to the book (based on the talk he had given at the 1955 symposium). Dichter not surprisingly made a vigorous case for psychology-based market research techniques, as only they (versus statistics) were capable of leading to, as he put it, "an understanding and scientific proof of the real causes of human behavior in the market place." Whereas descriptive research could tell someone how many people did what, diagnostic research could reveal why what happened did happen and was truly helpful in predicting future consumer behavior. "Studying human motivations is not unlike Herodotus' problem of studying the reason for the inundation of the Nile," he wrote in classic Dichterian style, the twentieth-century A.D. motivation researcher akin to the fifth-century B.C. Greek acknowledged as the first historian to collect materials systematically, test their accuracy, and arrange them in a compelling narrative. By focusing on interpretation rather than simple observation or meaningless facts, in other words, motivation researchers were simply better equipped to find the right answers to virtually any question involving human behavior. The social sciences were far from perfect, and good motivation research required discipline, Dichter concluded, though only a real understanding of consumers' current behavior could help marketers figure out why their own rivers overflowed.[21]

In his essay, Martineau also thoroughly endorsed using a psychological approach to provide new insights into marketing strategy, arguing that motivation research's emphasis on consumers' personalities didn't mean that economic considerations—often the focus of traditional research—had to be left out of the equation. When done competently, motivation research opened up directions for thinking otherwise left unopened, Martineau illustrated through a case study of the automobile category done by SRI, echoing Dichter's persuasive call to bring psychology into the research mix.[22]

Just as convincing, however, was Dichter's and Martineau's intellectual equal, Alfred Politz, his essay in the book "a powerful indictment of the validity of psychological methods as applied to marketing research," as the editors described it. Politz not only insisted on the need for quantification but also argued that the very lifeblood of motivation research—the depth interview and projective techniques—were deeply flawed methodologies when it came to understanding consumer behavior. Freud wouldn't recognize the depth interview as authentically psychoanalytic if his life depended on it, Politz implied, the three or so hours spent between interviewer and interviewee nowhere nearly enough for thoughts residing deep in the unconscious to emerge. Curing neuroses was an entirely different proposition from identifying consumer motivations, Politz reasonably maintained, seeing motivation research as a good "preresearch" tool to develop ideas and hunches but a bad way to test firm hypotheses.[23]

Playing the heavy in *Motivation and Market Behavior* was L. Edward Scriven, who made Politz's critique of motivation research seem like a light pat on the cheek. For the past few years, Scriven, along with his colleagues at the Philadelphia-based ad agency A. J. Wood, were on a mission to squash motivation research like a bug, fully convinced the whole affair was, in words I could not attempt to paraphrase, "a hodge-podge of jabberwocky." Even the phrase "motivation research" was wrong, Scriven thought; "motivation analysis" was a better choice of words if one had to use them at all. Fearing they'd be labeled old-fashioned and possibly put out to pasture, many market researchers were essentially being forced to use motivation research, he argued, while marketing executives were being taken by "glib psycho-salesmen," much as the fine folks of River City, Iowa, were taken by Harold Hill (*The Music Man* had just opened a few blocks from Madison Avenue, oddly enough). Using psychology to understand consumer behavior was actually a good thing, but "the attempt to apply the methods of the clinical psychologist to marketing research are [*sic*] irrational and doomed to failure," Scriven wrote, meaning that much if not all of motivation research should be driven out of town like a conman trying to sell something nobody really wanted or needed.[24]

Each camp fully believing it knew best how to get answers from consumers, the qualitatives and quantitatives appeared to be on a collision course. A few months after *Motivation and Market Behavior* was published, an all-star cast of market researchers gathered in Chicago to debate the pros and cons of motivation research, with an overflow crowd of more than 350 people crammed into the workshop, sponsored by *Advertising Age*. Included in the panel discussion, moderated by Steuart Britt (now not just a Northwestern University professor but managing editor of the *Journal of Marketing*), were Ernest Dichter, Burleigh Gardner, Alfred Politz, and the acacemic Richard Crisp, men so highly regarded in the field that one observer referred to them as "Matthew, Mark, Luke, and John." Politz led with an opening salvo against the term "motivational research," thinking that the research was more of a "special technique" and thus should be linguistically demoted (Britt agreed, suggesting the term "projective techniques"). Crisp's beef was more about users' tendency to call motivation research "new" when it had been around in some form or another for twenty years, while Dichter and Gardner tried to dismiss such pettiness and remind everyone that the technique was simply a useful tool for understanding human behavior. For the moment, the battle between the brainiacs was a draw.[25]

A Nation of Frustrated Breast Feeders

The growing antagonism among traditional market researchers toward motivation research was understandable given how successfully those fluent in the technique had invaded the field in less than a decade. Motivation researchers' reputation for knowing what questions to ask, how to ask them, and how to understand the answers was particularly vexing, their investigative chops often considered way beyond the number people's comfort zone of knowing just *who* to ask. "Clients sense the freshness and vitality of the answers to motivation researchers' new and penetrating questions," said *Printers' Ink* in 1958, and American business's love affair with the technique squelched most of the critics' whining. Despite the obvious flaws of motivation research—it was rarely systematic, often ambiguous, and occasionally just a waste of time and money—clients still considered the findings to be at the very least stimulating and provocative. "The MR fans tend to put their faith in plumbing the depths of the psyche, exposing the primal drives of the unconscious, tapping the irrational powers that sweep mere 'conscious' decisions before them like so much chaff," *Printers' Ink* rather poetically described the situation.[26]

Because of its generally perceived ability to go where market research had not gone before, motivation research continued to flourish in the late fifties despite the intense infighting within the field. In fact, ad agencies that were off the beaten track seemed only now to be getting word of motivation research, late to the party but intrigued nonetheless. Even late in the decade *Advertising Agency Magazine* frequently received letters like this one from a Pacific Northwest firm wondering if it wasn't too late to get in on the psychological action: "We are a little disturbed by all this talk about motivation research, subliminal advertising and the like. We don't feel that we know too much about psychology in this neck of the woods. Should we make an effort to study the subject? Are clients looking for it, do you think? And just how much do you feel we ought to know about it?—Oregon agency."[27]

A study by State Farm Insurance showed why motivation research was more than holding its own, illustrating how the use of indirect and projective techniques often provided a set of findings completely different from those obtained in traditional research. In addition to its motivation research study, State Farm did a standard market survey, which yielded information that was certainly important. The company learned, for example, that consumers were less aware of its low rates than executives thought, that husbands made the purchase decision when it came to auto insurance, and that a good portion of customers let their policies lapse because they simply didn't have the money to renew them.[28]

State Farm's motivation research study, however, revealed a very different collection of insights. The company discovered that insurance was paternalistic, meaning policy issuers held a fatherly kind of role for customers; that insurance was fraught with anxiety, because taking out a policy seemed an admission that something could go terribly wrong; that insurance was somehow magical, the mere act of buying it serving as a protective device; that insurance was empowering, enabling customers to in some way control the future; and that insurance was wasteful, in that nothing bad usually happened and thus one was throwing away good money. State Farm ended up combining some of the findings from the survey (low rates) with those from the motivation research study (emotional support) in a new ad campaign, and also used motivation research to train its agents and its claims adjusters in human relations. Blending findings from traditional and nontraditional research, like this was exactly the kind of yin-yang approach of which experts in the field dreamed.[29]

Other marketers proved how combining motivation research with "nose counting" could lead to synergistic results. The Pan-American Coffee Bureau had done a lot of market research to get a better understanding of Americans' attitudes toward coffee, but it was a motivation research study that shone the most light on the possibilities for the beverage. A first round of depth interviews was a caffeinated free-for-all, respondents asked to describe everything from how they felt about a cup of coffee (before and after drinking it) to personal stories of "the best cup of coffee I ever had in my life." A second round of motivation research interviews keyed in on opportunity areas identified in the first round, after which researchers quantified their findings with a questionnaire. Its cup running over with insights, the Bureau ditched its "coffee break" positioning in order to turn its product into, as the researchers' report advised, "an exciting beverage." A new advertising campaign presented coffee as part of an adventurous, even glamorous lifestyle, a far cry from its image of not being very healthy, the beverage transformed into a "positive, life-accepting product." Olé![30]

These studies were just a drop in the motivation research bucket as the technique made further gains despite or because of Vance Packard's exposé and the subliminal advertising hysteria. The public may have been uneasy about researchers poking around their collective unconscious, but the people that mattered the most—clients—were chomping at the bit for motivation research work. Motivation researchers could very well have retreated or even closed up shop, afraid of further antagonizing the public and media, but instead went on the offensive, taking full advantage of the greater awareness of their technique. One motivation research firm claimed in 1958 to have already helped various ad agencies win nine major accounts by pointing out to them that advertisers' current campaigns were, psychologically speaking, flawed, just the kind of ammunition to help them get even more business.[31] Agency old-timers, hoping that motivation research would prove to be just a short-lived fad, were disappointed. "Yesterday's adman, who carried his office in his hat and did his thinking standing up—most often at a bar," continued to be flummoxed by the army of Ph.D.s in agencies, as the *Washington Post* reported in 1959, rather bitter that their impressive drinking abilities, skill in picking out an appropriate necktie, and special touch of sending an orchid to a client's wife were no longer relevant.[32]

Even some church officials had by the late fifties come around to the idea that if you couldn't beat motivation research, why not use it? The Reverend R. Dean Goodwin, director of communications for the American Baptist Convention, believed just that, seeing motivation research as an ideal way to package his church to consumers of religion. Noting that many marketers of coffee had decided to put their product in brown packaging based on consumer preferences, Goodwin asked, "What color should the church walls be? I don't know." The right answer to that question (as well as to the color of the hymnals and seat cushions), he thought, resided in motivation research. In a church in Nebraska, Goodwin had tested putting the offering at the end of the service, and contributions increased, which made him even more interested in what probing people's unconscious could reveal. Goodwin seemed to be taking a cue from adman Bruce Barton, who, some thirty years before in *The Man Nobody Knows*, suggested that Jesus Christ was, first and foremost, a salesman extraordinaire. Goodwin was even open to the idea of putting Bible lessons on chewing gum wrappers if it made more people want to go to church, thinking that the sacred could learn a thing or two from the secular when it came to marketing a product or service.[33]

The boom in motivation research in the late 1950s was also a result of the gradual discounting of some of the claims that Packard and other critics had made. Writing in the *Harvard Business Review* in 1958, for example, Raymond A. Bauer assured readers there was "no reason to panic," that the more sensational aspects of motivation research were quite overblown. The commotion over motivation research was not that much different from that a generation earlier when many feared that people like George Creel and Ivy L. Lee held special powers, somehow able to manipulate the mass media to their constituents' advantage. Modern psychology simply didn't enable some people to control other people, Bauer argued; after all, the supposed controllees were just as savvy as the controllers. "As the persuaders become more sophisticated, so do the people to be persuaded," he explained, our ability to filter propaganda having come a long way since the beginning of broadcasting (radio) in the 1920s. Fears of being manipulated by Madison Avenuers without being aware of it via appeals to deeply seated motives were unfounded because consumers had the power to resist techniques of persuasion on both conscious and unconscious levels; this "see you and raise you" defense mechanism was an unbeatable hand. "The hidden persuaders are made of straw," Bauer insisted, and there was no cause for alarm that Orwell's *1984* had arrived a quarter century early.[34]

Even if they were made of straw, the hidden persuaders were, according to some market researchers, doing more damage than good to the field. Daniel Yankelovich, vice president of Nowland and Company in the late 1950s, was one of the most outspoken critics of motivation research, thinking it was only adding to the public's confusion and suspicion about marketing and advertising. Yankelovich strongly resented the fact that his occupation of choice was accused of sinister doings, specifically lifting psychoanalytic techniques for the purpose of mind control over consumers. "The public is presented with the idea of an unsavory alliance of symbol manipulators and depth probers," he wrote in 1958, decrying the fact that motivation research and its sidekick, subliminal advertising, was accused of brainwashing consumers into wanting things they would otherwise have no interest in.[35]

Some of the ideas that had sprung out of motivation research into cocktail party conversation, obviously influenced by Freudian psychology, perhaps proved Yankelovich's point. Americans chewed gum, one motivation research report about food went, because we were "a nation of frustrated breast feeders," the habit "a safety valve for impulses related to the infant's pleasure in sucking." Soup was even more regressive, returning the eater back to the uterus because it elicited "prenatal sensations of being surrounded by the amniotic fluid in our mother's womb." A wife baked a cake for her husband not because the big lug liked sweets but rather as a symbolic act of giving birth (leading Yankelovich to quip, "No wonder the poor dears get so upset when the cake falls!"). Yankelovich (who would turn out to be one of the premier market researchers in history via his monitoring of the American zeitgeist) thought such interpretations were not only ridiculous ("the language of psychoanalysis, invented and developed to deal with emotional problems of a neurotic character, cannot be applied with such carefree abandon to the consumption of products," he wrote), but were also doing serious damage to the reputation of market research and to that of its clients. "The great problem of the marketing research field is that its true potential is generally undervalued and misunderstood," he felt, hoping that all this "stale talk" could be squelched so that the profession could realize its full potential.[36]

Leave the Driving to Us

Most marketers believed that motivation research was much more than stale talk, however. Much of the business community saw nothing wrong whatsoever about motivation research, regarding it as just another, though especially effective, tool to identify consumer wants and needs. With motivation research, "the information comes from the world's best authority on the subject—the customer himself," thought *Nation's Business* in 1958, viewing the technique as simply a "better means of two-way communication" between marketer and consumer. In fact, if anyone was to blame for the motivation research dustup, it was consumers, because their failure to tell marketers what they needed to know essentially forced the latter to develop such a powerful technique. "In many cases, the consumer has been unable or unwilling to give meaningful answers," the magazine continued; Americans covered up their actions and preferences or were just oblivious to them.[37]

Seeing which way the wind was blowing in the field, and no doubt eager to keep his clients happy, Elmo Roper, the quintessential numbers man, had now gotten into the motivation research act, his firm helping Greyhound change its advertising to reflect the fact that the class of people who actually rode its buses was higher than people thought. Roper's motivation research study for Greyhound also revealed that automobile drivers disliked the hassle of long trips, leading the bus company to decide to tell Americans in its advertising, "Leave the Driving to Us." The campaign made advertising history and, not incidentally, led to Greyhound's best year to date.[38] Besides being used in all of marketing's "four Ps," motivation research's applications spread in the late 1950s, with companies finding the technique quite versatile. Human resources had adopted motivation research to train salespeople and evaluate employees, for example, a natural extension of their use of standard psychological tests.[39]

As motivation research settled in and made itself at home in the corporate world, market research methodology—typically not a subject that most businesspeople, much less the general public, found especially interesting—took on a certain cachet in the late 1950s as its huge economic implications became clear. "The current debate on subjective depth probing versus objective survey questionnaires is the latest conflict in the fast-changing field of market research," wrote Avron Fleishman in *Management Review* in 1958, quite sure that "the argument is of deep importance to business management." The "depth vs. breadth" issue had become a central concern not just because of the subliminal advertising phenomenon but also because consumers of the late fifties appeared to be a much different breed from customers of ten or even five years earlier. "Never before have buying patterns been more complex and more changeable," Fleishman concluded, and "never before have decision-makers so needed the guidance provided by reliable market research."[40]

Indeed, after ten years of prosperity and abundance for many Americans, the much anticipated feeding frenzy of consumerism—in part a response to a decade and a half of thrift and sacrifice during depression and war—seemed to be becoming more of a light snack. Americans were, quite simply, becoming satiated, many leading economists and sociologists believed, our horn of plenty now overflowing. "I suggest that there is a tendency for people, once they are accustomed to upper-middle-class norms, to lose zest for bounteous spending on consumer goods," explained David Riesman in 1958, thinking that consumption "no longer has the old self-evident quality." Riesman believed that the era of the mass market was ending and a new era of the specialized market beginning, meaning that businesses had to think differently if they were going to survive. Developing consumer "profiles" was the answer, Riesman suggested, and matching brands with customer personalities was the best way to keep Americans spending and the economy growing. Another leading sociologist, Rolf Meyersohn of the University of Chicago, concurred that simple demographics were no longer a good way to slice the American pie. "We, the social scientists as well as advertisers, perhaps must categorize consumers along more subtle lines, such as psychological classes," Meyersohn said with his marketing hat on, an idea that happened to fit motivation research like a glove.[41]

In fact, at America's biggest ad agencies, sorting consumers into more useful buckets based on motivation research findings was becoming a top priority. Arthur Koponen, the J. Walter Thompson psychologist, was now using "psychological needs" as the basis for classifying the five thousand families that composed the agency's Consumer Purchase Panel, for example, just the kind of "subtle" approach Meyersohn recommended. "In creating brand images we want a brand expression that will be appealing to and compatible with the personalities of our potential customer," said Koponen, finding consumer needs like "achievement," "compliance," "order," "autonomy," and "dominance" more useful than consumers' age and income.[42] Halfway across the country, Donald David, copy supervisor at Campbell-Ewald in Detroit, also was trying to match his client's corporate and brand personalities with those of consumers, this application of motivation research finally something creative people were excited about. To him, identifying consumers' dominant personality traits like "aggressive," "benevolent," "conscientious," "daring," and "zany" through motivation research offered a wonderful opportunity for what he described as "image building," a now commonly accepted approach to positioning products and services in the marketplace that half a century before was considered a rather revolutionary idea.[43]

Interestingly, however, while the advertising industry quickly and firmly grabbed onto motivation research, people in public relations were slow to embrace it, not immediately seeing its value for the field. At first glance, this was odd, given that PR was of course all about consumer psychology, as Edward Bernays had shown decades earlier. That PR people didn't do cartwheels over motivation research was especially surprising, given that they were already not nearly as statistically inclined as those in advertising. Unlike advertising, however, the field was mostly about relationships, the workings of publicity a proposition much different from the art of persuasion. "Generally, public relations people have preferred to rely on their intuitions and experience or to use older survey techniques," as Mackarness H. Goode explained in the *Public Relations Journal* in 1958. There was, however, one notable exception. SRI told a large, powerful trade organization that a motivation research study revealed that Americans felt big companies were essential to maintaining their way of life, this good news leading the industry to abandon its almost apologetic public persona and go on the PR offensive.[44]

Buoyed by such success stories, motivation researchers appropriately viewed their technique as the biggest and best thing to hit their field since Gallup's and Roper's opinion polls. Motivation research may have been less than scientific, but there was no doubt that it made great copy, its stars perfectly aligned with postwar America's obsession with all things psychological. For better or worse, the public was now talking about market research, something that certainly hadn't happened when the industry was almost all about numbers and dominated by, as they were sometimes known, the "slide rule boys." If it contributed to the field's overall growth and offered clients an alternative to less than scintillating data, wasn't motivation research good for market research?[45]

The fact that the University of Southern California drama department was dabbling with motivation research was a clear sign of its appeal to people who would otherwise have nothing to do with market research. Through something he called M-R Theater (not to be confused with Dichter's "Motivational Theater"), James H. Butler, chair of the department, thought he could possibly bridge the gap between the arts and sciences by having a psychiatrist analyze audience reactions to a play performed at the university's Art Linkletter Playhouse on two different nights. On June 6, 1958, and again on June 13 to the same audience, a professional Hollywood cast (including Marion Ross, later Mrs. Cunningham on television's *Happy Days*, and Ben Wright, perhaps best known as the Nazi Herr Zeller in *The Sound of Music*) performed *Table*

Number Seven, one of two plays from Terence Rattigan's *Separate Tables*. Audience reactions were documented during and after each performance via infrared photographs, tape recordings, and questionnaires, and Barnet Sharrin, M.D., was then asked to "give the actors and director his psychoanalytical interpretation of the play and its characters," as Butler explained. The kicker was that Sharrin offered his assessment to the ensemble after the first performance, meaning the actors and director could and did use that information in the second.[46]

The diagnosis? "A limited study of the data thus obtained shows a statistically significant shift in favor of the second performance," stated Butler in not very artistic language, with the second show "superior and more effective than the first." Would the psychiatrist's couch become a permanent feature of the stage given such findings? Not according to Philip K. Scheuer, a reporter for the *Los Angeles Times* who had been part of the experiment. "What of the imponderables involved—the players surer of themselves, the listeners more receptive, etc., etc.?" he asked, highly skeptical that motivation research would head to Broadway anytime soon. "I suppose it can be applied advantageously to industry, advertising and other mediums of communication," Scheuer wrote, but "it will take a good deal more to convince me that it can be used successfully to regiment the arts, control the emotions, condition reflexes, win friends and influence people generally."[47]

Motivation research even went Hollywood in 1959, hitting the big screen in *Ask Any Girl*, a feature film starring Shirley MacLaine. A "frothy spoof of motivation research," as Mae Tinee of the *Chicago Tribune* described it in her surprisingly positive review, *Ask Any Girl* was a classic innocent-girl-comes-to-big-city flick, with the usual hilarity—mostly involving martinis and men. Motivation research comes into the picture when MacLaine's character, Meg Wheeler, observes how appeals to the subconscious can persuade people to buy things they're not especially interested in, and then applies the same principles to her target market—Evan Doughton, played by Gig Young. Most interesting of all, at least in terms of how motivation research was depicted by Tinseltown, is when Evan's older brother, Miles (played almost inevitably by David Niven), does some research and plans a campaign to bring consumer (MacLaine) and product (Young) together, all this marketing mayhem making "bright, breezy entertainment for adults."[48]

Space World

Anything, in fact, that helped change researchers' image as the wet blanket of marketing and advertising would be a step in the right direction, many believed. Some of this negative image had to do with market researchers' role in evaluating advertising copywriters' work; in the process they were often blamed for sapping much of the creativity from campaigns-to-be. Given researchers' well-earned reputation as the killjoy of advertising, "is there any wonder that the entire field of market research is often looked upon as droll, mechanistic and unimaginative, a stumbling-block in the path of true expression?" wondered Irving White, motivation research supervisor for the Paper Mate Company. White astutely located the tension between researchers and copywriters within the long historical division between the arts and the sciences, but he argued that the brilliance of men like Freud and Jean Piaget illustrated that the two realms were by no means mutually exclusive. Likewise, White felt, motivation researchers, with their "theory-based sensitivity and inductive thinking," helped bring "fresh, exciting *and* valid advertising to the table," a best-of-both worlds set of skills that copywriters should appreciate rather than shun.[49]

For certain products, such as those sold in supermarkets, motivation researchers' thinking was considered especially useful because most shoppers didn't make their purchase decisions until they were in the store. Research showed that 16 percent of shoppers bought things based on (low) price and another 16 percent went for heavily advertised brands they knew and trusted. The remaining 68 percent of shoppers were, however, "fair game for the motivational researchers," as *Time* described the situation, "who took dead aim with all the analytical gimmicks under the supermarket sun." These two consumers out of every three weren't just neutral or even indecisive when it came to shopping in supermarkets, motivation research thinking went, but "emotionally insecure," and therefore the most open to persuasion. Two big factors thus came into play to snag the emotionally insecure at the point of purchase—packaging and shelf location. More than price or advertising, appealing to these shoppers' "impulses" through emotionally affirming packaging and easy-to-see and -read location on the shelf was the key to getting their attention and making the sale.[50]

Radio was another business that had a particularly keen interest in motivation research, more out of desperation than anything else. Struggling to survive as television became ever more popular in the late fifties, radio stations across the country brought in motivation researchers en masse to try to keep their sinking ships afloat. The goal among station managers was to find a well-defined personality that listeners found appealing, that is, to determine whether a broadcaster should be "young" or "old," "believable" or "fun." If part of a network, stations had the additional challenge of finding a format that struck a balance between the national "brand" and local tastes, not an easy thing to do. Fortunately, motivation research was there to save the day, its focus on listeners' emotions believed to be exactly what the doctor ordered, sometimes quite literally. Stations like Houston's KPRC sought out what manager Jack Harris called the "'Space World' of motivational research," specifically Dr. Dichter and his Institute for Motivational Research team to find just the right "image." "We have found in our work that when people tune in to a tv or radio program they are guided by basic psychological needs or need constellations," said Dr. Tibor Koeves, vice president of IMR in 1959, he claiming that "it isn't the story [or] even the star of a show which attracts them but the need to satisfy an inner drive." Westerns allowed listeners and viewers to release "pent-up feelings of aggression in a competitive society full of stress," for example, while news provided "orientation" and the arts "a heightened sense of life in the midst of a routine existence." Satisfying consumers' psychological needs was radio's best chance to not only survive but even thrive in the years ahead, motivation researchers like Koeves believed; this was the key to getting listeners to tune in.[51]

For industries in less dire straits, motivation research was more of a luxury, a nice add-on to an already robust market research program. Much of the appeal of motivation research to managers in consumer products was its ability to produce ideas and hypotheses, unlike after-the-fact (and, often, too-little-too-late) traditional research. A. R. Graustein, Jr., marketing director of Lever Brothers, explained in 1958 how his company used motivation research as a sort of launching pad: "We have come to think of motivation research as essentially an *idea* source. . . . Once we have developed an idea through motivation research, we can turn it over to the marketing people and say, in effect, 'Look, boys, does this idea intrigue you enough to make you want to take some new marketing action? If so, tell us what you'd like to do and how you'd go about doing it, and we'll then test the effectiveness for you with old-fashioned nose-counting techniques.'"[52]

Intrigued after reading about the method in business and general magazines, more industrial marketers and human resources people fell under its powerful spell in the late fifties. "At first glance, it may be difficult to see how subsurface motivations can influence industrial chemical sales, new product development, product improvement or employee productivity," wrote *Chemical Week* in 1958, but then provided a litany of examples of how motivation research was indeed being applied in those areas. Dow Chemical had had success using motivation research for its antifreeze, GE for its motors, DuPont for its automobile polish, and Corn Products Refining for its industrial starches, all of them illustrating how the technique had spread into the less sexier side of marketing. Other industrial fields such as steel, iron, and pigments too were gung-ho on motivation research, this second wave no doubt leading manly men to not only confront but actually talk about their feelings during depth interviews, quite a remarkable thing in postwar America.[53]

Considering how much more motivation research cost than regular research, managers in all industries must have felt it really did bring something new and different to the table. A single interview for a motivation research study cost as much as $30 in 1958, versus anywhere from $3 to $10 for a survey-type interview, which meant that marketing "boys" would choose to use motivation research only if they couldn't learn what they wanted from "old-fashioned nose-counting techniques." Clients' demand for motivation research, not to mention the much higher fees to be charged, made most traditional research firms offer it as a service, but their staffers usually lacked the spark of motivation research specialists. One reason for this was that "sample men" didn't truly believe in the technique, their passion residing in the hard proof of numbers; also, they simply didn't know how to deal with all of its many complexities and peculiarities. Motivation research specialists, with their interdisciplinary teams of behavioral scientists on staff, could not only take on the most challenging psycho-social issue but also offer clients one-stop shopping, something they readily pointed out to clients comparing services between big research firms and ad agencies.[54]

By the end of the decade, motivation research had become so familiar within industry circles that it was the stuff of satire, even among those who paid lots of money for it. "Sam Jones" weighed in on the subject for *Printers' Ink* in 1959, for instance, telling his story to E. F. Schmidt, merchandising manager of Anheuser-Busch. "I am here to warn you opinion and motivation research guys that you have been sticking your noses into my subconscious too much for your own good," Jones, an average man by any measure, "told" Mr. Schmidt. "When some bright young man with a notebook starts trying to trick me into disclosing my 'deepdown' (that's a phrase I picked up from a cake mix ad) yearnings, motives, prejudices, and fears. . . . I say watch out brother because I have a subconscious as tricky as foxy grandpa." Jones (a "self-appointed spokesman for us average consumers") was giving big marketers like Anheuser-Busch fair warning about the chameleon-like nature of people like himself. "Another thing that makes me such a slippery character for you id probers is I change my mind sometimes faster than you can add up your figures," he cautioned, his subconscious not only tricky but "about as loyal as an alley cat."[55]

A Psychological United Nations

No "id prober" was better known than Ernest Dichter, who was busier than ever sticking his nose into consumers' collective unconscious. By the late fifties, Dichter had achieved almost mythical status, with many in awe, if not a little afraid, of the ubershrink. In 1959, Dorothy Diamond, a writer for the advertising trade magazine *Tide*, wanted to see for herself what the motivation research fuss was all about, heading up to the IMR's offices for a personal look-see. Driving up the winding path (named Prickly Pear Hill Road for the irritation Dichter and his institute had caused) leading to the imposing castle, Diamond wasn't quite sure what was in store for her, feeling a bit like a character in a Grimm fairy tale. Upon her arrival, she was met not by a journalist-eating ogre but by Colin Kempner, the company's research coordinator, who promptly conducted an abbreviated depth interview with her. Rather than it being like an angst-filled therapy session or worse, Diamond felt the interview (about flatware) wasn't unpleasant in the least. "There was absolutely nothing sinister about the whole business," she later wrote, thinking in fact that Kempner's questioning was not much different from a reporter's. The only difference was that feelings were as important as facts in the depth interview, she surmised, with the conversation allowed, even encouraged, to go "off-script." "If there's anything wrong in finding out what people think about your product, in uncovering their resentments and meeting their needs, then I fail to see what it is," Diamond concluded, half relieved and half disappointed that her brush with Dichterian motivation research had left her entirely unscathed.[56]

Internationally famous after being cast as the protagonist in Packard's *The Hidden Persuaders*, Dichter began to aggressively pitch his company's services in Europe, confident his act would play well overseas. The IMR had in its hip pocket giant companies like General Foods, General Mills, Lever Brothers, and American Airlines as clients (who now paid $500 for a consulting session lasting a few hours), but for Dichter the world could and would be his oyster when it came to motivation research. "More and more countries throughout the world are switching to American psychological values which emphasize 'the good life,'" he told a group of journalists over lunch at the New York restaurant "21" in late December 1958, and he was perhaps better equipped than anyone else to export those values to Europe. Dichter claimed his company was already studying consumers in fifteen countries, this "inter-motivational" research not just a powerful selling tool but something that he believed would "help bring the world closer to a psychological United Nations."[57]

Dichter's firm was of course part of a large wave of American companies going overseas in the postwar years in search of new markets, the need to tailor products and communications to fit foreign tastes a bonanza for market researchers.[58] "The surge of participation by American companies in multinational operations in the late 1950s and 1960s was dramatic," observed Mira Wilkins in *The Maturing of Multinational Enterprise*, citing twenty-eight hundred U.S. businesses with a stake in about ten thousand enterprises abroad in 1957.[59] And as an American consultant, Dichter himself seemed to be in the right place at the right time. "American management consulting firms served as the primary institutional conduits for the transfer of American organization models to Europe in the 1960s and early 1970s," Christopher McKenna wrote in *The World's Newest Profession*, considering this the latest wave of exportation of U.S.-style business know-how. At home too Dichter and his competitors were enjoying the bounty of what McKenna called "the Gilded Age of consulting," with American management consultants (especially Booz Allen Hamilton, Cresap, McCormick and Paget, and McKinsey and Company) reaching the height of their power around 1960. There were twenty-five hundred separate firms and about thirty thousand active management consultants in the United States in 1962, according to the *Wall Street Journal*, their range of clients and assignments truly extraordinary.[60]

Naturally, it was ironic that Europe had to import motivation research expertise from America in the late fifties, given that Europe was where it had all begun a quarter of a century earlier. Their careers and often their lives in danger, social scientists had left European universities in droves before and during the war, with many more scholars recruited by American colleges after the conflict had ended. Faced with a shortage of behavioral psychologists and with few people left on the Continent fluent in motivation research, European market research organizations were now aligning themselves with American ones. The Hamburg-based Institut für Absatzpsychologie, for example, hooked up with Burleigh Gardner's SRI in 1959, the Americans brought in to help the German firm figure out Europe's complex, highly regional buying habits. More than two hundred brands of cigarettes were sold in Germany at the time, for instance, but only a few were nationally distributed, which meant that local preferences played a huge role in brand choice. The beer category was similarly fragmented, with the Germans hoping that Gardner, with his expertise in issues of class, could come up with a way to bridge the geographic differences.[61] Like Dichter, Gardner thought motivation research could take off in Europe much as it had in the United States as the Common Market encouraged the development of a large, consumer-oriented middle class.[62]

While Dichter was without question the world heavyweight champion of motivation research, Gardner was a worthy contender. A soft-spoken Texan, Gardner saw himself less as a market researcher and more as a social scientist working in the field of mass communication; unlike his more famous colleague, he had no European or psychoanalytic connections. Gardner and the fifteen other anthropologists on his staff "explore[d] the taboos, totems and voodoo rites of U.S. corporation executives, housewives and other bizarre indigenes," as *Printers' Ink* put it, helping marketers like Sears, CBS, and *Fortune* "understand more about the hopes, aspirations, self-doubts, daydreams and assorted emotional drives" that influenced consumer behavior. From his nondirective interviews, in which the interviewer didn't try to guide or control the conversation in classic motivation research style, Gardner and his fellow social anthropologists were able to extract how the interviewee felt about his or her station in life—prime fodder for determining how to position a product in the marketplace. Using SRI's findings, clients often advertised the same product differently to different consumers, for example, positioning something as offering validation for the working class, sophistication for the middle class, and elegance for the upper class; this social stratification sort of marketing strategy was Gardner's unique talent.[63]

It was Dichter, however, who was best able to capitalize on motivation research's day in the sun. Recognizing he now had the opportunity to fulfill his lifelong dream to do missionary work proclaiming the power and glory of consumerism, Dichter seized the day, setting up more than a dozen satellite offices in the United States and abroad. His project fees jumped from $20,000 to $60,000 and annual billings to a cool $1 million, allowing him to increase his staff to about sixty-five full-timers and fifteen hundred to two thousand part-time interviewers. His "Living Laboratory," in which he taped twelve to sixteen people watching television in a setting designed to look like a living room, must have been for Dichter a dream come true, an opportunity to study consumer behavior in a contained and controlled universe all his own. All of Dichter's dreams in fact seemed to have come true by 1960, with Packard's book the final stroke of luck that turned the impoverished Austrian émigré into the most famous market researcher in the world. Dichter kept a leather couch in his office, which added to the effect of what a reporter later described as, quite fittingly, "the consultation room of a prosperous psychiatrist."[64]

Although he was a psychiatrist and was often referred to as a "mass psychoanalyst," Dichter preferred thinking of himself as a doctor applying his skills to products that were, for lack of a better word, "ill." "Something isn't working—or selling," he said in 1959, so "I doctor it."[65] More than a quarter century later, in fact, Dichter still used a medical metaphor to describe his approach. "Like a good physician I can diagnose very quickly," he said very late in his career, the next step being "to prescribe a remedy."[66] In fact, consumers' inability to accurately answer researchers' direct questions—the whole basis for motivation research—was equivalent to a patient's typically ill-advised attempt at self-diagnosis. Dichter was especially adept at providing prescriptions for products afflicted with strong guilt associations like cigarettes, candy, and liquor, prescribing a spoonful of "moral permission" to make the medicine go down. Like other observers of the social scene in the late fifties, such as Riesman, Russell Lynes, and William H. Whyte, Jr., Dichter saw Americans as a particularly lonely crowd with a dire need for emotional support. The country's "puritan complex" was an unfortunate consequence of its prosperity, he thought, with many if not most Americans unable to fully enjoy the good things in life they had worked so hard to earn (himself included, ironically). From his immigrant perspective and impoverished background, Dichter viewed Americans as a decidedly insecure, needy bunch with fragile egos and even shakier self-worth. Women used nail polish, for example, not just to look attractive but, for Dichter, to "close off their extremities" in order to keep within "their own small, private world." Wrapping brands around such identity boosters as power, love, creativity, immortality, and, especially, security was marketers' best chance for success, Dichter consistently argued; it was the best therapy for a pretty sickly group of patients.[67]

Dichter's work was also very much about deconstruction, and he would break down a product into its operative parts like a literature scholar deciphering a James Joyce novel. Dichter was often summoned to Madison Avenue agencies for a half- or full-day session for this very reason, a gaggle of adpeople interested in the possible signifieds of a particular signifier. A cigar might occasionally have been just a cigar for Freud, but not for Dichter—its shape and color were key indicators for how it should be advertised. The context in which cigars were used—smoked with a glass of brandy in the other hand, say, or in front of a blazing fireplace—would be for Dichter another way to crack the product's code, leading to the appropriate "feeling" for an ad campaign. Like students listening to a brilliant professor lecture about the meanings embedded in *A Portrait of the Artist as a Young Man*, middle-aged men in gray flannel and black glasses gobbled up Dichter's analysis, receiving a free education in what would later be called postmodern theory.[68]

Dichter took full advantage of his new fame in the late fifties, his name seemingly in the Rolodex of every journalist looking for a quote about any aspect of advertising or marketing. "Far from being a luxury, they are involved in a man's struggle for survival, stability and security," he told the *Wall Street Journal* in 1958, speaking not of, say, burglar alarms or seat belts but of cigarettes, his firm one of many doing motivation research for tobacco companies. (Americans smoked "to prove that they are virile, to demonstrate their energy, vigor and potency," countered SRI, "a psychological satisfaction, moral censure, ridicule, or even the paradoxical weakness of 'enslavement' to a habit.")[69] Credit cards, another business his firm was studying, were "magic," Dichter thought, items that "provide the American consumer with a symbol of inexhaustible potency" because the cards were as good as money but could be used when one temporarily had none.[70] Dichter was also investigating the presumably drab world of carpet sweepers that year, digging up some pretty interesting findings. Women liked to do housework, his research showed, challenging the standard thinking that the more modern conveniences there were to make chores easier, the better. "There's no creativity in pushing a button," he told a group of reporters who had gathered at the Drake Hotel in Chicago to hear this surprising news; the "modern" American woman (55 percent of the adult female population, he estimated) considered housework an interesting and exciting kind of endeavor.[71]

Of course, some of Dichter's Dichterisms were completely lost on managers more concerned with their brand's bottom line than its semiotics. As his take on housework perhaps suggested, clients found Dichter's thoughts on women most puzzling and infuriating, as he typically limited the real reason for much of their behavior as consumers to some aspect of sexuality or fertility. ("The [male] consumer is trapped in a harem," Dichter once said, "lured and enticed by twenty good-looking women.")[72] His explanation for why women baked cakes—an act of fertility, he famously said—was widely ridiculed, a textbook example of why some felt motivation research to be all hot air. Dichter, however, stuck to his guns on his cake-as-baby metaphor, insisting that baking was inextricably linked to reproduction. Just as women immediately asked after giving birth if their baby was a boy or a girl, his thinking went (before ultrasound), the first questions they asked after removing a cake from the oven was, "Is it done? Is it good or bad?" This for Dichter was a "fertile moment." "Once the cake is actually on the table it is no longer hers—it belongs to her family," he later explained, "so I recommended that [clients] emphasize this 'creative, fertile' moment in their ads." He applied this idea of the "fertile moment" in all kinds of situations and for many different product categories, in fact, routinely recommending that clients first identify and then exploit it in their advertising.[73]

In between those who felt that every word Dichter uttered was a unique pearl of wisdom and those who listened to every word with a raised eyebrow were those who selectively applied his insights. The trick with Dichter was, as one anonymous client put it in 1959, "knowing how to use him," this wise client aware that "he can be a valuable gold mine if you know what to ask him and which of his contributions to pick up." The most important thing was to realize that even Dichter himself sometimes didn't take too seriously what he was saying. "Some of the psychological folderol he tosses off may come just because he expects that this is what his client wants to hear," this same client thought; "he may use this kind of lingo tongue-in-cheek." Besides liking to hear himself wax poetic on any subject imaginable, Dichter also was occasionally (and understandably, given how much he talked) just plain wrong. One notable blooper was his recommendation to executives at Japan Air Lines that they use only American pilots for flights to and from the United States, as that was what Americans "would feel most comfortable with." Further (or some?) research revealed, however, that exactly the opposite was true, something that Dichter readily admitted. "Most Americans are going to the Orient because they like it, and that means all things Oriental," he subsequently opined, doing a complete turnaround and recommending, "the more Oriental . . . , the better."[74]

In a period of American business heavily populated by "the organization man," Dichter's ability to, as we call it today, "think outside the box" must have been considered a welcome (or bone-chilling) gust of fresh air. Even from today's perspective, his ability to challenge status quo thinking was remarkable, with no aspect of consumer culture too sacred to be left as it was if he thought it could be improved in some way. In one typical stretch of 1959, for example, Dichter told the Australian government that its well-known "Down Under" nickname was all wrong ("bad semantics," he said), and that the country should be rebranded as "Hub of the South Pacific." During this same period, Dichter was working with the Greenbelt Cooperative Stores in Maryland, and he told the owners of the supermarket chain they should think about putting in comfortable chairs around the cash registers, because he had learned (through a brainstorming technique he called "Operation Day-dream") that housewives felt tired while they waited to pay for their groceries. (He also told them to put in a "splurge counter" filled with luxury items and an "economy counter" offering only inexpensive products.) Dichter was also continuing his work with the automobile industry, trying to get one company to offer "truer" and more "honest" models, advice based on his discovery that Americans wanted cars which "understood" them and didn't reveal "too much of [their] personalit[ies]." "Since he began, Dichter has aroused more storms, ire and conviction than any other market researcher," *Business Week* confidently stated as he worked on these and many other projects, his ideas often difficult to digest but never bland.[75]

Hot, Handsome, a Honey to Handle

While Dichter and his competitors rode the wave of interest in motivation research and expanded their empires around the world in the late fifties, troubling signs were beginning to appear on the horizon for them and their technique. For one thing, despite the phenomenal interest in motivation research among managers in all kinds of industries, few managers could really explain the technique. In 1958, *Tide* magazine asked a group of top marketing and agency people what they knew about motivation research, and only 5 percent claimed to have a "thorough understanding" of it (76 percent said they "knew something" about it). And in another study by Long Island University, 74 percent of those in advertising and, amazingly, 88 percent in market research itself said that top executives in their respective fields had absolutely "no understanding" of motivation research. Motivation research was, according to those who regularly used it, the best thing since sliced bread even if they had no idea as to how or why it worked.[76]

Its novelty perhaps wearing off, motivation research began to show chinks in its armor. More "sample men" were coming out of the woodwork to attack it as the magical aura surrounding it started to dissipate. Irving Penner, another naysayer at A. J. Wood, went on the speaking circuit to convince marketers that while motivation research was certainly "spectacular" and "entertaining," it was also the work of "medicine men."[77] Penner felt that because motivation research wasn't measurable, it just wasn't enough for businesspeople to use it by itself; some of them even said it was "tantamount to malpractice." Good research was, pure and simple, a combination of qualitative and quantitative information, with anything less than that a shortcut likely to lead decision makers down the wrong road. "I cannot blame a reporter for ignoring the more pragmatic type of research, however sound, when he can write about the sexual implications of dog food purchasing," Penner told a group of businesspeople at a conference at Michigan State University in 1959, but there was no excuse for marketers to be as dismissive about hard data.[78]

Others who had been neutral toward or even supportive of motivation research began to have serious doubts about the validity of the technique. Steuart Britt was now convinced that "some businessmen are suckers for buying so-called research because a man is called a doctor"—this from someone who himself had a Ph.D. (in psychology from Yale).[79] Similarly, S. I. Hayakawa, a noted semanticist, believed the motivation research faithful, "like other isolated people in underdeveloped areas[,] are devout believers in voodoo," especially those in the car business. While there is no shortage of irrationality in the real world, Hayakawa felt, most people "are reasonably well oriented to reality," making motivation research a flawed technique. Cigarette advertising was firmly packed with motivation research findings ("Some People Like Their Pleasure BIG," went one headline), but automobile ads (and even model names) were just as fully loaded, so to speak, with the technique, despite the belief that the crashing and burning of the Edsel would drive motivation research out of Detroit for good. Mercury's Marauder line, for example, "put 12,000 pounds of thrust behind every engine stroke," just the stuff to deliver on the carmaker's campaign theme, "Hot, Handsome, a Honey to Handle." If new car sales were booming, that would be one thing, Hayakawa argued, but they were in fact weak, suggesting that motivation research was not very effective where the rubber hit the road.[80]

Perhaps smarting from his own agency's unfortunate experience with motivation research as applied to the Edsel, Cornelius Du Bois, research director of FC&B, seized the opportunity to take a potshot at the technique. Du Bois maintained that even if what motivation researchers claimed was true—that consumers' attitudes toward brands were a function of deep-seated feelings,

often forged at an early age—there was little marketers could do about changing them. Better to "hire Drs. Spock and Gesell to develop attitudes now for
the 1985 model," Du Bois said in 1959, considering it a waste of marketers'
time and money to try to deal with heavy issues like inferiority complexes
stemming from having acne as a teenager, feelings of guilt and inadequacy re-
sulting from sibling jealousy or early toilet training, or the yearning to return
to the security and warmth of the womb.[81]

Also, a significant number of executives remained simply unwilling or unable to put their faith in Sigmund Freud and his followers. As anyone who has
ever worked in a big company could tell you, any new kind of research or new
thinking in general was an uphill battle in many organizations, with resistance
to change a common theme. Working with behavioral scientists (or "ologists,"
as Joseph W. Newman referred to them in a 1958 article in the *Harvard Business
Review*) was especially challenging for lots of managers, because of "their often
strange and upsetting theories of human behavior and their ideas of the best
ways to study it." Resistance to accepted ways of thinking and doing things, the
perceived threat of bringing in outsiders with their foreign jargon, unrealistic
expectations, and the low status of market research were just a few of the obstacles thwarting motivation research even at the peak of its popularity.[82]

Motivation research was now suddenly somewhat vulnerable, and it was
probably inevitable that new methodologies promising to be the next big thing
in market research materialized. One of these was "perception research," conceived by Saul Ben-Zeev and Irving S. White, directors of Creative Research
Associates. When it came to understanding consumers, the "what" was more
important than the "why," Ben-Zeev and White claimed, the two psychologists arguing that their technique was thus superior to motivation research.
Ben-Zeev and White were completely uninterested in the mysterious goings
on in the human subconscious, with perception research focusing instead
on how consumers experienced the products they chose to use. "It is more
important to know that a woman enjoys the sensation of applying a facial
lotion, for example, than to know that she has the fantasy of identifying with
a movie star when using the product," explained Ben-Zeev in 1959. Likewise,
he and White insisted, pipe smoking could very well at some level be about
satisfying dependency needs of asserting oneself, but it was elements of the
experience itself—lighting up or puffing, say—that offered marketers more
to work with. Emotional drives were varied and undefined, while perceptions
and experiences were specific and controllable, the two reasoned, their logic
another stone thrown at motivation research's house.[83]

One more new kid on the market research block—"operations research"—began to pick up steam in 1959, posing another threat to motivation research. "Motivation research, as the fad of the industry and the darling of its most 'advanced' practitioners, has already seen its best days," thought Martin Mayer in 1959, with operations research the new fad hot on its tail. Operations research (OR, naturally) was indeed gaining ground in business circles, its adherents (including Y&R) intrigued by the possibility to convert marketing problems into mathematical formulas, which could then be solved. Using game theory, Arthur D. Little was pioneering work in the field, and the consulting firm's physicists, mathematicians, and engineers were confident they could predict the result of a marketing effort such as an ad campaign. If true, motivation research's psychological and sociological noodling could very well be blown away by the mathematical certainty of operational research, an unfair match between speculation and calculation. One of Little's smarty-pants was already predicting that advertising copy would one day be written by electronic machines, turning the art into a science (and putting those crusty creative types out to pasture).[84] Was motivation research indeed doomed as newer, more precise research methods came down the pike? Certain events of the early 1960s would definitively answer that question.

5

The Psychology of the World of Objects

An empty sock drawer is a symbol of an empty heart.
—Ernest Dichter, in "Soxology: A Strategy for
Stimulating Sock Sales," a 1966 report for DuPont

A group of researchers at McCann-Erickson were understandably confused after talking with some low-income Southern women about insecticides. The women were convinced that roach killers which came in little plastic trays worked better and were less messy than sprays, even though they had never tried them. This kind of thinking kept market researchers up at night. Intent on solving the mystery to help their client develop a new product, the researchers asked the women to draw pictures of roaches and then write stories about what they had drawn. This exercise could reveal the women's subconscious feelings about roaches, the researchers believed, and perhaps explain why they preferred to use sprays when they knew the other kind of product was superior.[1]

The women's sketches and stories did indeed tell the agency what it needed to know. All the roaches the women drew were male, for one thing, the stories that went along with the drawings equally revealing. "A man likes a free meal you cook for him [and] as long as there is food he will stay," one woman wrote alongside her doodle of a particularly unsavory-looking insect, another mentioning in her roach story that "nothing is impossible with that guy." In short, the roaches were convenient surrogates for men who had treated these women badly, the researchers concluded, and this attitude accounted for the women's illogical preference for spray insecticides over the better but more passive product. "Killing the roaches with a bug spray and watching them squirm and die allowed the women to express their hostility toward men and have greater control over the roaches," explained Paula Drillman, McCann-Erickson's director of strategic planning. Such findings were a perfect example of how researchers were relying on psychology to understand the emotional bond between consumers and brands.[2]

Sound familiar? It should, given how extensively motivation research had been used to penetrate consumers' psyches in order to reveal the hidden truths behind their often unpredictable, irrational behavior. This Kafkaesque case study didn't take place in, say, 1958, however, but rather in 1988, a full thirty years after motivation research had peaked in popularity and crossed over into the discourse of American pop culture. The bug tale illustrates how deeply motivation research had penetrated the nation's subconscious, its legacy in fact still very much alive and kicking a full half century after it captured Americans' complete attention.

Magnificently Catalogued

As the 1960s began, however, many people were predicting that motivation research wouldn't be around by 1970, much less the twenty-first century. For one thing, the quiz show scandals of 1959 and subsequent government crackdown on all kinds of ethically questionable practices being pursued by marketers did not bode well for something admittedly predicated on probing Americans' unconscious. Over the course of the decade, a host of things would burst motivation research's 1950s bubble, the once celebrated and even feared technique turned into yesterday's news.

Based on what was going on within the world of market research in 1960, it would not have been unreasonable to assume that motivation research would have another great decade. American businesses were still investing in motivation research, hoping it would solve their problems despite its apparent loss of status, most importantly, with industries that had never used it. The Housing Industry Council sank $150,000 into motivation research in 1960 to try to figure out "what, down deep, makes someone want a new house," for example, the ultimate aim to get more Americans to buy a home, sweet home as demand for housing faltered.[3] Appliance manufacturers too were looking to motivation research for help, specifically for answers to why GE's and Hotpoint's introduction of kitchen ranges in various colors—rose, aqua, copper, green—went over like a lead balloon. (Only white equaled true cleanliness, the research revealed.) Cleanliness was also at the core of Chevron's red, blue, and—mostly—white color scheme based on a motivation research study with drivers, the oil company wanting a sparkly image. Motivation research was proving to be particularly useful for making brands appear more upscale. Smirnoff vodka, Parliament cigarettes, and Schweppes tonic water all went upmarket after motivation research studies told company executives that consumers looked to these product categories to express social status, a perfect use of the technique.[4]

Those making a living from motivation research were hardly ready to concede their good run was over. Louis Cheskin, now calling himself a "motivation specialist," believed that motivation research was more relevant and necessary than ever, in fact, its best days still to come. "The American public, for the most part, is bored with what it has and scared of new things," he told a group of journalists in 1962, with only the kind of deep insights afforded by motivation research able to overcome the double whammy of consumer malaise and paralysis.[5] Cheskin may have thought consumers didn't want anything new, but this didn't stop him from working with Brown and Bigelow the following year to change the centuries-old design of playing cards. Based on Cheskin's motivation research findings, the company introduced a "revolutionary new concept in playing card design," its Nu-Vue deck printed on aquatint paper and featuring modernized (longer and thinner) suit symbols and different looking face cards. Most people interviewed found the new cards more appealing, more elegant, and more distinctive than traditional ones, suggesting Americans were perhaps less frightened of change than Cheskin had believed.[6]

Another positive sign for motivation research in the early sixties was the pure venom some journalists and academics continued to spew at it, a sign that at least a portion of its symbolic power remained. "There are no secrets from the motivational research people," wrote Bill Gold of the *Washington Post* in 1961, adding that "they seem determined to learn every last detail about what we buy and when we buy it and why."[7] Gold was hardly alone in thinking that motivation research was overstaying its welcome, a houseguest perhaps who just wouldn't leave. "It's getting so a consumer needs to assemble his desired image before he opens his mouth, appears in public, or spends a nickel," chimed in Charles Neal, Jr., offering his opinion in the *Los Angeles Times* that same year. America and Americans were overresearched, Neal argued, with simply too many people asking too many questions in the pursuit of more effective advertising and marketing strategies. "You cannot buy a car, prefer a certain cigarette, or join a club without a researcher trying to type your personality and generalize on your hopes and dreams," he continued, coming to the reasonable conclusion that we were "magnificently catalogued."[8] Based on what was already going on, Neal half-seriously imagined a world in the not too distant future when motivation researchers might disguise themselves as supermarket cashiers in order to record a psychographic profile of a husband and wife much like this one: "Her husband went to Yale. He leans to blue suits, modified Homburgs, and button-down collars. He subscribes to *Time Magazine, Wall Street Journal, U.S. News and World Report*, and the *National Review*. She and her husband vote Republican and believe the country is going socialistic."[9]

Besides being invasive and obnoxious, a remnant of the evil intent that was once so much a part of motivation research remained. Rather than see motivation research as being in consumers' best interests, that is, as serving an individual by more fully understanding his or her wants and needs, some continued to see it as a weapon in a kind of battle. Motivation research "uses scientific techniques to find out which aspects will pull the buyer to product, make it tougher for him to get away," thought Joseph G. Phelan, an assistant professor in industrial psychology at Los Angeles State College, with marketers trying to "outguess the buyer by resorting to the course of action with the greatest payoff."[10]

Motivation research had shown that it could survive and even thrive on this sort of criticism from the intellectual elite, but attacks from within the field were an entirely different matter. The success of motivation research was now ironically damaging the technique's reputation as it became overused and as pretenders tried their hand at divining consumers' psyches. Writing for the *New York Times* in 1960, advertising columnist Robert Alden cautioned that seeking hidden meanings behind every purchase that a consumer made (or didn't make) was a bad idea, not the way motivation research should be used. "Misapplied Freudian techniques can have a kick like a mule, and the client is apt to be the person kicked," he warned, suggesting that such heady stuff be left only to experts.[11]

With motivation research on the ropes at least from a publicity perspective, the nose counters moved in for the kill, the biggest one of all being George Gallup. Gallup, "the unordained father confessor of the American body politic," according to *Printers' Ink*, had been reporting the opinions, attitudes, and preferences of the nation for three decades by 1960, his popularity greater than ever. His name was so synonymous with polling that some people thought his name was Gallup Poll, and the Greeks had adopted his last name as the verb "to poll." Although he was famous for his opinion poll, the preeminent market researcher in the world actually had three companies: Gallup and Robinson, which did copy testing; the Gallup Organization, which did general market research; and the American Institute of Public Opinion, which did the polling. After studying at Northwestern, Gallup joined Young and Rubicam as director of research, staying with the agency for fifteen years (and running the Gallup Poll as a sideline). As large a "large sample" man as they came, Gallup was now challenging the entire foundation of motivation research, arguing that "only five per cent of the buying decisions are made on the unconscious level," the subconscious of course being where the "id probers" spent most of their time. Gallup believed that it was simply impossible for consumers to say why they did what they did, which was of course the area of primary interest to motivation researchers. Gallup preferred a much more rational and methodical approach, taking consumers back to a particular buying decision and reconstructing the events leading up to it. The trick to market research was thus reporting, something consumers were very good at, he insisted; it was not to try to figure out what lurked in the nooks and crannies of our noggins.[12]

Others took sideswipes at motivation research as it gradually lost some of its luster. Walter A. Woods, who took Daniel Yankelovich's seat as director of research at Nowland, drew a distinction between motivation research and "psychological research," thinking the former was often "undisciplined and even capricious." Frustrated by the improvisational nature of motivation research, he called for a more systematic model to study consumer psychology, his 1960 article in the *Journal of Marketing* an attempt to bridge the loosey-goosey world of business and excessively buttoned-up academia.[13]

Soon Woods would get his wish as a new kind of market research steeped in anthropology and ethnography emerged in the early 1960s. Founded by motivation research refugees, "dynamic research" purported to not only understand but even anticipate the wants and needs of what *Business Week* in 1961 referred to as "that most mysterious and confusing of creatures, the consumer," this elusive quest nothing less than the holy grail of the field. If true, this would be history making, as the long view of the field suggested. The first generation of market research that developed between the two world wars could be described as direct, the assumption being that asking consumers straight questions would yield straight answers, with marketers using that numbers-oriented information to guide their plans. The second generation, which flourished in the 1950s, could be described as indirect, with motivation research based on Freudian psychoanalysis and Gestalt therapy promising to reveal what consumers felt rather than what they said. Dynamic researchers rejected the idea that the truth resided deep in the subconscious and had to be extracted like a bad tooth through psychological techniques, however, meaning a third generation was possibly coming into play. Firms such as Peekskill, New York–based Motivation Dynamics, Philadelphia-based Alderson Associates, New York–based Marplan, and Opinion Research in Princeton were ditching the proverbial analyst's couch to instead observe consumers in real or simulated settings, hence the "dynamic" in dynamic research. "These days we're more interested in motivations between the aisles of a supermarket than motivations between twin beds," summarily explained Albert Shepard, who had left Dichter to form Motivation Dynamics.[14]

Observing how people acted instead of probing their psyches was just one way dynamic research differed from its touchy-feely cousin, motivation research. Dynamic research, true to its name, encouraged consumers to offer their ideas on products, this more participative approach considered a pretty revolutionary approach in these top-down, leave-it-to-the-experts times. Had the Edselites used dynamic research rather than motivation research, subscribers to the former argued, Ford could have avoided the wreck, as the company would have learned about the softness of the medium-priced automobile segment before it introduced the model. Dynamic researchers even had consumers role-play to see how their products would be used in the real world through simulation, such as by asking children to "act out" breakfast rather than answer questions about their cereal preferences. "Freud dealt with the abnormal personality but the person we want to understand is the average consumer," said Richard Baxter, research director of ad agency Cunningham and Walsh, confirming the great psychologist's own famous attributed claim that sometimes a cigar is just a cigar.[15]

The much heralded, motivation-research intensive approach to arriving at product names also appeared to be waning in the early sixties. Chevrolet had no intention of going through all the sturm und drang of motivation research to come up with a good name for its new mid-size model in 1962, for instance, perhaps after seeing what Ford's exhaustive process ultimately produced a few years back. With production coming up fast, a group of Chevrolet's sales staff and Campbell-Ewald executives decided to simply get together in a room and bang out a good name for the new car intended to fill the gap between standard models and the smaller ones being introduced in the United States like the Volkswagen Beetle. "What we wanted to get across in the name was that this was a new kind of car in itself, not just a scaled down Chevrolet, and at the same time let the customer know that it was made by Chevrolet and had Chevrolet quality," explained Kenneth E. Staley, general sales manager for the company. This proved to be a more difficult task than expected. Name after name was offered for consideration and rejected when, frustrated after hours of misfires, the group decided to break for dinner. Inspiration struck at the restaurant when either Staley or the chairman of Campbell-Ewald, Henry G. Little (they reportedly weren't sure whom), observed that, "the name has to say that while it's a new car it's a Chevy also," this leading to the why-didn't-we-think-of-it-sooner "Chevy II." Napkin with perfect name in hand, Staley rushed to a phone to get approval from GM's top brass and, following that, made a call to Chevrolet's styling department to see how Chevy II looked in chrome.[16]

Critics were not hesitant to try to seal the lid on the coffin of motivation research as it lost some of its vitality. "MR quickly assumed the proportions of a fad, and its use has been indiscriminately applied, applauded, or condemned," said Warren Seulowitz of Arthur D. Little, the consulting firm, at a 1962 AMA meeting, not able to resist tossing in that "psychologists seem to know more about the psychopath than about our more normal citizenry."[17] Others were more direct as motivation research's days in the sun appeared to be over. "Whatever became of motivational research?" asked Peter Bart of the *New York Times* in late 1962, noting that the subject was no longer coming up at advertising conferences or, for that matter, bridge parties as it used to.[18] Psychoanalytic thinking, all the rage in the fifties, seemed to be becoming passé, and motivation research to be losing much of its shock value as it became increasingly fragmented and diluted.[19]

Motivation research's retreat from the limelight continued in the midsixties as it became more of a workhorse than a thoroughbred. "Rumor has it that motivational research . . . no longer enjoys the respect or popularity it had five years ago," wrote Mina Hamilton for *Management Review* in 1964, the irony being that motivation research in all its permutations was being used more than ever before but was less frequently referred to by that term as its methodologies blurred with others. Its strongest selling point a decade earlier, the Freudian component of motivation research was now regarded by some as its weakest. Psychoanalytic interpretations certainly revealed a lot about consumers' personalities but were now seen as not particularly relevant to most marketing situations, the fundamental practicality of "pure" motivation research in question. "The enormous amount of complex, dissimilar, random information collected through a series of rambling conversations does not lend itself to simple interpretations," Hamilton argued, the desire for more logic and order in all aspects of American business making motivation research seem more like a distraction than a useful tool.[20]

Logic and order could certainly be found in the latest research methodology to cast motivation research as too much art and not enough science. Also based on the belief that consumers couldn't or wouldn't articulate their likes and dislikes, pupil measurement was becoming the talk of the research town in 1964. In this technique an eye camera provided marketers with an "interest track" of advertising and packaging. With its Perception Lab, Marplan (Interpublic's research company) was proving that the eye, like the fingerprint, didn't lie, in this case meaning that the more consumers liked something, the more their pupils dilated. Other problems of qualitative research like faded memories or vaguely described feelings were also avoided with pupil tracking, Marplan was telling clients, biology able to trump psychology any day of the week.[21]

Posing the most serious threat to motivation research in the 1960s, however, was the elephant in the room, the computer. "The computer is the market researcher's latest toy," *Business Week* declared in 1964, a Mack-truck-sized IBM 7090 capable of sorting questionnaires much faster than a roomful of salary men. Making sense of what came out of the machine's back end—a ream of data thicker than the Manhattan phone book—was the challenge, of course, leading to a variety of mathematical and statistical techniques requiring a brain almost as big as the computer itself.[22] Because of their efficiency and mathematical "provability," vending-machine-sized computers were considered by many to be superior to all "psychosocial" methods, motivation research included. "A new group of researchers have recently pulled up seats to the conference table," George Christopoulos had observed way back in 1959, speaking of early "techies." The ability of "electronic data-processing" experts to simulate a market test that produced results more sophisticated than the real thing had come a long way over the intervening five years.[23]

Another thing hurting motivation research in the mid-sixties was American corporations' new love of MBAs, the quantitative orientation of business schools making qualitative research seem soft and, as Dichter himself might have suggested, "feminine."[24] Relatedly, researchers on the left-brain client side now had significantly more status than their colleagues on the right-brain agency side, a background in statistics and economics currently more

in favor than the social sciences.[25] Perhaps most damaging to motivation research, however, was the downgrading of the very concept of motivation as
a factor in consumers' behavior. As the rise of research methodologies like
pupil measurement suggested, "perception" was fast taking the wind out of
motivation research's sails, increasingly recognized as a better indicator of
consumers' decision-making process. "The preoccupation with the 'real reasons' why people purchase led to a vast overemphasis on the purchaser and
the brand image at the expense of the product identity itself as a marketing
and research variable," said Woods at an AMA meeting in 1965, having left
Nowland to head up his own consulting firm, Products and Concepts Research International. Woods was currently pushing what he called "concept"
research, another attempt to quantitatively measure consumers' reaction to
new products and advertising. Could motivation research survive without
motivation?[26]

The Strategy of Desire

Certainly hoping that it would survive were young people like John C. Philipp,
a seventeen-year-old Chicago newspaper carrier and freshman at Roosevelt
University majoring in sociology and psychology who was already planning
a career in motivation research.[27] Fortunately for Philipp, one man was doing
everything he could to counter the myriad threats to motivation research that
could possibly put it and him out of business. In 1960, Dichter published a
new book, *The Strategy of Desire*, which (along with two other books published that year, George Katona's *The Powerful Consumer* and Steuart Britt's
The Spenders) offered a response to Packard's *The Hidden Persuaders*, whose
impact still reverberated in the early sixties. In his new book, Dichter reas-
serted the case for motivation research, insisting once again that it was emotions, and emotions alone, that explained the why of human, and especially
consumer, behavior. "Whatever your attitude toward modern psychology or
psychoanalysis, it has been proved beyond any doubt that many of our daily
decisions are governed by motivations over which we have no control and of
which we are often quite unaware," Dichter stated, rebuffing all the doubt-
ing Thomases who were out to crush motivation research. Even with their
fancy computers, nose counters still were no match for Dichter and the kind
of insights he could bring to the table. "Too often, in my experience, I have
discovered that a helpless client, small or large, after having supposedly as-
sembled all the facts and having been given the diagnosis of his ills, still asks,

'What do I do now?'" he wrote; again, only an understanding of "motivational thinking" could provide the answer.[28]

Wisely, the *Journal of Marketing* asked Pierre Martineau—himself no slouch when it came to motivation research—to review *The Strategy of Desire* (with, ironically, a review of Packard's *The Waste Makers* appearing in the same issue). "This book is typical Dichter," Martineau wrote, impressive in the sheer amount of the ground it covered—the American doctor-patient relationship, why many Brazilian women didn't use sanitary napkins, Western Samoans' aspirations for independence, and, if that weren't enough, the meaning of horror films and literature. Martineau also noted Dichter's pronounced swing from psychology to sociology and cultural anthropology, his shift logically paralleling that which motivation research as a field had made in the 1950s. But with his call for Americans to reach for new goals and create new heroes, Dichter gone too far, thought Martineau. "He has allowed himself to be carried away with his facile scholarship and considerable experience with business research to the point where he assumes the mantle of a philosopher," Martineau worried, which was precisely the direction Dichter would take over the next three decades.[29]

The *New York Times* review of *The Strategy of Desire* was much less kind. John Keats went to town on Dichter's central premise that people were often illogical and that appealing to consumers' irrational sides was therefore not just sensible but essential for advertisers. Worse yet in Keats's view was Dichter's claim that his psychology-based approach was scientifically valid. "His science seems to be compounded of two parts Barnum to one part Freud," Keats wrote, thinking that Packard had done a very good job in assessing the man's philosophy and methods.[30] Dichter took the opportunity to respond to Keats's review, however, in a letter to the editor published in the newspaper about a month later. Keats was just the latest in a long line of "morality hucksters," Dichter wrote, hypocrites who decried consumerism but drove fancy sports cars and owned expensive homes in Connecticut filled with new appliances. (Packard himself had quite the cushy lifestyle.) The Packards and Keatses would come and go, Dichter suggested, while strategies of desire would be around for a very long time.[31]

The following year, Dichter landed a feature story in, of all publications, *Sports Illustrated*, in which the writer Robert W. Boyle called him "the big daddy" of this "relatively new and spooky specialty" called motivation research. Dichter had, not surprisingly, done some work within sports, exploring the emotional factors behind a wide range of recreational activities and leisure pursuits. Golfing and fishing were substitutes for the baseball and football one played as a kid, a way to make oneself believe one wasn't getting older. Golfers also had an urge to fly, their long drives standing in for flying. Bowlers were really knocking down people, a release of pent-up frustrations. More hardcore sportswriters, not used to such thinking, were not amused to see their beloved activities presented as mere psychological fodder. "They used to put a net over you for making studies like that," sneered Jim Murray of the *Los Angeles Times*, but "now they hire you as consultant at a fat fee."[32] Interestingly, another Freudian psychologist, Arnold Bessier, was dipping his toes into sports, he too believing that there was much more going on than appeared on the surface. Bessier, once a top tennis player, had recently published an article about Oedipal conflict at Wimbledon in the journal *Psychoanalysis and the Psychoanalytic Review*, arguing that the id was running amok at this most genteel of sporting events. Dichter, however, remained what one critic called "the most prominent retailer of Freud going today," his forays into the sporting world another opportunity for him to sell his intellectual wares.[33]

The variety of sports-related projects Dichter weighed in on was typically impressive. For a boat maker, he found boating to have "deep, underlying emotional meaning," specifically "pleasant memories of one's first childhood experiences via a toy sailboat." Another watery project for Dichter was with the Esther Williams Pool Company, the competitive swimmer turned Hollywood starlet now in the swimming pool business. Finding swimming pools to be a "fertile psychological market," Dichter came up with no fewer than thirty-two recommendations for his client. One of them was to tell potential buyers that the water in Esther Williams swimming pools was specially treated with an additive ("XQ35," Dichter suggested), another that the company should odorize the water ("The pool with the smell of the sea!" he proposed as an advertising headline). That the client was in the business of selling swimming pools, not water, and that consumers would invariably fill them up with whatever came out of their garden hose seemed to be, for Dichter, beside the point.[34] Equally interesting was that during the press conference to announce the findings of the study, Williams took Dichter aside to grumble that he had overlooked what she believed to be one of the best reasons to own a pool: the opportunity to make love under water. Almost impossible to faze, Dichter was admittedly stunned (and delighted) by Williams's personal motivations.[35]

These were just a drop in the bucket compared to his thoughts on baseball, however. Although he had never seen the game played until he arrived in the United States when he was thirty-one, Dichter seemed to know more about the national pastime than any American. For a baseball glove marketer, he filled his Living Laboratory with a bunch of Little Leaguers, asking them to pretend they were buying a glove in a store. "Tactile sensory satisfactions are a major appeal of gloves," went one of Dichter's key findings from this session. Home base (or plate) seemed to be particularly fascinating to the émigré from Austria, who wrote that it is "not too difficult to find the parallel between the home in which you live and home plate on a baseball diamond." One of the men behind home base, the umpire, too held special significance for one trained in Freudian theory. Wearing "a sinister-looking outfit," the ump was "a perfect target for hostile feelings," representing, need we say it, "the stern father figure."[36]

If Dichter had a lot to say about baseball, he was positively verbose when it came to the sport of harness racing. Hired by the Western Harness Racing Association, the doctor for ailing products wrote a 103-page report on the subject, its title alone quite a mouthful: *A Motivational Research Study Aimed at Increasing Public Interest in Harness Racing and Building Attendance at the Los Angeles Racing Tracks*. Finding that Los Angelenos had a less than favorable view of harness racing, Dichter recommended his client present the sport as youthful, hip, and, above all, masculine. "The important thing is to dispel a man's fear that his wife will nag him about his gambling and a woman's fear that, instead of enjoying herself, she will worry about his losing too much," Dichter made clear, which lead to his mandate that women be left out of all advertising for the track. "Many of our studies have shown that women find any activity which is supposedly for men twice as appealing," he explained, one of many comments that did not endear him to those calling for a more equal playing field along gender lines.[37]

If anything, Dichter stepped up his claim that men were "better" consumers than women despite the fact that the latter accounted for far more spending (largely because of traditional gender roles in the family, of course). This was particularly true for anything new. "A man is apt to be a much better customer for the many new products on the market today," Dichter said in the same year he made his comments regarding harness racing, asserting that men were not only more curious than women but also "more fascinated by imported goods and impressed by ingenious packaging and new inventions." Men were, in short, open to change, while women were, in his words, "likely to go on doing what they've always done."[38]

More famous, if not controversial, than ever, Mr. Dichter went to Washington in 1961, having been asked to testify before a Senate Antitrust and Monopoly subcommittee investigating deceptive packaging and labeling. It made sense that the Senate would ask the person arguably better equipped than anyone else to explain why people bought what they did to help in its crackdown on a wide variety of ethically questionable practices being used by marketers. Dichter testified that it was consumers' emotions, not their logic, that ruled the show, which accounted for them frequently being duped into buying big boxes with relatively little product inside. "What people actually spend their money on in most instances are psychological differences, illusory brand images," he informed the subcommittee presided over by Philip A. Hart (D-Michigan), and he stated that even a proposed law to make manufacturers prominently feature the weight of products would not be likely to change this fundamental rule of consumer behavior. The average American didn't really want to know what was inside a package or how it was made, Dichter told the senators; the mythology surrounding the product was much more important. "About the only label[s] most Americans look at closely are those disclosing the proof of the liquor they buy," he added, the wonks receiving a free, advanced education in marketing from one of the masters of the game.[39]

My Name Is Betsy

Despite his fame and lucrative consulting business, Dichter was by 1962 fighting a losing battle, at least in the United States. Now fifty-five and more than a few pounds heavier than he was at the peak of the motivation research boom, Dichter conceded that American market research had changed considerably over the past decade: "My innovation is no longer an innovation." The world, however, could yet be Dichter's oyster, with many companies in many countries still unfamiliar with the ways of motivation research. Dichter was in fact now spending about half of his time overseas, his foreign assignments ranging from how to help companies sell beer in South Africa, gasoline in France, and candy in Spain. Interestingly, Dichter was also helping European ad agencies fight back the invasion of competitors from the United States, who seemed to have a better understanding of consumers. German hausfraus, for example, were increasingly buying low-calorie soups and choosing soap not for how well it cleaned but according to what Dichter called "Hollywood standards of beauty," things that puzzled the country's advertising people. Dichter was keenly aware that American-style consumerism was becoming the global standard, and was in a unique position to help marketers around the world adapt before they got gobbled up by U.S. companies.[40]

His own target market redefined, Dichter turned up the international volume on his PR machine. "Knowledge of the basic differences, as well as basic similarities, among consumers in different parts of the world will be essential," Dichter wrote in a 1962 article in the *Harvard Business Review*, correctly predicting that "the successful marketer of the future will have to think not of a United States customer . . . but of *a world customer*" (his emphasis). Now positioning himself as an international cultural anthropologist, Dichter already had a working knowledge of this world customer, or was at least familiar with some of the basic differences among consumers in different parts of the world, he made clear in the article. Only one Frenchman in three brushed his teeth, Dichter had purportedly discovered, and four of five Germans changed their shirts only once a week. (Dichter would later catch flack for this latter claim.) Whether or not such insights were true, Dichter saw big opportunities for marketers willing to go the extra mile to sell their products overseas. Best of all, not just Western Europe but developing markets in South America, Africa, and Asia were there for the plucking as the desire for the good things in life broke through "the barricades of centuries," as Dichter poetically put it.[41]

A year later, Dichter was convinced motivation research had entered a new stage, moving beyond what he called "the psychology of products," again an opportunity for international marketers (himself included). Rather than just explain how and why consumers felt about certain things or brands, motivation research was now being used to create new products, redesign existing ones, and solve many other marketing problems. A good example of this new, broader role of motivation research was a project Dichter had recently completed for Britain's National Coal Board. Despite concerted efforts to make mines safer in the country through posters and films emphasizing safety, accidents continued to rise, and Dichter got the call. Believing that, as the *New York Times* described it, "miners regarded the automatic machinery with great hostility and took pride in how roughly—and carelessly—they could treat them [*sic*]," Dichter decided to make the machines more endearing by making them more like women. "My name is Betsy," went one coal crusher, which had been fitted with a loudspeaker that had a feminine voice. "You are a lot more intelligent than I am so handle me with care," cooed another, such friendly chatter designed to make the burly men exercise more caution around the dangerous equipment.[42]

"Betsy" and her coal-mining friends were just one example of this new, more applied kind of motivation research that Dichter was pursuing in the early 1960s. He was juggling a typically disparate collection of projects in late 1963, including the sources of tension (for a company marketing tranquilizers), the reasons why people dined out (for a restaurant group), and, for a real estate developer, how people chose where to live. One other area Dichter was working on was the matter of race, studying the motivations of African American consumers for a number of clients. As part of the escalating civil rights movement, black leaders were calling for more African Americans in advertising (and TV shows), the tricky issue landing in Dichter's lap. Despite his own experience with discrimination as a Jew in 1930s Austria, Dichter was hardly sympathetic to blacks' struggle for equal rights, seeing racism on a far too theoretical and psychological level for pretty much everyone's comfort. "Throughout his career, Dichter had paid minimal attention to African Americans, focusing instead on the groups his clients targeted: white, mostly suburban, middle-class Americans," Daniel Horowitz wrote in *Anxieties of Affluence*, a neglect that did not help his cause when it came to the issue of race.[43]

It wasn't surprising, then, that Dichter told his clients to think twice about featuring more blacks in advertising despite the pressure they were getting, believing that by doing so sales to African American consumers would fall rather than rise. As evidence, Dichter cited the recent example of a French dairy company that, wanting to sell more milk in Morocco, switched to a label printed in Arabic. Instead of going up, sales reportedly plummeted, Dichter explaining that "Arabs wanted French milk, and the label made them believe they were getting something Arabic, not French." Likewise, Dichter was saying in not so many words, black consumers actually wanted to see white models in advertising, the same sort of racial and class associations in play as in the milk instance.[44]

Racial and gender politics did little (actually nothing) to slow Dichter down, however. In 1964, he published *Handbook of Consumer Motivations: The Psychology of the World of Objects*, the book "a sort of contemporary cultural anthropology of modern man"—that is, another attempt to use motivation research as a bridge to interpreting everyday life. The conceit of the book was to view mid-1960s Western society as a strange, foreign land (which of course it was), something that had a lot in common with "primitive" cultures. Dichter said of the modern Western man that "his customs, motivations, desires, and hopes are often not too far removed from the rituals and fetishes of the New Guineans"; while the latter might "carve their [fetishes] out of the skulls of their enemies" the former simply "buys his . . . in the department store."[45]

Drawing upon the more than twenty-five hundred motivational studies his firm had conducted to date, Dichter traversed the landscape of consumer culture, explaining the real reasons Americans did the things they did. The range of projects the IMR had been assigned was truly astonishing, "from providing an understanding of the use of contraceptives to explaining why people prefer to be buried in one cemetery rather than another," as he put it.[46] Coffee drinkers added cream and sugar not because of taste but as a rebellion against having food served to them by "Mother" as she preferred it. Indigestion may be unpleasant but, in contrast, serves as a status symbol signifying that one is a responsible and sophisticated person. Both buying life insurance and taking out a loan are proof of adulthood and masculinity, perhaps analogous to the hunter of centuries past bringing home meat for his family. Whatever it was, Dichter continued to find deeper meaning lurking underneath it, his latest book perhaps his strongest argument that routine behavior and ordinary things were much more than what they seemed to be.[47] While Dichter would go on consulting and writing the occasional book for another quarter century, *Handbook of Consumer Motivations* was in some respects the capstone to his career, an encyclopedia of knowledge based on his studies of American consumer culture for the previous quarter century.

Reviewing *Handbook of Consumer Motivations* for the *Journal of Marketing Research*, Donald F. Blankertz found what he considered a "non-book" frustratingly enjoyable, both mocking and praising Dichter's ability to turn the ordinary into the remarkable. Describing some of Dichter's loftier observations (e.g., "esthetic appreciation [of art] is to a large extent a re-experiencing of the original birth of the artist's concept" and owning a dictionary is also proof of adulthood) as not only pretentious but "hilarious," Blankertz, a professor at the University of Pennsylvania, couldn't help but conclude the book was worth the ten bucks it cost. Dichter's latest book may have had no identifiable school of psychological theory, little real technique, negligible bibliography, no footnotes besides one in which the author cited himself, and many inconsistencies ("it is about as satisfactory as a composite picture of the average consumer as a *Nude Descending a Staircase*"), but it remained of considerable value all the same. "He who cannot find satisfactions and truths and benefits certainly lacks curiosity, utilitarian drives or other motivations," Blankertz concluded, his take on what he called "Dichter Deductivism" quite typical of reviewers' realization that, when it came to critiquing his books, they were simply in over their heads.[48]

Not everyone found Dichter's handbook of motivations motivating, however. Russell Baker, writing for the *New York Times* in 1964, thought that, at "478 disturbing pages," it "may be the most depressing book of the year." He was peeved that Dichter had reduced everyday life to a psychological meta-analysis. Baker just had no patience at all for Dichter's sorting of the universe of consumer goods into the emotionally positive (e.g., fresh spaghetti, which "suggest[ed] family fun and conviviality") and the emotionally negative (canned spaghetti, because it was "a blatant symbol of a lack of efficient planning"), the whole exercise making humans appear subject to the symbolic power of the things they used. Did shaving really have to be a "masochistic ritual" that both negated and reaffirmed men's masculinity, as Dichter wrote? That it happened to be a useful way to get the hair off one's face was perfectly fine for Baker and, probably, a fair share of readers.[49]

Likewise, in his review for the *Journal of Marketing*, A. B. Blankenship suggested that a good subtitle for the book would have been "Freud in Consumerland." He was clearly upset by some of Dichter's more visceral psychological interpretations. Beets were disliked by many people, wrote Dichter, because they suggested blood, an example made only that much more disturbing for Blankenship when Dichter illustrated his point by describing one man's childhood exposure to menstrual blood. "This is a potentially dangerous book for communications experts, with decisions to make," argued Blankenship (who happened to be one), "the half-truth and no-truth . . . so intermingled with the truth that it would take a Philadelphia lawyer to sort it all out."[50] Another reviewer was even more dismissive of *Handbook of Consumer Motivations*. "The book is most likely to attract the advertising man who is desperately short of creative ideas for a particular product and wants to hear about somebody else's," wrote Philip L. Short in his pithy review for *Occupational Psychology*, a British publication, not realizing this was exactly Dichter's intent.[51]

I Love You the Way You Are

In the mid-1960s, Dichter stepped up his writing of articles, which, like his books (he ultimately published seventeen, including one for children) were a means to spread his philosophy beyond consulting. He wrote a few more articles for the *Harvard Business Review*, one of them entitled "Discovering the 'Inner Jones,'" in which he made the case that the days of keeping up with the Joneses were over, meaning that consumers were now interested in satisfying internally directed wants and needs rather than in impressing others.[52] He then gave specific examples of how that could play out, some of them no doubt surprising readers expecting more traditional management fare. "I can imagine a supermarket having special departments corresponding to different consumer needs," he wrote, which is where it began to get interesting: "One of them, for example, might be entitled 'Feeling Depressed Today? Here are all the articles you can buy which will help you get rid of your depression'; another might be identified, 'Feel Like Splurging? This is what you can do and buy.'"[53]

In another article, published in the *Harvard Business Review* the following year, Dichter told readers how word-of-mouth advertising works, anticipating in some respects the viral and guerrilla communications phenomena of a few decades hence. In the article, he made the interesting argument that most advertising should be directed at current customers rather than potential ones, as the former acted as "propagandists" for products they used and liked, unbiased authorities spreading the good word. Because both the talker and the listener were voluntarily involved in word-of-mouth communication, this was an underutilized resource for advertisers, Dichter argued, something that marketers of the twenty-first century have been quick to change. He also mentioned the role of "influencers," "experts," and "aficionados," anticipating by about three decades Malcolm Gladwell's "mavens" who, in his theory of social epidemics in *The Tipping Point*, act as knowledgeable information specialists who shape consumer behavior.[54]

Of course, Dichter was hardly done helping clients out with their problems. In 1965 he took on the House of Louis Feder, a maker of men's hairpieces, as a client, adding a PR twist to the project by inviting a bunch of the interviewees to a press conference where they could reveal their motivations for wearing or not wearing a rug. Naturally, Dichter took the opportunity to analyze the men's comments, and his take was typically different from what the interviewees themselves said. In response to one man's explanation that he decided not to purchase a toupee after his wife had told him, "I love you the way you are," Dichter wondered aloud if the wife wanted to keep him bald so he would be less attractive to other women. Dichter also didn't buy another man's story that he wore a hairpiece only because he worked outside and perspired too much for a hat, making a wig necessary to protect his scalp from sunburn. "Men think they have to give a practical reason, when the real reason is vanity," Dichter suggested, his dismissal of the merely rational fully intact.[55]

Clothing manufacturers were very happy to hear Dichter's announcement that a "Peacock Revolution" had begun in America, the idea that the other half of the population had finally become fashion-conscious extremely exciting news.[56] Sock makers in particular had hopes that the Peacock Revolution could turn things around for them. The average American man was buying eighteen pairs of socks a year but, with more wearers choosing synthetics, which lasted a lot longer, things were looking down, so to speak, for the industry. Sock-lessness too was fast gaining favor among both the chic set and the hippie set, making manufacturers very nervous as they relied more than ever on the mysterious one-sock-gone-missing-in-the-laundry phenomenon for sales. In 1966, DuPont—which was largely to blame for all those non-holey synthetic socks—brought in Dichter to try to figure out how to get the knitted-sock category back on its feet. Dichter promptly produced a seventy-three-page report on the "fascinating new science of soxology," his study a tour de force of the psychological underpinnings of the soft, knitted things worn inside shoes. For one thing, there was a lot of sex in sox, Dichter found, as 86 percent of wives surveyed bought socks for their husbands, establishing a direct connection between a woman and a man's feet. Furthermore, feet themselves were positively loaded with sexuality, Dichter said in his report, something that sock people should take full advantage of in their advertising.[57]

Size too mattered when it came to socks, apparently. Over-the-calves meant that the wearer, usually an executive, was successful, while ankle-lengths were associated with the "unsuccessful middle-aged man." Dichter's "Soxology: A Strategy for Stimulating Sock Sales" for DuPont was filled with other pieces of podiatric wisdom ("The general tendency for men [is] to buy their socks too large, indicating a hidden desire for longer, more potent feet" and "The sock user should be reminded . . . that while he has a close attachment to his socks, he doesn't love all of them equally," to name just a couple), and the company used the report to fix issues like "the DuPont stomp" (men pounding their feet on the floor after standing up because of static cling). Another issue—the dreaded "calf gap" (the patch of hairy skin between the top of the sock and the bottom of the trousers that showed when a man crossed his legs)—remained, but DuPont was hopeful it could eventually solve that riddle as well.[58] Dichter's "Soxology" report made such a splash that he wound up on the *Tonight Show* to tell America about it, meeting Sonny and Cher backstage while waiting to chat with Johnny Carson.[59]

Because he knew so much about men's fashion sense or lack thereof, Du-Pont brought Dichter to Scottsdale, Arizona, in 1966 to speak with a group of menswear manufacturers and retailers. The big issue of the conference was the exploding "youth market." Rather suddenly, it was young men—sixteen-to twenty-nine-year-olds—who were setting clothing styles, the gender blur-ring of the bourgeoning counterculture making those in fashion try to, as one of them said, "get hep and get with youth." Dichter had definite thoughts on the matter, looking to the recent tremendous growth in men's fragrances as a clear sign that men were becoming more—not less, as others might conclude—confident of their masculinity. "Men are frustrated animals but they're now becoming more secure," he told DuPont and its guests, his rea-soning being that "only a man who feels completely secure as a man can allow himself to wear anything with feminine overtones."[60]

Even after decades of explaining consumers' behavior to businesspeople in psychological terms, meeting planners still probably didn't know what they were getting into when they booked Dichter for a talk. Lodging industry ex-ecutives at their annual convention in 1967 certainly didn't expect to hear that the typical traveler was "uprooted in a psychological sense, somewhat afraid," according to Dichter, which explained why he or she wanted four or five tow-els in the bathroom when only one was perfectly fine at home. Because "he regresses to a more infantile level," he continued, extra doses of pampering were in order for the hotel and motel guest. One of Dichter's recommen-dations was to put into rooms "small refrigerators stocked with drinks and snacks, with the guest paying for what he uses." Should we thank (or blame, given how much that bag of pistachios costs) Dichter for the minibar?[61]

Marketing and advertising conferences too were opportunities for Dichter to develop new ideas and see how well they played before an audience. (De-spite having made thousands of presentations all over the world, he still got nervous before speaking in public.) Going after whatever was the hot thing in market research was a perfect opportunity to restate his core beliefs and make motivation research seem fresh and relevant. As a case in point, "gut feeling" was more powerful than the computer when it came to market research, Dich-ter told the Southern California chapter of the American Marketing Associa-tion in 1969, a true understanding of the motivations of a single individual more valid than the results from an electronically processed questionnaire completed by thousands of demographically alike respondents. "Each prod-uct has a soul—a deeper meaning—and it is only when this deeper meaning is grasped that a real communication takes place between the advertiser and

the consumer," he suggested to the group, which was not exactly sure what
he was talking about; only a psychological probing of human desires was able
to dig that far down. Easier to understand no doubt was his point that iconography was an ideal way to tap into a soul of a particular product and, in
the process, create great advertising. Needless to say, Dichter loved the white
knights, talking tigers, green giants, and other mythic entities that populated
1960s TV commercials, seeing them as unsophisticated but powerful forms
of nonverbal communication not unlike the tribal rituals, totems, and taboos
common to many primitive cultures.[62]

Studying the Savages

What's the first thing a younger and decidedly groovier generation of researchers does after staring blankly at reams of statistics purportedly revealing deep insights into the human condition? Toss them out and start talking
to real-life consumers again, one at a time, to find out what's really on and
in their minds. Despite the ever-increasing role of computers, qualitative
research made a major rebound in the late sixties, again believed to be the
only way to mine meaningful thoughts and opinions lurking in the subconscious. Ulric Neisser's theory of cognitive psychology became all the rage in
market research just as the Beatles' *Sgt. Pepper* album hit the shelves, suggesting that countercultural thinking ran a lot deeper than bell-bottoms and
tie-dyed shirts. Not surprisingly, the self-help movement of the seventies fueled psychology-based market research techniques, including motivation research, a phenomenon that could only be described as the happy facing of the
field. Various forms of pseudo-research, such as "psychophysics," ran amok
throughout the decade, evidence perhaps that the inmates were running the
asylum.

One sign that motivation research was on the way back was not how
professionals continued to use methodologies that sprang from the field but
rather how otherwise average businesspeople had integrated it into their
thinking and approach to selling. William A. Alter, president of Chicago-
based Realty Company of America, for example, was a self-acknowledged
amateur motivation researcher, a firm believer that subconscious desires
played a major role in homebuyers' decision-making process. "If you had a
happy childhood, you will try to repeat that experience thru your choice of
a home," Alter explained in 1969, but "if your childhood was unhappy, you
would look for a house that is completely different from the one in which you

grew up." Alter wasn't just repeating something he had read but was instead offering what he had learned from firsthand experience. He had recently and separately sold homes to a brother and sister in a development in Arlington Heights, and the thing he found interesting about this was that the siblings had no idea that the other had purchased a house in the same area.[63]

Others might have dismissed this as a strange coincidence, but not Alter. The homes the brother and sister bought were, in fact, precisely the same, specifically the Vernon model, a four-bedroom Georgian colonial (for $47,600, rather depressingly). As Alter would learn from his own form of depth interviewing, the Vernon was essentially a larger version of the home the two had grown up in, accounting for what had appeared to be an odd, random event. "We didn't realize it at first, but after visiting the house a couple of times, the similarity occurred to us," the brother said, neither he nor his sister conscious of the resemblance until they had decided to buy their homes. Pressing them further, in classic motivation research style, Alter learned from the siblings that the layout of the Vernon was nearly identical to the floor plan of the house they had lived in as children, which confirmed the developer's conviction that the subconscious was a powerful force and, if harnessed, a useful marketing tool. "Whether they are aware of it or not, their mutual choice was probably as much affected by a pleasant recollection of their youth as any feature the house has to offer," the amateur shrink concluded, his interpretation of human motivation in this case every bit as good as any interpretation from Ernest Dichter.[64]

There were other indications that the world, especially the market research world, was finally catching up with Dichter's brand of "mass psychology." As an ardent nose counter, Daniel Yankelovich (who had a Ph.D. in psychology) had been one of Dichter's most vocal critics in the late 1950s but had gradually come around to the idea that measuring the temperature of the American zeitgeist from a sociological viewpoint would be of considerable value to marketers. In 1970, Yankelovich was tracking no fewer than thirty-one trends that he believed revealed the nation's mood, with clients like Coca-Cola and CBS gobbling up every morsel contained in his "Lifestyle Monitor." "A few years ago we began to get different kinds of requests," he explained, with traditional types of research no longer considered enough for companies trying to anticipate where the consumer was headed rather than document where he or she had been. Soon Yankelovich was talking about things like the "psychology of affluence," the "reaction against complexity," and trends that "move away from Puritan values" in his Monitor, with a growing list of marketers willing to fork over $10,000 for the annual report. Although the Monitor was decidedly more sociological in scope than psychological, there was no doubt that Yankelovich and other top researchers were now embracing Dichter's prescription to see the forest rather than just count the trees. "You can't take a market problem and isolate it from social change," said a spokesman for the IMR speaking for Dichter, reminding people that "we've been doing social research right along."[65]

Seeing American business continue to move away from the strictly quantitative model of the 1960s, Dichter had no difficulty finding work with international clients, nonprofits, and companies interested in his perspective on managerial (versus market research) issues. Based on conversations with his leftish son, Dichter divided his work into "A-projects"—those that were humanitarian or socially responsible in some way—and "B-projects"—those that made money for companies.[66] Through the 1970s and 1980s, the man who had revolutionized the way consumers were studied kept a busy schedule speaking, consulting, teaching, and writing, shifting his focus to A-projects (often on a pro-bono basis). "I am an anthropologist, studying the savages right here," Dichter said in 1969, his imposing castle on Prickly Pear Road now described by a reporter as "a rambling old house."[67] The next year, he had a major heart attack (which occurred while he was verbally sparring about racism with the head of Malcolm X College), but this did not even come close to making him want to retire. Against his doctors' advice (one told him flat out after taking a look at his EKG, "You are going to die"), Dichter continued to travel around the world and churn out book after book on at least the same level as before. "Maybe this was an attempt on my part to disprove the predictions of the physicians," he mused, the possibility of a premature death not about to get in the way of his contrarian instincts.[68]

Clearly on a mission after the latest of his close calls, Dichter in 1971 published *Motivating Human Behavior*, in which he made the bold (too bold, in fact) claim that continuous economic growth could solve all the world's ills. Poverty, nationalism, racism, war, and even destruction of the environment were no match for the happiness to be found in consumerism, he wrote, going directly against the grain of early 1970s "limits to growth" thinking.[69] In these decidedly antiscientific times (Alvin Toffler's best seller *Future Shock* had just been published), Dichter defended the need for progress in all its forms, with "motivating human behavior" our best opportunity to achieve individual and collective happiness and fulfillment.[70] He now boasted in his book of having done four thousand research studies for clients, including one in which he told the Florida Celery Growers' Association to feature in its advertising the crackling noises made while eating the vegetable because people enjoyed the experience despite its being socially unacceptable.[71]

Reviewers of *Motivating Human Behavior* were no less flummoxed than reviewers of his previous books. "This is a rather peculiar book for an academic to review by the usual criteria," wrote a decidedly puzzled Bernard P. Indik of Rutgers University, completely thrown by Dichter's improvisational style. Indik thought a good subtitle of the book would be "How I Tried to Influence People for My Various Clients," for Dichter's positivism in the spirit of Dale Carnegie was what stood out the most. Somewhat taken aback by Dichter's self-professed role as a social engineer doing whatever he could to make people happier, Indik was more than a little skeptical that he was able to do that better than the people themselves. Dichter's ever-expanding role of philosopher too was not lost on Indik, who found the author's six-page section "How to Produce Unification of the World and Peace" arrogant beyond belief. Again, however, the book was not at all a lost cause, containing "some very interesting insights" for a reader able to negotiate his or her way through Dichter's gung-ho attitude and larger-than-life personality.[72]

Total Environmental Immersion

Despite the occasional mixed (or scathing) book review, Dichter's almost single-handed effort to save motivation research from the dustbin of history was literally paying off. With two million dollars in the bank in 1972, Dichter was now financially secure, the even better news being that his brand of research was experiencing a revival after its near-death experience (not to mention his own). Part of motivation research's comeback was due to purely economic factors during recessionary times. Once comparatively very expensive, motivation research was now a lot cheaper than nose counting, and the skyrocketing costs of large-scale, analysis-heavy quantitative studies made many marketers take another look at different kinds of qualitative research. Over the previous two or three years, Dichter had landed gigs with dozens of big companies, including DuPont, Alcoa, General Mills, Procter and Gamble, Colgate-Palmolive, and Johnson and Johnson, making the early 1970s his best days since the late 1950s.[73] As always, Dichter made himself very available to journalists looking for a pithy quote. Of the apparent end of the love affair between Americans and the VW Beetle in 1972, for example, Dichter said: "It was a protest against Detroit [but] if you own a VW today, you can't boast about it. . . . It isn't an adventure anymore." (Dichter himself owned a Beetle but, no longer in love with it, was thinking about trading it in for a Toyota.)[74]

A good chunk of Dichter's wealth had resulted from the 1971 sale of his Institute of Motivation Research to Lehigh Valley Industries, a New York–based conglomerate. In addition to the cash payment, Dichter remained president of the company, allowing him to do what he did best. Even his windfall, however, did not provide Dichter peace of mind. "I was very poor in my childhood, so I still suffer from insecurity," he confessed to a *Wall Street Journal* reporter, his wife Hedy "always asking me when I will stop worrying about going hungry."[75] The venture between Dichter and Lehigh Valley would prove short-lived. In 1973, Dichter severed all ties with the company, deciding to go solo as an independent consultant and "conceptualizer."[76] "It was a bad marriage," he said that year of the partnership with Lehigh Valley (the company was in deep debt, it turned out); it was difficult to imagine Dichter being happily married to anyone (except Hedy). At his new company, the impressively named Ernest Dichter Creativity Ltd., he and a small staff planned to apply the "alpha" state of biofeedback to motivation research and employ what he called "total environmental immersion," something which involved the use of colors, shapes, and 3-D stimuli in order to discover the "mantra" or "leitmotif" of a consumer. At sixty-five, Dichter had apparently tuned in and/or turned on.[77]

Dichter's almost stream of consciousness way of addressing savages near and far continued to flow. Well into the 1970s, Dichter published a newsletter for his clients (*Findings* superseding the earlier *Motivations*), which provided him with an opportunity to further spread his gospel of identity-affirming consumerism. One newsletter in 1974 was a diatribe against consumer ignorance, in which, for example, Dichter took issue with the ways in which people were not in control of their own desires and needs. "What we need is a systematic campaign in order to motivate people in such a way that they do those things that are really better for them," he wrote, the solution being an "organization which works not only with legislation and coercive measures but one that uses modern methods . . . to educate people better." More than a bit vague and dogmatic, perhaps, but an idea that anticipated the flood of consumer rights groups that sprang up in the 1980s and 1990s.[78]

Dichter's next book was about packaging, an area he had dabbled in for years as part of his 360-degree insight into consumer behavior. Like many if not most of his books, *Packaging: The Sixth Sense?* published in 1975 was not particularly well received, although Dichter may be having the last laugh. "Many of Dichter's ideas seem impractical or just downright undesirable," wrote Roy R. Grundy and Wayne R. Stuetzer in their review in the *Journal of Marketing*, the two asking, "Would consumers really find it more appetizing to apply jelly to their morning toast by squeezing it out of a tube?" Maybe not more appetizing but certainly more convenient, as users of Welch's or Smucker's squeezable jelly would today report.[79] Dichter also predicted in his book that we would one day buy basic products like paper towels and toilet paper in bulk, envisioning this a decade or two before such products were available at Costco or Sam's Club. Another forecast by Dichter—that we'd bring our empty whiskey bottles to be refilled at liquor stores—has yet to come to pass, however, our current mantra of reduce, reuse, recycle notwithstanding.[80]

In the late 1970s, Dichter started to think about writing his memoirs, knowing he had the classic Horatio Alger story on his hands (with Nazis to boot). "I listen for the messages behind what they [advertisers] are saying," he told a reporter for the *Los Angeles Times*, having soap on his mind that particular day, as he was working on a project for Dial. (He also had turtles on the brain, currently advising farmers in the Caribbean how they could possibly persuade Americans to switch from beef to turtle steaks.) As in his project for Ivory almost four decades earlier, bathing and showering were at least as much about pleasure as about cleanliness and, if joined by a partner, to "feel a sense of absolution after sex." Dichter had suggested to Procter and Gamble that it use a contoured shape for Dove after observing that people liked to fondle soap ("I think of a man as a higher ape, an animal who loves to grasp, whose palm is an erogenous zone," he explained), a recommendation that has obviously served the brand well.[81]

Up to that point, Dichter admitted to having just one failure in his career, advising General Mills, the maker of Wheaties, to put their cereal in a package with loud colors to wake people up in the morning ("people were frightened by seeing such a box at breakfast," he confessed). (He had apparently forgotten about his psychological blessing of the jumpsuit, the fitted, one-piece garment that had a brief moment of popularity on the West Coast in the late 1960s. "Apparel requirements in the supersonic era of speed may include clothing that can be put on in 30 seconds or less," he told the *Wall Street Journal* in 1967, the jumpsuit offering the additional advantage of acting "as if it is another skin.")[82] In any case, he had had much better luck with "the whole crispy flake idea," as he described it, taking credit for the birth of crunchy cereal. Believing that consumers find mushy cereals "disheartening" and that fibrous cereals "make people feel like losers," Dichter came up with his theory of "conquerable resistance," his story went, leading to the crispy flake—"a test of potency that reassures you that you won't flop during the day." The "breakfast of champions" really was, apparently, a breakfast for champions.[83]

Having covered virtually every topic imaginable in his writings, Dichter finally decided to tackle the toughest one of all—himself. In his 1979 autobiography, *Getting Motivated: The Secret Behind Individual Motivations by the Man Who Was Not Afraid to Ask "Why?"* he traced his life story, arranging his recollections not as a traditional narrative but (fittingly enough) as "psychological chain reactions." Although he was proud of virtually all the projects he had worked on for forty years, he seemed most happy to write about recent assignments that had contributed to society (the A-projects) rather than to a corporation's bottom line (the B-projects). Not long before, Dichter had written a monograph, *Why Is the United Nations Not More Effective?* an attempt to use his expertise in human motivations on a larger stage, and in *Getting Motivated* he emphasized social issues like the need for greater voter participation and the possibility of raising prejudice-free children (both of which could be achieved through motivation research, not incidentally). Other worthy goals, such as crime prevention and fighting drug addiction, could be achieved if parents, teachers, and professionals had a better grasp of what motivated bad behavior, he believed, and he attempted to use his intellectual platform to try to make the world a better place. In *Getting Motivated,* Dichter confessed that his own dreams involved going off with aliens à la *Close Encounters of the Third Kind* and, after a few months of observing the natives on a remote star, returning to Earth with amazing abilities. "I could cure cancer, solve international conflicts eliminating wars, or to put it very modestly, become a messiah who can use his talents in almost all areas," he wrote, quite a fantasy even for a man like Ernest Dichter.[84]

Dichter's autobiography contained a host of other interesting insights that made the man seem that much more extraordinary. While Dichter usually studied the motivations of humans, for one project he had explored the subconscious of dogs, his mission to understand the psychology of their eating habits. (Unfortunately, he didn't mention what depth interviews with them revealed.) Executives should be sent to Las Vegas as part of their management training, he also believed, as there were valuable lessons in flexibility and adaptability to be gained from learning how to gamble. The boundaries of "Dichter Deductivism" seemed limitless. Pants were creased because they made men feel as though they had an erection, something especially valuable for militaries wanting courageous men. As "Hidden Persuader Number 1," he was hired by Hubert Humphrey in 1968 to help the vice president win the presidency, but, as it turned out, "Nixon came through as the fox." Stanley Kubrick asked him to collaborate on *Dr. Strangelove,* but the two couldn't reach a mutually agreeable financial arrangement, making one speculate how the film would have turned out had Dichter had the chance to "doctor" it. Most interesting, perhaps, was that he and Hedy had what he described as "a half-open marriage," meaning it was Ernest who got to engage in "middle-age escapades" (most of them at the office with his "very sexy secretary"). At the end of the day, however, it was Dichter's own motivations that stood out in the book. "I have acted as a discoverer, as a general on the battlefield of free enterprise," he wrote, proud and admittedly a little surprised that he had been the victor.[85]

I'm the Hidden Persuader

Although the publication of his autobiography provided closure in some ways and perhaps allowed him to exorcize some of his demons, new challenges and opportunities awaited him in the 1980s, and Dichter was ready to seize them. His company now called Dichter Motivations Incorporated, he dismissed the 1980s near obsession with sorting consumers into buckets based on values and lifestyles, reasserting that psychology played a more important role in making people who they were. "The emphasis on values and lifestyles has become very popular of late, though it is actually the latest in a long line of attempts to pigeonhole people into different personality types or 'styles of behavior,'" Dichter sniffed in a 1986 article in *Psychology and Marketing* entitled "Whose Lifestyle Is It Anyway?" seeing it as not much more than dumb-as-a-box-of-hammers demographics. Terms like "baby boomers" or "yuppies" were certainly clever and cute, Dichter admitted, but represented unduly simplistic attempts to make sense of the chaos that was human behavior. Rather, it was things like childhood experiences (such as being poor, as he knew all too well) or the relationship with one's spouse (another thing close to home) that offered marketers a rich and deep well to draw insights from, he insisted, not about to let the research trend du jour diminish his legacy. "Consideration of complex individual and familial psychological factors provides a more complete understanding of the consumer and a more accurate prediction of buyer behavior," he made clear, which was news to a new generation of businesspeople perhaps not familiar with his work over the preceding decades.[86]

Dichter had little to worry about. Fueled by product parity and the statistics-driven New Coke disaster of 1985, which rivaled the Edsel campaign as the marketing faux pas of the century, psychology-based research thrived in the late eighties as companies tried to tap into consumers' emotional connections to brands. "Brands are not just commercial products we buy and use; they're our companions in life as well," said Rosalind Rago, director of advertising research at Ogilvy and Mather in 1988, sounding a lot like Ernest Dichter circa 1939. Her agency was just one of many keeping Freud quite busy on Madison Avenue a century or so after the father of psychoanalysis came up with his core concepts about the workings of the human mind. McCann-Erickson, for example, was pursuing a variety of psychology-based projects in addition to its ne'er-do-well-husband-or-boyfriend-as-roach research study for its insecticide client. Besides asking consumers to draw pictures, the agency was having them write obituaries for particular products, how and when a certain brand died (old age? tragic accident? beheaded by a competitor, perhaps?) chock-full of interesting insights. Foote, Cone and Belding, meanwhile, was giving consumers stacks of photos of people's faces and then asking them to sort them as hypothetical users of designated brands, yet another revealing portrait of product personalities. And down the block at N. W. Ayer, researchers were having consumers record their reactions to new product ideas by making them draw shapes with their left hand, one more way to get around the limitations of logic. "Since the right hemisphere of the brain is visual, symbolic and emotional and it controls the left half of the body, this technique taps into perceptions better expressed as images rather than words," explained Fred Posner, a senior vice president at the agency, sounding not too unlike, dare I say it, James Vicary in his presubliminal days.[87]

Although there were skeptics, just as there had been in motivation research's heyday ("the subconscious techniques of clinical psychologists have yet to prove their utility," insisted Peter Kim, head of consumer behavior at J. Walter Thompson), Freudian-style psychoanalysis was again having a field day on "Ad Alley." Another big agency, Saatchi and Saatchi DFS Compton, kept no fewer than seven practicing clinical psychologists on retainer to analyze consumers' reactions to ads it created, the less the shrinks knew about market research, the better. "We prefer practicing doctors who do true psychoanalysis with patients and really know what makes people tick," said Penelope Queen, director of planning and research at the agency. One such therapist was even brought in to parse consumers' underlying feelings toward cold medicine. (One consumer's image of a "gurgling waterfall" signified the soothing effect of the cold medicine, the therapist suggested, again something right out of Dichter's mid-century playbook.) A recent, well-received campaign developed for Philips light bulbs drew heavily on what Saatchi's shrinks brought to the conference table, the agency going back to Dichter's #1 theme—security—for inspiration. Saatchi might have gone to the psychological well once too often in pitching the $200 million Burger King account, however, its competitive analysis a bit too bizarre for the fast food chain. Burger King was a "sly, unfriendly cat," while McDonald's was a "cute, friendly baby chick," Saatchi told its potential client on the basis of one of its psychologist's research findings, and the account was promptly awarded to N. W. Ayer.[88]

Now that his body of work was fully integrated into the DNA of Madison Avenue, Dichter continued to hold forth on issues that intrigued him. Interested in political market research since the "Dewey Defeats Truman" fiasco, Dichter believed that pollsters were still asking the wrong kind of questions when it came to predicting the outcome of elections. Rather than simply ask people who it was they planned to vote for, Dichter explained he would ask them what kind of animal the candidates would be. "I would have got back answers that [Mondale] would be a tame rabbit, maybe a mouse," he conjectured, while "Reagan would be a jaguar, a fox, a much more aggressive animal." Using his kind of analysis, he said, the outcome of the elections would be as clear as day.[89] A book he published in 1986, the unfortunately titled *How Hot a Manager Are You?* actually received rave reviews from *Public Personnel Management*, which considered it a "highly practical guide" offering "solid advice and helpful examples." At seventy-nine, had Dichter finally learned how to satisfy critics?[90] Either way, he claimed to have done more than five thousand research studies, ranging from the psychological dynamics of life (birth control) to death (cemeteries). "We're doing work on how to sell health, how to get people to be fit, to exercise, how to get people to stop smoking for the [American] Cancer Society, how to get people to give money for charitable funds, and the approach is exactly the same," Dichter told Rena Bartos that year.[91]

At the top of Dichter's list of A-projects, however, were those that promoted the American Way of Life or, not mutually exclusively, promised to bridge cultural differences. "The whole free-enterprise system suffers from the lack of an appropriate image," Dichter griped in a 1985 article in the *Journal of Consumer Marketing*, thinking that we were far behind (at least in branding terms) the Communists with their hammer and sickle iconography, red packaging, and clearly delineated (if not executed) reason for being. "The so-called 'capitalist' society, in itself a rather negative term, has failed to invent not only a convincing color and trademark, but even a clear-cut, sharp image," he continued, suggesting the United States adopt "self-renewal" as its unique selling proposition to export around the world.[92] While Dichter thought the Soviets' branding was better than that of the United States, he believed both sides could do a much better job in achieving the ultimate objective—world peace. "Disarmament is the wrong word," he told Eric Clark, author of 1989's *The World of Advertising: How They Make You Buy*. "No one wants to be disarmed," he explained, recommending that both superpowers "call it something else."[93]

Dichter received many honors in the eighties, being named a fellow of the American Psychological Association and a member of the Halls of Fame of both the American Marketing Association and the Market Research Council. Even more impressive, his very first client, Compton Advertising, was still a client a half century after he decoded for Ivory soap the psychologically charged ritual that was bathing.[94] In 1989, at the age of eighty-two, Dichter was teaching marketing at the Westchester campus of Long Island University when he got what was arguably the call of his life: to bring motivation research to the Soviet Union. He landed the project just as the country was falling apart, and it was probably the first real attempt to understand Russian consumers. He had actually been hired by an Austrian communications company in partnership with a Soviet publisher, hence the need to do, as he put it, "a survey on the Russian soul." Dichter's hypothesis was that Russians "like to suffer" and were "somewhat masochistic" but, with the right approach, could be turned into excellent consumers. "For 50 years, Soviet citizens have been told, 'Don't buy from capitalist devils! They will tempt you with hidden persuaders!'" he told a *New York Times* reporter (who called him "the patron saint of motivational research") just before he left, unable to resist adding, "*I'm* the hidden persuader!"[95]

Epilogue

Ernest Dichter may indeed have been the hidden persuader, but his method of persuasion was now part of a much more competitive research marketplace. With remote controls, VCRs, and dozens of new channels to watch on cable TV, the American consumer was proving to be more elusive to the advertiser than ever, pushing marketers to try different kinds of research methodologies. Many marketers decided to fight technology with technology, using UPC scanners, "people meters," and computers now far smaller than a vending machine to gather and compile all sorts of data about consumers. The amount of information being gathered and compiled was truly startling. One research firm, JFY Audit America, tracked which products were being used in twenty-four million of the country's eighty-four million households, while another, Claritas, used census data to segment every one of the nation's 240,000 neighborhoods into forty demographic groups. And with its BehaviorScan service, Information Resources linked shopping behavior to television viewing habits, this "single source data" allowing marketers to know, for example, whether heavy users of Cool Whip were fond of watching *The Cosby Show*.[1]

Right alongside the rise of high-tech consumer research was psychographics, which had been kicking around in one form or another since the late 1960s. Psychographics hit its stride in the eighties, however, as marketers increasingly looked to values and attitudes as the most important determinant of consumer behavior. Driving the interest in psychographics was the growing number of specialty retailers and products aimed at niche markets, these kinds of efforts beyond the nuts-and-bolts statistics and demographics gleaned from technology. "Demographics tell you what he [the customer] looks like and what he does but it doesn't tell you why he does things," said Peter Stisser, vice president at Yankelovich Clancy Shulman—a familiar tune. Also called "lifestyle research," psychographics consisted of sorting people into attitudinal buckets, with SRI leading the pack with its Values and Life

Styles (VALS) program. Should an advertiser go after "actualizers," "fulfilleds," "achievers," "experiencers," "believers," "strivers," "makers," or "strugglers"? SRI had the answer, telling its clients which hot buttons to push for which kind of consumer archetype.[2]

Clearly influenced by the pop psychology movement of the 1970s, psychographics brought the complex universe of feelings, emotions, and perceptions to an easy-to-understand, commonsense level, used by ad agencies as much to attract and keep clients as to shape strategy. More "me-too" products were prompting advertisers to appeal to consumers' emotional sets, the image of a brand considered more marketable than its features. Also, with broad consumer affluence, the physical needs of many Americans (especially those of aspirant baby boomers) had been met, which meant they were ready to march up Maslow's hierarchy by satisfying unfulfilled psychological needs. By the late 1980s, emotional benefits were deemed not just as important as physical ones but just as real, implying that in many cases the advertising *was* the product to be consumed rather than the product itself.[3] Much as Packard had argued thirty years earlier, advertisers were "portray[ing] products as symbolic solutions to people's deep emotional cravings," as Jonathan Rowe wrote in the *Christian Science Monitor* in 1987, the sizzle at least as important as the steak.[4]

With psychographics, marketers truly believed that the sizzle had been turned into a science. More than two hundred clients were paying $7,500 to $20,000 or more for access to VALS reports and seminars in 1986, well worth the money considering the amount of research that went into VALS. The program had its origins in a 1983 book by Arnold Mitchell, *The Nine American Lifestyles*, in which the social scientist built on Maslow's well-known theories with a quantitative survey. Within a few years, SRI was asking twenty thousand Americans per year to describe their lives in considerable detail, confirming the compelling idea that there were nine basic types of people in the nation, each type warranting its own approach to marketing. (The number and description of the archetypes were continually refined.) Yankelovich Clancy Shulman used a different methodology for its Lifestyle Monitor, measuring the changing attitudes of Americans every year since 1971. Whatever the methodology, who one was was now accepted to be what one bought, an understanding of consumers' inner needs the primary goal of market research.[5]

With psychographics planting the seed for more psychological market research methodologies, a rather unexpected turn of events took place:

Freud began to make his way back to Madison Avenue. Psychographics were fine but were a mass approach, ignoring individuals and, correlatively, their unconscious, where many had once again come to believe where the real "why" of decision making resided. Since Dichter's death in 1991, other researchers, obviously influenced and inspired by his work, have appeared on the scene, eager to claim the title of "hidden persuader." Clotaire Rapaille has definitely come the closest, using his theory of "culture codes" to parse why we do the things we do and, as important, buy the things we buy. Rapaille has cracked culture codes for dozens of Fortune 100 companies over the past couple of decades, his client list—Chrysler, Procter and Gamble, GE, AT&T, Boeing, Honda, Kellogg, L'Oréal, and many others—as impressive as Dichter's in his prime. By putting on "'a new set of glasses' with which to view our actions and motivations," as he wrote in his 2006 book *The Culture Code*, everything from why we are disillusioned by love to why fat is a solution rather than a problem becomes as clear as day, his decoding process (not to mention his theory about our reptilian brains) "reveal[ing] the hidden clues to understanding."[6]

As the anecdote in my Introduction suggests, my personal experience with one of Rapaille's "discovery sessions" was something less than miraculous. Somewhere in motivation research heaven, Ernest Dichter is either laughing his head off or crying his eyes out at how some of his theories have been turned into such silliness, all uncredited of course. (Freud and Jung are each mentioned exactly once in his book, but their respective theories about the individual and collective unconscious are summarily dismissed.) Fortunately, other aspirant hidden persuaders have done more justice to the body of work laid down by Dichter and other motivation researchers of the past. Proudly carrying on the motivation research tradition, most notably, is Olson Zaltman Associates with its Zaltman Metaphor Elicitation Technique (ZMET), the first patented market research tool in the United States. Cofounder Gerald Zaltman, a marketing professor at Harvard and member of the university's Mind, Brain, Behavior Initiative, began tinkering with the technique in the early 1990s by combining neuroscience with plentiful servings of semiotics and Jungian theory. Like Dichter, Zaltman was convinced that consumers couldn't tell you what they think because they simply didn't know, their deepest thoughts residing in the unconscious. Either on his own or through his consultancy, Zaltman had completed more than two hundred ZMET studies by 2002 for companies like DuPont, GM, Reebok, AT&T, P&G, Coca-Cola, and Hallmark. Although the secret sauce of the technique was and is as closely guarded as KFC's recipe, Zaltman acknowledges that using visual images rather than words is the key to revealing people's hidden thoughts about the products they use.[7]

Not surprisingly, given Olson Zaltman's success, a number of other marketing professors around the country are now using ZMET-inspired methodologies to probe consumers' subconscious for clients. "There's a huge amount of interest in new market research techniques . . . trying to uncover the motivation behind people's actions," said Tim Calkins, clinical professor of marketing at Northwestern University, in 2008, confirming that psychoanalytic models have been gaining traction against both focus groups and quantitative research as more marketers realized that, as another current ZMET practitioner put it, "You can't measure what you can't understand."[8]

While motivation research has enjoyed a revival in the past two decades, subliminal advertising has fallen into further disrepute. "Subliminal Delusion" went the title of a 1985 *Psychology Today* article about the subject, for example, followed a year later by "Subliminal Foolishness" in the *Los Angeles Times* and a few years later by *New York*'s "From the Subliminal to the Ridiculous." Former professor William Bryan Key (who quit his teaching job in 1975 to write more books and work the college lecture circuit after his success a few years earlier with *Subliminal Seduction*) was undeterred, however, still making the case that advertisers were using the technique by embedding images of skulls in ice cubes and spelling out the letters S-E-X in crackers. While there was no doubt that some marketers, particularly those in the alcohol and tobacco business, were appealing to consumers' unconscious in their advertising through emotion-laden language and imagery, by the early 1990s the idea of subliminalism had become largely a running joke despite Key's populist appeal. Some advertisers had in fact begun to parody subliminal advertising in their actual advertising, turning the whole concept into wink-wink, nudge-nudge sardonic fodder. With the help of arrows, vaguely sexual images—a couple dancing? a woman floating in an inner tube?—could be detected amid the bubbles and gin in a series of Seagram's ads, for instance, the subliminal connotations a humorous cultural reference rather than a dangerous weapon of propaganda. (The campaign was called "Hidden Pleasure," riffing on Packard's book, and was a response to Key's claim that the word "sex" was planted in the ice of a Gilbey's gin ad.) Commercials for the 1992 Toyota Paseo flashed images of bikinis and the words "wild," "hot," and "sexy" while the announcer drolly talked about how practical the car was, this too a tongue-in-cheek homage to the phenomenon that once scared Americans out of their wits. Kevin Nealon's "Subliminal Man" on *Saturday Night Live* in the 1990s pushed the joke even further, as the character interjected what he *really* thought or wanted (e.g., "Have sex") into normal conversation.[9]

Paradoxically, however, many people continue to believe that advertisers are (nonironically) using subliminal techniques and, more amazingly, that they work. (Nearly two-thirds of Americans believed subliminal advertising existed in 1991, according to an Ogilvy & Mather telephone survey, and more than half of those asked felt it could make them buy things they didn't want.) Although proved ineffective more than four decades ago and despite little new research to suggest otherwise, subliminalism has turned out to be quite a resilient mythology, at least for the more gullible. Since the mid-1980s, marketers of self-help products have cleverly traded on these persistent beliefs, splicing subliminal messages of positive affirmation into audio and video formats to purportedly improve listeners' and viewers' mental or psychological health. Low self-esteem? Poor memory? Not quite successful, rich, or popular enough? Just pop a CD or DVD into a player and let the hidden messages work their magic by getting you to think more creatively, these marketers have told consumers wanting to do everything from lose weight to stop smoking—a compelling proposition despite the fact that there is precious little evidence that the messages work.[10]

Even if subliminal advertising did work, it would pale in comparison with the next generation of marketing rapidly taking shape. As scientists explore the deep recesses of the human brain, it's now becoming possible to biologically read people's minds, offering an exponential leap in understanding what and how consumers think. MRI scans of the prefrontal cortex along with biometrics are revealing our very thoughts and feelings, the Holy Grail for those trafficking in the business of information and knowledge. "Neuromarketing" emerged as a legitimate field in the early 2000s, when brain scientists began to make a convincing case they were now the best market researchers in town. Exploring "the neural dynamics of the perception and production of rhythmic sensorimotors patterns," as one neuromarketer put it in 2003, is increasingly being used as the basis for decision making in business, with activity in the medial prefrontal cortex perhaps the skeleton key to marketing success.[11] Today's researchers ask them themselves why one should bother talking with consumers at all when one can go directly to the source—a very good question as such technology improves and the practice becomes more accepted.

And just like motivation research half a century ago, brain scans are being touted as a way to avoid the dishonesty and incompleteness that often comes with standard market surveys and focus groups, a case of déjà vu all over again.[12] Not surprisingly, however, the same concerns that hounded motivation research and subliminal advertising surrounds neuromarketing—that peering into our brains is an Orwellian invasion of privacy and potentially dangerous stuff.[13] Until these fears are allayed and the MRI rules the marketing roost, more conventional means will have to do, meaning Freud will likely remain on Madison Avenue for some time to come.

Notes

Introduction

1. Ernest Dichter, *Getting Motivated: The Secret Behind Individual Motivations by the Man Who Was Not Afraid to Ask "Why?"* (New York: Pergamon Press, 1979), 138.

2. Danielle Sacks, "Crack This Code," *Fast Company*, April 2006, 96–101.

3. Sacks, "Crack This Code."

4. Sacks, "Crack This Code."

5. Barbara B. Stern, "The Importance of Being Ernest: Commemorating Dichter's Contribution to Advertising Research," *Journal of Advertising Research*, June 2004, 165–69.

6. Eric Clark, *The World of Advertising: How They Make You Buy* (New York: Viking, 1989), 65–66.

7. Pamela Walker Laird, *Advertising Progress: American Business and the Rise of Consumer Marketing* (Baltimore: Johns Hopkins University Press, 1998), 179, 224.

8. Laird, *Advertising Progress*, 225, 281–84, 288–90.

9. Charles F. McGovern, *Sold American: Consumption and Citizenship, 1890–1945* (Chapel Hill: University of North Carolina Press, 2006), 32.

10. Robert Bartels, *The History of Marketing Thought* (Columbus, Ohio: Grid, 1976), 126, 129.

11. Roland Marchand, *Advertising the American Dream: Making the Way for Modernity, 1920–1940* (Berkeley: University of California Press, 1985), 35.

12. McGovern, *Sold American*, 33.

13. Marchand, *Advertising the American Dream*, 74–76.

14. Regina Lee Blaszczyk, *Imagining Consumers: Design and Innovation from Wedgwood to Corning* (Baltimore: Johns Hopkins University Press, 2000), 229–35.

15. Regina Lee Blaszczyk, *American Consumer Society, 1865–2005: From Hearth to HDTV* (Wheeling, Ill.: Harlan-Davidson, 2009), 123–25.

16. Blaszczyk, *American Consumer Society, 1865–2005*, 130–31.

17. Roland Marchand, *Creating the Corporate Soul: The Rise of Public Relations and Corporate Imagery in American Big Business* (Berkeley: University of California Press, 1998), 229–35.

18. Lisa Jacobson, *Raising Consumers: Children and the American Mass Market in the Early Twentieth Century* (New York: Columbia University Press, 2004), 8.

19. Martin Mayer, *Madison Avenue, U.S.A.* (New York: Pocket Books, 1958), 216–18.

20. Mayer, *Madison Avenue, U.S.A.*, 218–19, 221–22.

21. Clark, *The World of Advertising*, 67–68.

22. Joseph W. Newman, *Motivation Research and Marketing Management* (Cambridge, Mass.: Harvard University Press, 1957), 17.

23. Rena Bartos, *Qualitative Research: What It Is and Where It Came From* (New York: Advertising Research Federation, 1986), 2, 5.

24. Newman, *Motivation Research and Marketing Management*, 506.

25. Newman, *Motivation Research and Marketing Management*, 507–9.

26. Edith Witt, "The Personal Adman," *Reporter*, May 14, 1959, 36–37.

27. Newman, *Motivation Research and Marketing Management*, 52–54.

28. Newman, *Motivation Research and Marketing Management*, 64–65.

29. Jack Patterson, "Invisible Salesman," *Commonweal*, April 18, 1958, 71–73.

30. "'Action' Research, Aimed at Decision-Making, Seen as Dominant in the 1960s," *Advertising Age*, July 20, 1959, 78.

31. George Christopoulos, "What Makes People Buy?" *Management Review*, September 1959, 5–8 and following.

32. Christopoulos, "What Makes People Buy?" 5–8 and following.

33. Stephen Fox, *The Mirror Makers: A History of American Advertising and Its Creators* (New York: Vintage, 1984), 184, 186.

34. Thomas Cudlik and Christoph Steiner, "'Rabbi Ernest': The Strategist of Desire: A Portrait," in Franz Kreuzer, Gerd Prechtl, and Christoph Steiner, eds., *A Tiger in the Tank: Ernest Dichter: An Austrian Advertising Guru* (Riverside, Calif.: Ariadne Press, 2007), 79–82.

35. Vance Packard, "The Ad and the Id," *Reader's Digest*, November 1957, 118–21.

36. Joseph Seldin, "Selling to the Id," *Nation*, May 21, 1955, 442–43.

37. Vance Packard, *The Hidden Persuaders* (Brooklyn, N.Y.: Ig Publishing, 2007), 10–12.

38. Cudlik and Steiner, "'Rabbi Ernest,'" in *A Tiger in the Tank,* 63–64.

39. Fox, *The Mirror Makers*, 186–87.

40. Franz Kreuzer and Patrick Schierholz, "Dichter Lives On: Motivational Research and Advertising Today," in *A Tiger in the Tank*, 126.

41. Gerd Prechtl, "Kick-Off: Ernest Dichter, a Man from Vienna," in *A Tiger in the Tank*, 201.

42. Clark, *The World of Advertising*, 69–70.

43. Cudlik and Steiner, "'Rabbi Ernest,'" in *A Tiger in the Tank*, 45–46; Dichter claimed in 1972 that only 5 percent of his recommendations were based primarily on sex, something difficult to believe. Roger Ricklefs, "Psyching Them Out," *Wall Street Journal*, November 20, 1972, 1.

44. Franz Kreuzer, "The Secret Freudian: Ernest Dichter as a Witness of His Work," in *A Tiger in the Tank*, 35; Dichter was expert enough on sex to be able to write an article called "Why Men Like Breasts" for *Playboy*. Hefner ended up rejecting the article because it was too much of a "clinical analysis of their two main sell-

ing points," as Dichter put it, but *Cosmopolitan* happily picked it up. Dichter, *Getting Motivated*, 94.

45. Dichter, *Getting Motivated*, 164–65.

46. Kreuzer and Schierholz, "Dichter Lives On," in *A Tiger in the Tank*, 126.

47. Cudlik and Steiner, "'Rabbi Ernest,'" in *A Tiger in the Tank*, 47, 90–91, 93.

48. Barbara Ehrenreich, *The Hearts of Men: American Dreams and the Flight from Commitment* (Garden City, N.Y.: Anchor Press/Doubleday, 1983), 45.

49. Bill Osgerby, *Playboys in Paradise: Masculinity, Youth and Leisure-Style in Modern America* (New York: Berg, 2001), 175.

50. Cudlik and Steiner, "'Rabbi Ernest,'" in *A Tiger in the Tank*, 64–72, 87–88, 94.

51. Marina Moskowitz, *Standard of Living: The Measure of the Middle Class in Modern America* (Baltimore: Johns Hopkins University Press, 2004), 2.

52. Stern, "The Importance of Being Ernest," 165–69.

53. Dichter, *Getting Motivated* 18, 49.

Chapter 1. The Psychology of Everyday Living

1. George Christopoulos, "What Makes People Buy?" *Management Review*, September 1959, 5–8 and following.

2. Lewis A. Coser, *Refugee Scholars in America: Their Impact and Experience* (New Haven: Yale University Press, 1984), 110–12, 120; one of Lazarsfeld's coauthors of the study was his first wife, Marie Jahoda.

3. Paul F. Lazarsfeld, "An Episode in the History of Social Research: A Memoir," in Donald Fleming and Bernard Bailyn, eds., *The Intellectual Migration: Europe and America, 1930–1960* (Cambridge, Mass.: Harvard University Press, 1969), 272.

4. Anthony Heilbut, *Exiled in Paradise: German Refugee Artists and Intellectuals in America from the 1930's to the Present* (New York: Viking, 1983), 95–96.

5. Coser, *Refugee Scholars in America*, 110–14, 118–19; Heilbut, *Exiled in Paradise*, 96.

6. Lazarsfeld, "An Episode in the History of Social Research," 297.

7. Heilbut, *Exiled in Paradise*, 95.

8. Coser, *Refugee Scholars in America*, 114–16.

9. Lazarsfeld, "An Episode in the History of Social Research," 320–21.

10. Christopoulos, "What Makes People Buy?" 5–8.

11. Jean Converse, *Survey Research in the United States: Roots and Emergence, 1890–1960* (Berkeley: University of California Press, 1987), 131–36.

12. Joseph W. Newman, *Motivation Research and Marketing Management* (Cambridge, Mass.: Harvard University, 1957), 35.

13. Converse, *Survey Research in the United States*, 131–42, 258, 267.

14. Lazarsfeld, "An Episode in the History of Social Research," 332.

15. Coser, *Refugee Scholars in America*, 117–19.

16. Heilbut, *Exiled in Paradise*, 98.

17. "Peoria: Yardstick for Sales," *Business Week*, December 7, 1946, 50–52.

18. McGovern, *Sold American*, 272.

19. "Peoria: Yardstick for Sales," 50–52.

20. "Ford Asks Some Questions," *Business Week*, May 29, 1948, 74–77.

21. "Rush to Researchers Is On," *Business Week*, April 29, 1950, 63–64.

22. Harold Isaacs, "Market Research Helps Chart Course for Business . . . Spectacular Growth Highlights Need for Standards," *Newsweek*, March 29, 1948, 70–71.

23. George Cable Wright, "Gallup and Roper Acclaim Gains in Scientific Status of Poll Taker," *New York Times*, April 21, 1963, III, 12; Martin Weil, "Elmo Roper, Opinion Pollster, Dies," *Washington Post*, May 1, 1971, B8. Although the photo of the triumphant president-elect holding the newspaper with the "Dewey Defeats Truman" headline became an iconic image, pollsters had actually made an even more egregious political blunder when *Literary Digest* predicted a win for Alfred M. Landon over FDR in the 1936 election. The magazine polled only owners of automobiles and those with telephone service, a classic case of economic bias.

24. Hugh S. Hardy, ed., *The Politz Papers: Science and Truth in Marketing Research* (Chicago: American Marketing Association, 1990), 9; Politz himself did just one opinion poll during his career, but it was a memorable one. Before a meeting between President Eisenhower and Winston Churchill, Politz polled Americans on a number of issues. The information was used by Eisenhower in his meeting with Churchill, thus shaping international diplomacy.

25. Isaacs, "Market Research Helps Chart Course for Business," 70–71; standards in opinion polling improved over the next few years but still had a long way to go. In 1952, both Gallup and Roper (as well as a third major pollster, Crossley, Inc.) correctly picked Eisenhower to win but thought the race would be much closer than it turned out to be, again not a particularly stellar performance for the nation's elite researchers. Joseph J. Seldin, "Market Research is a Mess," *American Mercury*, April 1957, 19–26.

26. "Why Do They Buy?" *Business Week*, January 7, 1950, 34–36.

27. Daniel Horowitz, *The Anxieties of Affluence: Critiques of American Consumer Culture* (Amherst: University of Massachusetts Press, 2004), 51–52.

28. Thomas Cudlik and Christoph Steiner, "'Rabbi Ernest': The Strategist of Desire: A Portrait," in Franz Kreuzer, Gerd Prechtl, and Christoph Steiner, eds., *A Tiger in the Tank: Ernest Dichter: An Austrian Advertising Guru* (Riverside, Calif.: Ariadne Press) 47, 82; Ernest Dichter, *Getting Motivated: The Secret Behind Individual Motivations by the Man Who Was Not Afraid to Ask "Why?"* (New York: Pergamon Press, 1979), xi. Dichter considered himself even more of an outcast because he was a capitalist while his two younger brothers and many of his classmates were leftists. Yet another reason Dichter felt different from others was that he was circumcised, which caused him great embarrassment while taking his weekly shower among Gentiles as a child in the public baths in Vienna. *Getting Motivated*, 2, 4.

29. Cudlik and Steiner, "'Rabbi Ernest,'" 53.

30. Gerd Prechtl, "Kick-Off," in *A Tiger in the Tank*, 12–13.

31. Peter Scheer, "The Clock of Life: Memories of a Friend," in *A Tiger in the Tank*, 100–101.

32. Cudlik and Steiner, "'Rabbi Ernest,'" 56; Lynne Ames, "Tending the Flame of a Motivator," *New York Times*, August 2, 1998, WE2; Dichter, *Getting Motivated*, 11. Aichhorn is perhaps best remembered for saving Freud's library during the Anschluss.

33. "Ernest Dichter of Croton: 'A Doctor for Ailing Products,'" *Printers' Ink*, June 26, 1959, 72–80; Dichter's office was at Berggasse 20, Freud's at Berggasse 19. Although he never met Freud, Dichter did take a public-speaking course from Esti Freud, his daughter-in-law. In his autobiography, Dichter explained that while at the Sorbonne he decided to drop "literature, philosophy and other impractical subjects" after developing a crush for a girl, Tassja, who was studying psychology at the university. "She tried a Rorschach inkblot test with me and told me about her studies," Dichter remembered, and "the inevitable happened. I switched and chose, out of a burgeoning love, psychology as my object of study. As is often the case, I wanted to find solutions for my own problems and I wanted to please my girl friend at the same time." *Getting Motivated*, 9.

34. Hedy Dichter, "A Life with Ernest: Episodes from a Jewish Emigrant's Story Between Hope and Fulfillment," in *A Tiger in the Tank*, 115; Barbara B. Stern, "The Importance of Being Ernest: Commemorating Dichter's Contribution to Advertising Research," *Journal of Advertising Research*, June 2004, 165–69. Dichter also tried writing novels, no doubt acquiring some good material during a brief stint writing a romance column in a magazine read by Catholic Austrian housewives. Roger Ricklefs, "Psyching Them Out," *Wall Street Journal*, November 20, 1972, 1.

35. Horowitz, *The Anxieties of Affluence*, 52–53.

36. Scheer, "The Clock of Life," 102.

37. Dichter, "A Life with Ernest," 118.

38. Horowitz, *The Anxieties of Affluence*, 52–53.

39. Scheer, "The Clock of Life," 103; Sally Helgesen, "Sighting the Giant of Madison Avenue," *Los Angeles Times*, July 17, 1977, R87; Dichter, *Getting Motivated*, 33–34.

40. Cudlik and Steiner, "'Rabbi Ernest,'" 57–58. Much more encouraging was Margaret Mead, whom Dichter met soon after he arrived in America. "I have been studying the natives in New Guinea and Samoa and you have become fascinated with the natives of New York," Dichter remembered her telling him, the anthropologist remarking, "We use comparable methods to the ones that you have discovered in your work." *Getting Motivated*, 46.

41. Franz Kreuzer, "The Secret Freudian: Ernest Dichter as a Witness of His Work," in *Tiger in the Tank*, 35. In 1977, Dichter said he first applied the term "image" to a proposed TV commercial for Green Giant in the early 1950s, but all other accounts (including one by Dichter himself) suggest it happened much earlier.

42. Cudlik and Steiner, "'Rabbi Ernest.'" 58; Ames, "Tending the Flame of a Motivator," WE2; Rena Bartos, "Ernest Dichter: Motive Interpreter," *Journal of Advertising Research*, February–March 1986, 15; Dichter thought that his once a week visits to the public baths in Vienna as a child may well have inspired his study for Ivory decades later as well as those for shampoos and hair conditioners. "I not only washed away the

physical dirt, but also all the moral dirt accumulated during the week," he wrote in his autobiography; "it gave me a feeling of a fresh start." *Getting Motivated*, 3.

43. Horowitz, *The Anxieties of Affluence*, 53; Helgesen, "Sighting the Giant of Madison Avenue"; Dichter, *Getting Motivated*, 37. Dichter had yet to own a car, it might be added.

44. Louis Cheskin, the package designer, claimed that he was actually the first to use motivation research in the United States. And in *The Hidden Persuaders*, Packard credited Cheskin as a worthy rival to Dichter as "the father of MR, " noting that Packard claimed to have had pursued the technique as early as 1935—three years before Dichter arrived in America. Cheskin was not shy about claiming an impressive number of firsts, including his bold assertion that he was the "first to apply psychoanalytic techniques" (assuredly false given admen's widespread interest in behavioral psychology in the 1920s). Vance Packard, *The Hidden Persuaders* (Brooklyn, N.Y.: Ig, 2007), 47.

45. Cudlik and Steiner, "'Rabbi Ernest,'" 58; Dichter, *Getting Motivated*, 45. At CBS, Dichter also had what must have been a distinct pleasure in interviewing Milton Berle on the nature of comedy, concluding that "a comedian very often acts as a psychotherapist." *Getting Motivated*, 45.

46. Ernest Dichter, "Psychology in Market Research," *Harvard Business Review*, Summer 1947, 432–43.

47. Cudlik and Steiner, "'Rabbi Ernest,'" 74–75. The psychodrama was originally developed by Jacob Moreno, a Viennese psychiatrist, to whom Dichter gave full credit.

48. Franz Kreuzer and Patrick Schierholz, "Dichter Lives On: Motivational Research and Advertising Today," in *A Tiger in the Tank*, 125.

49. Cudlik and Steiner, "'Rabbi Ernest,'" 76–77. As one of the "tiger in your tank" stories goes (there are a number), Dichter inadvertently came up with the slogan when he told an Esso executive that the company should advertise more heavily. "You need a tiger in your tank," Dichter told the man, the metaphor completely missed by the oilman who replied, "But how could a tiger fit in the tank?" Dichter explained he was talking about power, and the phrase eventually turned into advertising history. Ames, "Tending the Flame of a Motivator," WE2. Dichter has also said that the roots of "tiger in the tank" went all the way back to a psychoanalytic session with one of his patients who had dreamed of ferocious animals (surrogates for his father, of course). *Getting Motivated*, 80.

50. Scheer, "The Clock of Life," 104–5.

51. Kreuzer and Schierholz, "Dichter Lives On," 127.

52. Cudlik and Steiner, "'Rabbi Ernest,'" 83–86, 89–90. The working title of Dichter's autobiography was *My Bloodless Autopsy*; "an autobiography is like an autopsy except the corpse is still breathing," he explained in *Getting Motivated* (x).

53. Ralph Goodman, "Freud and the Hucksters," *Nation*, February 14, 1953, 143–45.

54. "A New Language for Madison Avenue," *Business Week*, September 5, 1953, 40–44.

55. "A New Language for Madison Avenue," 40–44.

56. "A New Language for Madison Avenue," 40–44.

57. "A New Language for Madison Avenue," 40–44.

58. George Horseley Smith, *Motivation Research in Advertising and Marketing* (New York: McGraw-Hill, 1954), 222.

59. Smith, *Motivation Research in Advertising and Marketing*, 221–31.

60. Robert Graham, "Adman's Nightmare: Is the Prune a Witch?" *Reporter*, October 13, 1953, 27 and following.

61. Smith, *Motivation Research in Advertising and Marketing*, 207.

62. Lydia Strong, "They're Selling Your Unconscious," *Saturday Review*, November 13, 1954, 11–12.

63. Goodman, "Freud and the Hucksters," 143–45.

64. Graham, "Adman's Nightmare," 27 and following.

65. Graham, "Adman's Nightmare," 27 and following.

66. Graham, "Adman's Nightmare," 27 and following.

67. Packard, *The Hidden Persuaders*, 55.

68. Graham, "Adman's Nightmare," 27 and following.

69. Graham, "Adman's Nightmare," 27 and following.

70. Graham, "Adman's Nightmare," 27 and following.

71. Graham, "Adman's Nightmare," 27 and following.

72. Graham, "Adman's Nightmare," 27 and following.

73. Smith, *Motivation Research in Advertising and Marketing*, 224–26. Decades later Dichter recalled having seen prunes as "the old maids of the fruit world," but by adding the juice back to them they could be "fleshy young girls again, like peaches." Helgesen, "Sighting the Giant of Madison Avenue."

74. Graham, "Adman's Nightmare," 27 and following.

75. "People: What's Behind the Choices—in Buying, in Working," *Business Week*, August 14, 1954, 50–61.

76. Thomas E. McCarthy, "Psyche & Sales," *Wall Street Journal*, September 14, 1954, 1.

77. "Motivation Research," *Wall Street Journal*, September 14, 1954, 10.

78. Packard, *The Hidden Persuaders*, 49.

79. "Behavior Research: To Get Answers, Ask the People," *Business Week*, August 21, 1954, 130–43.

80. "Behavior Research," 130–43.

81. "Behavior Research," 130–43.

82. "Behavior Research," 130–43.

83. Strong, "They're Selling Your Unconscious," 11–12.

84. Smith, *Motivation Research in Advertising and Marketing*, 211, 18.

85. Smith, *Motivation Research in Advertising and Marketing*, 19–20.

86. Newman, *Motivation Research and Marketing Management*, vii, 12–16, 34.

87. Newman, *Motivation Research and Marketing Management*, iii, 28, 31, 36, 48–49.

88. Strong, "They're Selling Your Unconscious," 11–12. By "digging" down into consumers' subconscious, Dichter felt he was like a "psychological archaeologist," as he put it in his autobiography. *Getting Motivated*, 159.

89. Strong, "They're Selling Your Unconscious," 11–12.

90. Strong, "They're Selling Your Unconscious," 11–12.

91. "You Either Offer Security or Fail," *Business Week*, June 23, 1951, 68–76.

92. Strong, "They're Selling Your Unconscious," 11–12.

Chapter 2. The Sophisticated Sell

1. John P. Sisk, "Freud in a Gray Flannel Suit," *America*, August 10, 1957, 480–82.

2. Quoted in Sisk, "Freud in a Gray Flannel Suit," 480.

3. Sisk, "Freud in a Gray Flannel Suit," 480–82.

4. "Inside the Consumer: The New Debate: Does He Know His Own Mind?" *Newsweek*, October 10, 1955, 89–93.

5. "Inside the Consumer," 89–93.

6. Martin Mayer, *Madison Avenue, U.S.A.* (New York: Pocket Books, 1958), 123–24, 238, 242.

7. Mayer, *Madison Avenue, U.S.A.*, 221–24, 237–39. Consistent with Freudian theory postulating that deeply held feelings could be extracted only through considerable pain, even a two- or three-hour session sometimes wasn't enough to get the kind of answers Dichter was looking for, this unfortunate situation forcing the client to take another marketing tack.

8. Mayer, *Madison Avenue, U.S.A.*, 239–40.

9. Mayer, *Madison Avenue, U.S.A.*, 235–38.

10. Mayer, *Madison Avenue, U.S.A.*, 244, 247.

11. Mayer, *Madison Avenue, U.S.A.*, 247–49.

12. Carter Henderson, "Name Game," *Wall Street Journal*, August 24, 1956, 1.

13. Henderson, "Name Game."

14. Henderson, "Name Game."

15. Mayer, *Madison Avenue, U.S.A.*, 244–45.

16. Mayer, *Madison Avenue, U.S.A.*, 245–46.

17. Vance Packard, *The Hidden Persuaders* (Brooklyn, N.Y.: Ig Publishing, 2007), 51, 119.

18. Packard, *The Hidden Persuaders*, 67.

19. Packard, *The Hidden Persuaders*, 53, 65.

20. Packard, *The Hidden Persuaders*, 54, 56.

21. Perrin Stryker, "Motivation Research," *Fortune*, June 1956, 144–47 and following.

22. Display Ad 29, *Wall Street Journal*, April 30, 1956, 7.

23. Display Ad 9, *Wall Street Journal*, November 9, 1956, 3.

24. Classified Ad 5, *Wall Street Journal*, April 30, 1057, 16.

25. Classified Ad 8, *Wall Street Journal*, October 16, 1956, 18.

26. Stryker, "Motivation Research," 144–47 and following.

27. Newman, *Motivation Research and Marketing Management*, 51.

28. Stryker, "Motivation Research," 144–47 and following.

29. Stryker, "Motivation Research," 144–47 and following.

30. Anthony Heilbut, *Exiled in Paradise: German Refugee Artists and Intellectuals in America from the 1930s to the Present* (New York: Viking, 1983), 121–22. A "woman's perspective" was indeed a rare thing within the field. There were plenty of women in junior market research positions but precious few senior analysts and probably no directors at major corporations. Furthermore, "at all levels the rates of pay for women are well below those paid to men," the *New York Times* reported in 1959. (Carl Spielvogel, "Advertising: Outlays for Marketing Research Studied," *New York Times*, June 30, 1959, 41).

31. Packard, *The Hidden Persuaders*, 50–51, 55; Mayer, *Madison Avenue, U.S.A.*, 268. McCann and Y&R, of course, weren't the only agencies to have social scientists on staff. "It is a poor agency that can't afford at least one house psychologist," wrote Spencer Klaw for *Fortune* in 1961. Key executives on Madison Avenue or "Ad Alley" also often had some academic background in psychology (Marion Harper, president of McCann-Erickson, for example, had an A.B. in the subject from Yale), which created an organizational climate that was friendly to virtually anything that fell within the realm of behavioral science. Spencer Klaw, "What Is Marion Harper Saying?" *Fortune*, January 1961, 122–26 and following.

32. Mayer, *Madison Avenue, U.S.A.*, 69, 220–21.

33. Rena Bartos, *Qualitative Research: What It Is and Where It Came From* (New York: Advertising Research Federation, 1986), 3; Lynne Ames, "Tending the Flame of a Motivator," *New York Times*, August 2, 1998, WE2.

34. Stryker, "Motivation Research," 144–47 and following.

35. George Christopoulos, "What Makes People Buy?" *Management Review*, September 1959, 5–8 and following. By the early 1960s, Herzog had become part of a small, elite group of McCann-Erickson executives freed of administrative duties in order to focus on high-level problem solving. This team, working under the name Jack Tinker and Partners (after the former head of creative services), was happily ensconced in a luxurious duplex apartment at the Dorset Hotel in midtown Manhattan, making its big thinking somewhat less taxing. Klaw, "What Is Marion Harper Saying?" 122–26 and following.

36. "Psychology and the Ads," *Time*, May 13, 1957, 51–55.

37. Stryker, "Motivation Research," 144–47 and following.

38. Stryker, "Motivation Research," 144–47 and following.

39. Stryker, "Motivation Research," 144–47 and following.

40. Joseph J. Seldin, "Market Research Is a Mess," *American Mercury*, April 1957, 19–26.

41. "Motivation Research Requires Review," *Christian Century*," April 3, 1957, 412.

42. Stryker, "Motivation Research," 144–47 and following.

43. "Research Rivals Trade Blows," *Business Week*, October 29, 1955, 56 and following.

44. "Research Rivals Trade Blows."

45. Seldin, "Market Research Is a Mess."

46. "Inside the Consumer: The New Debate: Does He Know His Own Mind?" *Newsweek*, October 10, 1955, 89–93.

47. Stryker, "Motivation Research."

48. Mayer, *Madison Avenue, U.S.A.*, 225, 249–51, 256, 279.

49. Stephen Fox, *The Mirror Makers: A History of American Advertising and Its Creators* (New York: Vintage, 1984), 185.

50. Hugh S. Hardy, ed., *The Politz Papers: Science and Truth in Marketing Research* (Chicago: American Marketing Association, 1990), 1–2.

51. Hardy, ed, *The Politz Papers*, 4, 10; Mayer, *Madison Avenue, U.S.A.*, 170.

52. Hardy, ed, *The Politz Papers*, 4–5.

53. Bartos, *Qualitative Research*, 5.

54. Stryker, "Motivation Research."

55. Hardy, ed., *The Politz Papers*, 9–10; Mayer, *Madison Avenue, U.S.A.*, 185, 253–54, 256–57. Dichter also had the habit of mistaking calling his young son Thomas "Oscar," the name of his younger (by ten years) brother, which perhaps also did not endear Thomas to his dad. Later on, Dichter would berate Thomas for taking so long to finish his doctoral thesis (he had joined the Peace Corps), telling him that he himself had needed just a few months to get his own done, this too no doubt creating a situation that any Freudian analyst would have a field day with. On the "cheapskate" claim, Dichter defended his frugality by saying, "It reassures me," a reminder that "if needed, I could still do without." Thomas couldn't resist throwing away Dichter's old suits when he was on the road, however, something the old man actually appreciated because he couldn't do it himself. In 1979 (when Thomas was thirty-eight), Dichter viewed their relationship as "far from perfect, although it seems to be continuously improving." Dichter got along perfectly well with his daughter Susie, who was two years younger than Thomas. Ernest Dichter, *Getting Motivated: The Secret Behind Individual Motivations by the Man Who Was Not Afraid to Ask "Why?"* (New York: Pergamon Press, 1979), 1, 11, 51, 55, 130.

56. Daniel Horowitz, *Vance Packard and American Social Criticism* (Chapel Hill: University of North Carolina Press, 1994), 197, 208, 104.

57. Horowitz, *Vance Packard and American Social Criticism*, 105.

58. "Psychology and the Ads." Built in 1912, the mansion, which the Dichters lived in for many years, contained eleven bathrooms and a pipe organ. Seeing his garage as a waste of space, Dichter converted it into an indoor swimming pool, and he also installed an "elevator chair" in which people could ride between floors (saving the money and space needed for a staircase).

59. Vance Packard, "The Ad and the Id," *Reader's Digest*, November 1957, 118–21.

60. Horowitz, *The Anxieties of Affluence*, 51–53; Packard, *The Hidden Persuaders*, 67.

61. Horowitz, *Vance Packard and American Social Criticism*, 133–35, 151.

62. Gilbert Seldes, "What Makes the Customer Tick?" *Saturday Review*, June 1, 1957, 29–30.

63. "Psychology and the Ads."

64. "College Favorites," *Chicago Daily Tribune*, August 10, 1958, F24.

65. Packard, "The Ad and the Id."

66. "Psychology and the Ads."

67. Display Ad 47, *Wall Street Journal*, June 3, 1957, 12.

68. Robert H. Boyle, "Not-So-Mad Doctor and His Living Lab," *Sports Illustrated*, July 24, 1961, 50–56.

69. Vance Packard, "The Growing Power of Admen," *Atlantic Monthly*, September 1957, 55–59.

70. Thomas Cudlik and Christoph Steiner, "'Rabbi Ernest': The Strategist of Desire: A Portrait," in Franz Kreuzer, Gerd Prechtl, and Christoph Steiner, eds., *A Tiger in the Tank: Ernest Dichter: An Austrian Advertising Guru* (Riverside, Calif.: Ariadne Press, 2007), 92.

71. Horowitz, *The Anxieties of Affluence*. 59; Horowitz, *Vance Packard and American Social Criticism*, 162; Dichter and Packard considered having a *mano a mano* debate, but the battle between the heavyweights never happened.

72. "Market Motivator," *Los Angeles Times*, November 1, 1957, A4.

73. A. C. Spectorsky, *New York Times*, April 28, 1957, 3.

74. Harold Lancour, *Library Journal*, April 15, 1957, 1059; Robert R. Kirsch, "The Book Report," *Los Angeles Times*, May 8, 1957, B5.

75. Jerome Spingarn, "The 'Manipulation' of Buyers, Voters," *Washington Post*, April 28, 1957, E6.

76. "Ad Men and the Id," *Atlantic Monthly*, June 1957, 97–98.

77. Charles Winick, *Christian Science Monitor*, April 30, 1957, 9.

78. R.F.H., *Springfield Republican*, June 2, 1957, 7C.

79. Seldes, "What Makes the Customer Tick?"

80. Leo Bogart, *Management Review*, July 1957, 89.

81. Henry Greene, *Chicago Sunday Tribune*, May 12, 1957, 7.

82. Ernest van der Haag, "Madison Avenue Witchcraft," *Commonweal*, November 29, 1957, 230–32; Henry Greene, "Selling Your Subconscious," *Chicago Daily Tribune*, May 12, 1957, G7.

83. Elmo Roper, "How Powerful Are the Persuaders?" *Saturday Review*, October 5, 1957, 19. Other critics considered motivation research a lightweight version of psychoanalysis, and worthless as a research tool because its "sample size" was too small. Some agency men weren't afraid to express their feelings toward motivation researchers in much stronger terms. Charles Brower of BBDO called motivation research consultants "outside witch doctors and head shrinkers," for example, while Charles Adams of Mac-Manus, John and Adams called them "Freud-happy figures" (headed by "Herr Doktor Dichter"). Packard, *The Hidden Persuaders*, 161, 165.

84. Horowitz, *Vance Packard and American Social Criticism*, 202.

85. Carl Spielvogel, "Advertising: Recession? It's All in the Mind," *New York Times*, March 19, 1958, 43.

86. Packard, "The Growing Power of Admen."

87. Packard, "The Growing Power of Admen."

88. Fairfax Cone, "Advertising Is Not a Plot," *Atlantic Monthly*, January 1958, 71–73.

89. Vance Packard, "The Advertising 'Plot,'" *Atlantic Monthly*, February 1958, 28.

90. Vance Packard, "The Mass Manipulation of Human Behavior," *America*, December 14, 1957, 342–44.

91. Packard, "The Mass Manipulation of Human Behavior."

92. "What Sways the Family Shopper," *Business Week*, November 30, 1957, 46–48 and following.

93. Fairfax M. Cone, "Advertising Nefarious? That's Bunk!" *Chicago Daily Tribune*, December 22, 1957, B4.

94. Lucy Key Miller, "Front Views & Profiles," *Chicago Daily Tribune*, November 5, 1957, A3.

95. Van der Haag, "Madison Avenue Witchcraft."

96. Van der Haag, "Madison Avenue Witchcraft."

97. Guy Shipler, Jr., "The Hidden Reasons Why You Buy a Car," *Popular Science*, November 1957, 89–92.

98. "What Sways the Family Shopper."

99. "What Sways the Family Shopper."

100. Seldin, "Market Research Is a Mess."

Chapter 3. The Secret Pitch

1. Richard P. Barthol, "The Subliminal Rabbit," *Nation*, November 15, 1958, 356–58.

2. Edward S. Aarons, "The Communicators," *Magazine of Fantasy and Science Fiction*, June 1958, 52–53.

3. Loyd Ring Coleman, "Subliminal Advertising Is 'Scientific Absurdity' Like Table Rapping, Ouija Boards: Irate Adman," *Advertising Age*, June 30, 1958, 67–68.

4. Gay Talese, "Most Hidden Hidden Persuasion," *New York Times*, January 12, 1958, 22. The word "subliminal" was used for the first time in 1938 in a *Journal of Psychology* paper by A. C. Williams, Jr., with research in the area picking up after World War II. William H. Kalis, "The Phantom of the Soap Opera," *Public Relations Journal*, March 1958, 6–8.

5. E. B. Weiss, "Next—Advertising by Electrical Stimulation of the Brain?" *Advertising Age*, February 10, 1958, 64–65 (reprint of an article originally published in the same publication on May 21, 1956).

6. "Ads You'll Never See," *Business Week*, September 21, 1957, 30–31.

7. Carter Henderson, "A Blessing or Bane? TV Ads You'd See Without Knowing It," *Wall Street Journal*, September 13, 1957, 1.

8. "Devilish," *Newsweek*, October 17, 1957, 98–99.

9. Henderson, "A Blessing or Bane?"

10. "Devilish," 98–99.

11. "Unseen TV Gets Exposure on Both Coasts," *Broadcasting*, January 20, 1958, 98–99.

12. Henderson, "A Blessing or Bane?"

13. Fred Danzig, "Subliminal Advertising—Today It's Just Historic Flashback for Researcher Vicary," *Advertising Age*, September 17, 1962, 72–74.

14. Norman Cousins, "Smudging the Subconscious," *Saturday Review*, October 5, 1957, 20.

15. Al Geller, "Truth About Those 'Invisible Ads,'" *Science Digest*, December 1957, 16–18.

16. Talese, "Most Hidden Hidden Persuasion."

17. Geller, "Truth About Those 'Invisible Ads.'"

18. "What Sways the Family Shopper," *Business Week*, November 30, 1957, 46–48 and following.

19. Cousins, "Smudging the Subconscious."

20. "Diddling the Subconscious," *Nation*, October 5, 1957, 206–7.

21. Gerald W. Johnson, "The Unconscious Itch," *New Republic*, November 11, 1957, 8.

22. Marya Mannes, "Ain't Nobody Here but Us Commercials," *Reporter*, October 17, 1957, 35–37.

23. Vance Packard, "The Mass Manipulation of Human Behavior," *America*, December 14, 1957, 342–44.

24. Geller, "Truth About Those 'Invisible Ads.'"

25. Larry Wolters, "Psychologist Creates New Ad Technique," *Chicago Daily Tribune*, September 22, 1957, SW14.

26. Phyllis Battelle, "'Invisible Commercials' Stir the Subconscious," *Washington Post and Times Herald*, September 18, 1957, D8.

27. Battelle, "'Invisible Commercials' Stir the Subconscious."

28. Donald Craig, "Threat of the Hidden Persuader," *Los Angeles Times*, February 24, 1958, B5.

29. Danzig, "Subliminal Advertising."

30. James Staver, "Subliminal Advertising" (letter to editor), *Washington Post and Times Herald*, October 1, 1957, A16.

31. Larry Wolters, "Where to Dial Today," *Chicago Daily Tribune*, December 10, 1957, C13.

32. "The Invisible Monster," *Christian Century*, October 2, 1957, 1157.

33. "Quicker Than the Eye," *New Republic*, January 27, 1958, 5–6.

34. Mannes, "Ain't Nobody Here but Us Commercials."

35. "Ads You'll Never See."

36. Jack Patterson, "Invisible Salesman," *Commonweal*, April 18, 1958, 71–73.

37. "What Sways the Family Shopper."

38. "The Ad That Isn't There," *New York Times*, January 23, 1958, 26.

39. "Ads You'll Never See."

40. "Devilish."

41. "Devilish."

42. Talese, "Most Hidden Hidden Persuasion."

43. Cousins, "Smudging the Subconscious."

44. "The Ad That Isn't There."

45. Talese, "Most Hidden Hidden Persuasion."

46. Jack Gould, "A State of Mind: Subliminal Advertising, Invisible to Viewer, Stirs Doubt and Debate," *New York Times*, December 8, 1957, 15.

47. "Proponent of SP Deprecates Effect," *Broadcasting*, March 24, 1958, 47–48.

48. Talese, "Most Hidden Hidden Persuasion."

49. Kalis, "The Phantom of the Soap Opera."

50. R. M. Kidd, "Subliminal Stimuli a 'Monster'? Don't Worry—Mass Public's Individual Differences Blunt Its Power, Says Agency Man," *Advertising Age*, August 11, 1958, 56–58.

51. Kalis, "The Phantom of the Soap Opera."

52. Talese, "Most Hidden Hidden Persuasion."

53. Talese, "Most Hidden Hidden Persuasion."

54. Gould, "A State of Mind."

55. Gould, "A State of Mind."

56. "The Ad That Isn't There."

57. Barthol, "The Subliminal Rabbit"; Kalis, "The Phantom of the Soap Opera."

58. Gould, "A State of Mind."

59. Oscar Godbout, "'Subliminal' Ads over Air Studied," *New York Times*, November 13, 1957, 70.

60. Val Adams, "3 Networks Ban Subliminal Ads," *New York Times*, December 4, 1957, 79.

61. "Subliminal Advertising, Banned by TV Chains, May Hit Movie Houses," *Wall Street Journal*, December 5, 1957, 19.

62. "What Sways the Family Shopper."

63. "Psychic Hucksterism Stirs Call for Inquiry," *New York Times*, October 6, 1957, 38.

64. "Subliminal TV Cited as Dangerous to Youth," *New York Times*, January 29, 1958, 24.

65. Godbout, "'Subliminal' Ads over Air Studied."

66. "Subliminal: Plans for Using, Controlling It," *Printers' Ink*, January 31, 1958, 3–4.

67. "Hold It, Lady! Sure You Need a Mink Coat?" *Chicago Daily Tribune*, February 16, 1958, 3.

68. "N.Y. State Senate Okays Subliminal Ban," *Advertising Age*, March 24, 1958, 42.

69. "Bill to Ban Subliminal Advertising Offered," *Los Angeles Times*, April 1, 1959, 13. Richards's bill died in June after Robert E. Corrigan, a psychologist from Garden Grove, California, told the committee that a law prohibiting subliminal advertising was unnecessary because the technique "probably wouldn't work anyway." "Subliminal Ad Ban Measure Loses Out," *Los Angeles Times*, June 10, 1959, 6.

70. "Subliminal Ads Lose," *New York Times*, March 13, 1958, 20.

71. "British Ad Group Sets Probe of Subliminal Ads," *Advertising Age*, January 13, 1958, 71.

72. "British Ad Group Bans Subliminal Communication," *Advertising Age*, July 28, 1958, 2.

73. "British TV Row Breaks Over Alleged 'Subliminal' Message," *Advertising Age*, November 3, 1958, 107.

74. "Huxley Fears New Persuasion Methods Could Subvert Democratic Procedures," *New York Times*, May 19, 1958, 45; John Chamberlain, "Reading for Pleasure," *Wall Street Journal*, November 12, 1958, 16; Interestingly, Huxley seemed a lot less peeved about the methods of motivation research a few years later. In his *Brave New World and Brave New World Revisited* published in 1965, Huxley wrote that Packard's *Hidden Persuaders* was something to be "more amused than horrified" by and "more resigned than indignant" about. "Given the mass producer's obnoxiously desperate need for mass consumption," he continued, "this [motivation research] is the sort of thing that is only to be expected" (p. 39).

75. "Subliminal: Plans for Using, Controlling It."

76. "TV's 'Invisible' Ads Called 'Ineffective,'" *Science Digest*, May 1958, 22–23.

77. "Canadians Brood over Subject of Subliminal Pitch," *Advertising Age*, January 27, 1958, 3 and following.

78. "TV's 'Invisible' Ads Called 'Ineffective.'"

79. "'Phone Now,' Said CBC Subliminally—but Nobody Did," *Advertising Age*, February 10, 1958, 8.

80. Patterson, "Invisible Salesman."

81. Carter Henderson, "The Phantom Sell," *Wall Street Journal*, March 7, 1958, 1.

82. "Non-Coffee-Using Housewife Made Fresh Coffee After Hint in Subliminal Radio Test," *Advertising Age*, February 3, 1958, 3 and following.

83. "Non-Coffee-Using Housewife Made Fresh Coffee After Hint in Subliminal Radio Test."

84. Patterson, "Invisible Salesman."

85. Val Adams, "Subliminal Ads Shown in Capitol," *New York Times*, January 14, 1958, 66.

86. Patterson, "Invisible Salesman."

87. "Subliminal Has a Test; Can't See if It Works," *Printers' Ink*, January 17, 1958, 4–5.

88. "Subliminal Bees in Your Bonnet," *Chicago Daily Tribune*, January 19, 1958, 24.

89. "Subliminal Silver Lining," *Wall Street Journal*, March 14, 1958, 8; "Subliminal Advertising," *Wall Street Journal*, September 17, 1957, 12.

90. "Banned in Britain," *Printers' Ink*, August 8, 1958, 12.

91. Patterson, "Invisible Salesman."

92. "Psychologists Hit Subliminal Ads as 'Chimera,' Laud Clarity, Repetition," *Advertising Age*, September 8, 1958, 1 and following.

93. "The Invisible Sell," *Scientific American*, August 1958, 52 and following.

94. "Psychologists Hit Use of Subliminal Methods in Ads as 'Unprofessional,'" *Advertising Age*, June 16, 1958, 85.

95. "Vicary 'Delighted' at Academic Criticism," *Advertising Age*, June 16, 1958, 85.

96. Coleman, "Subliminal Advertising Is 'Scientific Absurdity' Like Table Rapping, Ouija Boards."

97. "Unconscious Sell Theme Tops '58 Ad Conference," *Advertising Age*, April 21, 1958, 1 and following.

98. "Unconscious Sell Theme Tops '58 Ad Conference."

99. "Unseen TV Gets Exposure on Both Coasts."

100. "Subliminal: Plans for Using, Controlling It."

101. Henderson, "The Phantom Sell."

102. "Hollywood TV Station Cancels Plans to Use Subliminal Ads," *Wall Street Journal*, March 12, 1958, 15.

103. "Subliminal Ads Blocked on Coast," *New York Times*, March 7, 1958, 49.

104. Wesley S. Griswold, "TV's New Trick: Hidden Commercials," *Popular Science*, April 1958, 95–97 and following.

105. Barthol, "The Subliminal Rabbit."

106. Henderson, "The Phantom Sell."

107. Barthol, "The Subliminal Rabbit."

108. Patterson, "Invisible Salesman."

109. Henderson, "The Phantom Sell."

110. Clara S. Logan, "Hidden Pitch Fight Urged," *Los Angeles Times*, March 10, 1958, B4.

111. "Nucoa Uses New Subliminal Twist: It's 'Contrapuntal,'" *Advertising Age*, March 24, 1958, 2 and following.

112. "ARF Checks on Subliminal Ads; Verdict: 'Insufficient,'" *Advertising Age*, September 15, 1958, 50.

113. "SP Can Tell, but Not Necessarily Sell," *Broadcasting*, April 13, 1959, 42.

114. Roy Gibbons, "Fear of Mass Brain Washing Is Ruled Out," *Chicago Daily Tribune*, February 4, 1961, A10.

115. Fred Farrar, "Advertising News," *Chicago Daily Tribune*, March 15, 1962, D9.

116. Danzig, "Subliminal Advertising."

117. Danzig, "Subliminal Advertising."

Chapter 4. The Fertile Moment

1. Martin Mayer, *Madison Avenue, U.S.A.* (New York: Pocket Books, 1958), 110.

2. Thomas E. Bonsall, *Disaster in Dearborn: The Story of the Edsel* (Stanford: Stanford University Press, 2002), 112.

3. Bonsall, *Disaster in Dearborn*, 113–14.

4. Bonsall, *Disaster in Dearborn*, 115.

5. E. B. Weiss, "Ed Weiss Flays Away at Researchers and Economists," *Advertising Age*, March 10, 1958, 65–66 and following.

6. Weiss, "Ed Weiss Flays Away at Researchers and Economists."

7. Weiss, "Ed Weiss Flays Away at Researchers and Economists." Dichter had a different take on the fundamental problem with the Edsel, putting most of the blame on

a motivationally challenged Ford designer. As Dichter explained in his autobiography, "He castrated the car. It had a gaping hole at the front end. Our survey showed that the otherwise inhibited Americans were referring to this oval shaped opening either as a lemon or, the more outspoken ones, as a hole which needed a bit of pubic hair around it to make it more real. This was a major reason for the flop." Ernest Dichter, *Getting Motivated: The Secret Behind Individual Motivations by the Man Who Was Not Afraid to Ask "Why?"* (New York: Pergamon Press, 1979), 94.

8. Bonsall, *Disaster in Dearborn*, 109–10.

9. Mayer, *Madison Avenue, U.S.A.*, 111–13.

10. Franz Kreuzer and Patrick Schierholz, "Dichter Lives On: Motivational Research and Advertising Today," in Franz Kreuzer, Gerd Prechtl, and Christoph Steiner, eds., *A Tiger in the Tank: Ernest Dichter: An Austrian Advertising Guru* (Riverside, Calif.: Ariadne Press, 2007), 127.

11. Joseph J. Seldin, "Market Research Is a Mess," *American Mercury*, April 1957, 19–26.

12. Peter Bart, "Advertising: A Critic Lays About," *New York Times*, November 15, 1961, 58. One ad agency in the early sixties came up with an interesting alternative to the diaries, surveys, and questionnaires that many Americans were completing rather haphazardly. Marsteller handed out an alarm clock to a group of consumers, the thing randomly ringing day or night, at which point the consumer was to record the name of any publication he or she was reading at the time. Subjects were also expected to write down what page they were on, where they got the publication, and why they were reading it, a lot to ask perhaps, but a good way to get around the inaccurate reporting that was said to be rampant in the field.

13. Weiss, "Ed Weiss Flays Away at Researchers and Economists." Bill Bernbach of Doyle Dane Bernbach, rather famously, also didn't much care for any kind of research, motivation or otherwise. "It's a nice, safe way to do business, but who the hell wants to be safe?" he asked, viewing research as even less necessary since advertising was about persuasion—an art versus a science, he believed. Mayer, *Madison Avenue U.S.A.*, 68.

14. B. Gimbel, Jr., "Market Research 'Isn't Worth a Damn': Gimbel," *Advertising Age*, November 3, 1958, 3 and following.

15. Donald R. Longman, "Competitive Pressures are Corrupting Market Research," *Advertising Age*, December 1, 1958, 61–62.

16. Carl Spielvogel, "Advertising: Cuts During Recession Scored," *New York Times*, October 16, 1958, 63.

17. "You Can't Escape MR," *Advertising Agency Magazine*, January 3, 1958, 20–33.

18. Robert Ferber and Hugh G. Wales, eds., *Motivation and Market Behavior* (Homewood, Ill.: Richard D. Irwin, 1958).

19. Ferber and Wales, eds., *Motivation and Market Behavior*, 4–11.

20. Ferber and Wales, eds., *Motivation and Market Behavior*, 11–21.

21. Ferber and Wales, eds., *Motivation and Market Behavior*, 21–31.

22. Ferber and Wales, eds., *Motivation and Market Behavior*, 36–49.

23. Ferber and Wales, eds., *Motivation and Market Behavior*, 50–64.

24. Ferber and Wales, eds., *Motivation and Market Behavior*, 64–72.

25. "Top Researchers Say MR Misnamed, Misused," *Advertising Age*, July 28, 1958, 1 and following.

26. "Sampling-Motivation Research Merger: How Will It Aid Ad Men?" *Printers' Ink*, November 28, 1958, 23–29.

27. Kenneth Groesbeck, "Knowledge of Psychology Is Needed by Agency People," *Advertising Agency Magazine*, January 3, 1958, 34–36.

28. George Christopoulos, "What Makes People Buy?" *Management Review*, September 1959, 5–8 and following.

29. Christopoulos, "What Makes People Buy?" 5–8 and following.

30. Christopoulos, "What Makes People Buy?" 5–8 and following.

31. Mackarness H. Goode, "Motivation Research in Public Relations," *Public Relations Journal*, February 1958, 9–14.

32. Frank C. Porter, "Psychologists Replace Hucksters as Agencies Battle for Accounts," *Washington Post and Times Herald*, April 12, 1959, C14.

33. "Bible Lessons Proposed for Gum Wrapper Use," *Los Angeles Times*, February 1, 1958, 14.

34. Raymond A. Bauer, "Limits of Persuasion," *Harvard Business Review*, September 1958, 105–10.

35. "A Marketing Concept Should Be the Sum of Psychoanalysis and Nose-Counting," *Printers' Ink*, April 25, 1958, 75–76.

36. "A Marketing Concept Should Be the Sum of Psychoanalysis and Nose-Counting."

37. "You Can Gauge Customers' Wants," *Nation's Business*, April 1958, 76–84.

38. Goode, "Motivation Research in Public Relations."

39. "You Can Gauge Customers' Wants."

40. Avron Fleishman, "Depth vs. Breadth," *Management Review*, April 1958, 56–58.

41. "Advertising's Enigma," *Tide*, March 14, 1958, 22–31.

42. "Advertising's Enigma."

43. Donald David, "Image Building Is an Unexplored Advertising Horizon," *Advertising Agency Magazine*, January 3, 1958, 12–16.

44. Goode, "Motivation Research in Public Relations."

45. "Researchers Want to Compare Techniques, Cautious Clients Want Them Classified," *Printers' Ink*, June 13, 1958, 62 and following.

46. Philip K. Scheuer, "On with the Play: Enter Psychiatrist," *Los Angeles Times*, July 28, 1958, C11.

47. "On with the Play."

48. Mae Tinee, "Breezy Film About Girls Lots of Fun," *Chicago Daily Tribune*, June 10, 1959, A6.

49. "Researcher Asks More Discipline for Idea Men, Creativeness for Statisticians," *Printers' Ink*, October 3, 1958, 86 and following.

50. "Impulse Buying: New Assault on the Consumer," *Time*, July 7, 1958, 66.

51. "How Do You Program With MR?" *Sponsor*, June 20, 1959, 46 and following. The psychological dynamics of radio listening was one of the earliest applications of motivation research, both in Europe and in the United States, as I discuss in chapter 1.

52. David S. R. Leighton, "Using MR in Your Marketing Program," *Management Review*, July 1958, 47–49; Sally Helgesen, "Sighting the Giant of Madison Avenue," *Los Angeles Times*, July 17, 1977, R87.

53. Audrey Langdon, "Motivation Research," *Chemical Week*, April 19, 1958, 85–92.

54. Leighton, "Using MR in Your Marketing Program."

55. "What's the Fastest Route to Man's Subconscious?" *Printers' Ink*, September 18, 1959, 106. Dichter believed that the basis of women painting their fingernails was the "almost animal-like original desire to make one's extremities appear longer and to frighten the enemy by putting his expected blood on your fingernails." Lipstick, incidentally, was an attempt to "simulate youth and permanent life," explaining why the clear favorite color remained red. *Getting Motivated*, 105–6.

56. Dorothy Diamond, "The Woman's Viewpoint," *Tide*, March 1959, 38.

57. "Meaningful Patterns," *New Yorker*, January 3, 1959, 17–19.

58. Mitchell Gordon, "Overseas Selling," *Wall Street Journal*, July 13, 1956, 1.

59. Mira Wilkins, *The Maturing of Multinational Enterprise: American Business Abroad from 1914 to 1970* (Cambridge, Mass.: Harvard University Press, 1974), 374.

60. Christopher D. McKenna, *The World's Newest Profession: Management Consulting in the Twentieth Century* (New York: Cambridge University Press, 2006), 166–67, 145–53.

61. "Europe Is Importing What It Invented: Motivation Research," *Advertising Age*, October 12, 1959.

62. William Clark, "Explores Motivation Research—A Boss' Tool," *Chicago Daily Tribune*, August 4, 1959, B5.

63. "Burleigh Gardner: Selling the U.S. By Class," *Printers' Ink*, March 25, 1960, 77–80.

64. Horowitz, *The Anxieties of Affluence*, 59.

65. "Ernest Dichter of Croton: 'A Doctor for Ailing Products,'" *Printers' Ink*, June 26, 1959, 72–80.

66. Eric Clark, *The World of Advertising: How They Make You Buy* (New York: Viking, 1989) 71–73.

67. Vance Packard, *The Hidden Persuaders* (Brooklyn, N.Y.: Ig, 2007), 74–94. Dichter, like Freud, believed that people were born and died insecure, never fully recovering from being expelled from the womb (Kreuzer, in Franz Kreuzer, Gerd Prechtl, and Christoph Steiner, eds., *A Tiger in the Tank*, 36).

68. "Ernest Dichter of Croton."

69. Richard L. Madden, "Cigaret Psychology," *Wall Street Journal*, November 11, 1958, 1.

70. Dave Jones, "Credit Card Climb," *Wall Street Journal*, February 21, 1958, 1.

71. Jacquelin Southerland, "Find Women Like to Work in Own Home," *Chicago Daily Tribune*, January 18, 1958, 7.

72. Seldin, "Market Research Is a Mess." Women inclined to do so can also blame Dichter for the proportions of the Barbie doll, as he did motivation research on the project which led to the production of America's plastic sweetheart. "He interviewed girls about what they wanted in a doll [and] it turn[ed] out that what they wanted was someone sexy looking, someone that they wanted to grow up to be like," Hedy Dichter recalled in 1998, the specifics being "long legs, big breasts, glamorous." Lynne Ames, "Tending the Flame of a Motivator," *New York Times*, August 2, 1998, WE2.

73. "Ernest Dichter of Croton."

74. "Ernest Dichter of Croton."

75. "Ernest Dichter of Croton."

76. Christopoulos, "What Makes People Buy?"

77. "Because 'Imprecise,' Motive Research Misleads, Penner Tells Marketers," *Advertising Age*, January 6, 1958, 69.

78. "Qualitative Data Okay, but Numbers Necessary: Penner," *Advertising Age*, October 5, 1959.

79. "Be Wary of Motive Researchers, Britt," *Advertising Age*, February 17, 1958, 68.

80. "Semanticist Hayakawa Blames Motivationists for Ills of Automobile Makers," *Advertising Age*, May 12, 1958, 111–12.

81. "Despite Motive Studies, Ads Alter Attitudes: DuBois," *Advertising Age*, October 26, 1959, 23.

82. Joseph W. Newman, "Working with Behavioral Scientists," *Harvard Business Review*, July 1958, 67–74.

83. "Perception Studies More Practical Than Motivation: Ben-Zeev," *Advertising Age*, October 19, 1959, 58.

84. Mayer, *Madison Avenue, U.S.A.*, 257–58.

Chapter 5. The Psychology of the World of Objects

1. Ronald Alsop, "Advertisers Put Consumers on the Couch," *Wall Street Journal*, May 13, 1988, 21.

2. Alsop, "Advertisers Put Consumers on the Couch."

3. "Home Builders Shape Fresh Sales Appeal as Basic Demand Appears to Be Faltering," *Wall Street Journal*, November 16, 1960, 5.

4. Joseph G. Phelan, "Motivation Research for Retail Use," *Journal of Retailing*, Winter 1962–1963, 17–20.

5. George Schreiber, "Housewares Trade Show Opens in McCormick Pl," *Chicago Daily Tribune*, June 16, 1962, C5.

6. Fred Farrar, "Marketing," *Chicago Tribune*, April 10, 1963, C6.

7. Bill Gold, "The District Line," *Washington Post*, May 6, 1961, C18.

8. Charles Neal, Jr., "Research Phobia Irritates," *Los Angeles Times*, January 17, 1961, A3.

9. Neal, Jr., "Research Phobia Irritates."

10. Phelan, "Motivation Research for Retail Use," 17–20.

11. Robert Alden, "Advertising: The Hunt for Buyer Motives," *New York Times*, January 24, 1960, III, 13.

12. "Dr. Gallup: Don't Ask Consumers 'Why,'" *Printers' Ink*, June 24, 1960, 53–55.

13. Walter A. Woods, "Psychological Dimensions of Consumer Decisions," *Journal of Marketing*, January 1960, 15–19.

14. "New Way to Size Up How Consumers Behave," *Business Week*, July 22, 1961, 68 and following.

15. "New Way to Size Up How Consumers Behave."

16. Fred Farrar, "The Name, Chevy II, Pulled 'Out of a Hat,'" *Chicago Daily Tribune*, July 16, 1962, C6.

17. Warren Seulowitz, "Social Science in Market Research," *Sponsor*, January 7, 1963, 36–37.

18. Peter Bart, "Advertising: 'M.R.' Use Is Dwindling," *New York Times*, December 18, 1962, 11.

19. Thomas Cudlik and Christoph Steiner, "'Rabbi Ernest': The Strategist of Desire: A Portrait," in Franz Kreuzer, Gerd Prechtl, and Christoph Steiner, eds., *A Tiger in the Tank: Ernest Dichter: An Austrian Advertising Guru* (Riverside, Calif.: Ariadne Press, 2007), 78.

20. Mina Hamilton, "Weak Spots in Market Research," *Management Review*, August 1964, 58–61.

21. " . . . In the Eye of the Beholder," *Sponsor*, December 28, 1964, 25–29.

22. "Scouting the Trail for Marketers," *Business Week*, April 18, 1964, 90–114.

23. George Christopoulos, "What Makes People Buy?" *Management Review*, September 1959, 5–8 and following.

24. Daniel Horowitz, *The Anxieties of Affluence: Critiques of American Consumer Culture* (Amherst: University of Massachusetts Press, 2004), 62–63.

25. Eric Clark, *The World of Advertising: How They Make You Buy* (New York: Viking, 1989), 78.

26. "Emphasize Buyer's Perception, Not Motivation: Woods," *Advertising Age*, December 13, 1965, 106.

27. "Carrier Boys Look Forward to College," *Chicago Daily Tribune*, June 14, 1962, N A1.

28. Ernest Dichter, *The Strategy of Desire* (Garden City, N.Y.: Doubleday, 1960).

29. Pierre D. Martineau, "Respectable Persuasion," *Journal of Marketing*, April 1961, 108–9.

30. John Keats, "To Persuade Is to Sell," *New York Times*, September 11, 1960, BR22.

31. Ernest Dichter, "Hucksters," *New York Times*, October 9, 1960, BR53.

32. Jim Murray, "Freud in the Sulky," *Los Angeles Times*, September 29, 1961, C1.

33. Robert H. Boyle, "Not-So-Mad Doctor and His Living Lab," *Sports Illustrated*, July 24, 1961, 50–56.

34. Boyle, "Not-So-Mad Doctor and His Living Lab."

35. Ernest Dichter, *Getting Motivated: The Secret Behind Individual Motivations by the Man Who Was Not Afraid to Ask "Why?"* (New York: Pergamon Press, 1979), 52.

36. Boyle, "Not-So-Mad Doctor and His Living Lab."

37. Boyle, "Not-So-Mad Doctor and His Living Lab."

38. Lester David, "What Do You Really Know About Men Vs. Women?" *Los Angeles Times*, July 2, 1961, TW11.

39. Alvin Shuster, "Consumers Held Led by Emotions," *New York Times*, June 30, 1961, 10.

40. Bart, "Advertising: 'M.R.' Use Is Dwindling."

41. Ernest Dichter, "The World Customer," *Harvard Business Review*, July–August 1962, 113–22.

42. Peter Bart, "Advertising: A Talk With a Motivation Man," *New York Times*, November 5, 1963, 49.

43. Horowitz, *The Anxieties of Affluence*, 62–63; Bart, "Advertising: A Talk with a Motivation Man."

44. Bart, "Advertising: A Talk with a Motivation Man."

45. Ernest Dichter, *Handbook of Consumer Motivations: The Psychology of the World of Objects* (New York: McGraw-Hill, 1964), v.

46. Dichter, *Handbook of Consumer Motivations*, vii.

47. "What Makes Them Buy," *Sponsor*, August 24, 1964, 36–37.

48. Donald F. Blankertz, "Handbook of Consumer Motivations," *Journal of Marketing Research*, November 1964, 73–74.

49. Russell Baker, "The Observer," *New York Times*, July 26, 1964, E8.

50. A. B. Blankenship, "Freud in Consumerland," *Journal of Marketing*, January 1965, 116.

51. Philip L. Short, "Handbook of Consumer Motivations," *Occupational Psychology*, January 1965, 71–72.

52. Ernest Dichter, "Discovering the 'Inner Jones,'" *Harvard Business Review*, May–June, 1965, 6–8 and following.

53. Dichter, "Discovering the 'Inner Jones.'"

54. Ernest Dichter, "How Word-of-Mouth Advertising Works," *Harvard Business Review*, November–December 1966, 147–66; Edward Boggs, "Lend Me Your Ears," *Journal of Advertising Research*, December 1966, 46–47; Malcolm Gladwell: *The Tipping Point: How Little Things Can Make a Big Difference* (New York: Little Brown, 2000).

55. Everett Mattlin, "Bald Facts About Wig Wearers," *Chicago Tribune*, July 7, 1969, B7.

56. Dichter, *Getting Motivated*, 129.

57. Marilyn Bender, "Men's Socks: Onward and Upward . . .," *New York Times*, June 4, 1970, 50.

58. Bender, "Men's Socks"; "Some 'Soxology' Theories," *New York Times*, June 4, 1970, 50.

59. Dichter, *Getting Motivated*, 52. Dichter met a number of celebrities, such as Pat

Boone, Sammy Davis, Jr., Shelley Winters, and Gig Young, on other television appearances, and even demonstrated his psychodrama technique on David Frost's show.

60. Leonard Sloane, "Youth Sets Style in Men's Clothing," *New York Times*, February 18, 1966, 45.

61. Charles Ball, "Lodging Industry Briefed on Faults," *New York Times*, October 29, 1967, XX5.

62. Martin Rossman, "Marketing Men Told to Dig for Motivations," *Los Angeles Times*, September 11, 1969, D14.

63. "Childhood Memory Shapes Home Buying Choice," *Chicago Tribune*, May 10, 1969, W-A10.

64. "Childhood Memory Shapes Home Buying Choice."

65. Marilyn Bender, "'Tracking' the Trends of Social Change," *New York Times*, November 29, 1970, 168.

66. Dichter, *Getting Motivated*, 158; Kreuzer, in Franz Kreuzer, Gerd Prechtl, and Christoph Steiner, eds., *A Tiger in the Tank*, 32–33.

67. Mattlin, "Bald Facts About Wig Wearers."

68. Dichter, *Getting Motivated* 121.

69. Thomas R. De Gregori, "Motivating Human Behavior," *Journal of Economic Issues*, September 1973, 501–3.

70. Ernest Dichter, *Motivating Human Behavior* (New York: McGraw-Hill, 1971). Toffler actually mentioned Dichter in *Future Shock*, not particularly flatteringly.

71. Colston E. Warne, "Motivating Human Behavior," *Journal of Economic Issues*, September 1973, 503–4.

72. Bernard P. Indik, "Motivating Human Behavior," *Personnel Psychology*, Autumn 1972, 598–9.

73. Roger Ricklefs, "Psyching Them Out," *Wall Street Journal*, November 20, 1972, 1.

74. Greg Conderacci, "End of an Affair?" *Wall Street Journal*, February 17, 1972, 36.

75. Ricklefs, "Psyching Them Out."

76. Philip H. Dougherty, "Advertising: Finding Statistics," *New York Times*, January 17, 1973, 58.

77. "Dichter Leaves Institute but Takes Jargon with Him," *Advertising Age*, January 29, 1973, 60.

78. Gay Pauley, "Consumer Ignorance Abounds Behavioral Expert Claims," *Atlanta Daily World*, August 29, 1974, 14.

79. Roy R. Grundy and Wayne R. Stuetzer, "Packaging: The Sixth Sense?" *Journal of Marketing*, July 1976, 130.

80. Donald Holland, "Packaging: The Sixth Sense?" *Journal of Advertising*, Spring 1976, 38–39.

81. Sally Helgesen, "Sighting the Giant of Madison Avenue," *Los Angeles Times*, July 17, 1977, R87.

82. Clarence Newman, "Mod Is Dead: Arbiters of Fashion Now Say the Jump Suit Is In," May 19, 1967, 1. Dichter also later admitted he erroneously advised presidential

candidate Adlai Stevenson to smile more often during his campaign, something the intellectual just couldn't do very convincingly.

83. Helgesen, "Sighting the Giant of Madison Avenue."

84. Dichter, *Getting Motivated*, ix–xi, 6, 13. In his nightmares, on the other hand, Dichter dreamt he was poor again, with nothing to eat. "During sleep, the childhood dreams come back," he wrote in his autobiography, explaining that "they sit on my chest, probably one of the reasons why I keep working although I would be entitled to retire, because of age and income." *Getting Motivated*, 138.

85. Dichter, *Getting Motivated*, 32, 70, 89, 98, 147, 156.

86. Ernest Dichter, "Whose Lifestyle Is It Anyway?" *Psychology and Marketing*, Fall 1986, 151–63.

87. Alsop, "Advertisers Put Consumers on the Couch."

88. Alsop, "Advertisers Put Consumers on the Couch."

89. Clark, *The World of Advertising*, 73–76.

90. "How Hot a Manager Are You?" *Public Personnel Management*, Winter 1986, 475.

91. Rena Bartos, "Ernest Dichter: Motive Interpreter," *Journal of Advertising Research*, February–March 1986, 15.

92. Ernest Dichter, "What's in an Image?" *Journal of Consumer Marketing*, Winter 1985, 75–81.

93. Clark, *The World of Advertising*, 73.

94. Clark, *The World of Advertising*, 73–76.

95. Randall Rothenberg, "Advertising," *New York Times*, February 15, 1989, D19.

Epilogue

1. David Clark Scott, "Finding Out What Makes Us Tick," *Christian Science Monitor*, January 27, 1987, 1 and following.

2. Jesus Sanchez, "Consumer Psychographic Research Examines the Why Behind the Buy," *Los Angeles Times*, June 5, 1990, 6.

3. Scott, "Finding Out What Makes Us Tick."

4. Jonathan Rowe, "Gauging the Impact of Advertising," *Christian Science Monitor*, January 28, 1987, 14–15.

5. Brad Edmondson, "Who You Are Is What You Buy," *Washington Post*, October 26, 1986, B3.

6. Clotaire Rapaille, *The Culture Code: An Ingenious Way to Understand Why People Around the World Live and Buy as They Do* (New York: Broadway Books, 2006).

7. Emily Eakin, "Penetrating the Mind by Metaphor," *New York Times*, February 23, 2002, 9.

8. Rick Romell, "Getting to Heart of Market Research," *Milwaukee Journal Sentinel*, January 6, 2008.

9. Timothy E. Moore, "Subliminal Delusion," *Psychology Today*, July 1985, 10–11; Herbert Rotfeld, "Subliminal Foolishness," *Los Angeles Times*, April 1, 1986, B5; Bernice Kanner, "From the Subliminal to the Ridiculous," *New York*, December 4, 1989, 18 and

following; John Leo, "Hostility Among the Ice Cubes," *U.S. News and World Report*, July 15, 1991, 18; Michael Lev, "No Hidden Meaning Here," *New York Times*, May 3, 1991; Marshall Schuon, "Selling Paseo's Sizzle Between the Lines," *New York Times*, June 16, 1991, S12.

10. Anthony R. Pratkanis and Elliot Aronson, "Subliminal Sorcery: Who Is Seducing Whom?" *USA Today*, September 1991, 64–66; Joshua Levine, "Search and Find," *Forbes*, September 2, 1991, 134–35; Timothy E. Moore, "Subliminal Perception: Facts and Fallacies," *Skeptical Inquirer*, Spring 1992, 273–81; Anthony R. Pratkanis, "The Cargo-Cult Science of Subliminal Persuasion," *Skeptical Inquirer*, Spring 1992, 260–72; Bryan C. Auday, "Subliminal Tapes: Controlled Tests (with Bogus Tapes)," *Skeptical Inquirer*, Summer 1992, 349–51.

11. Clive Thompson, "There's a Sucker Born in Every Medial Prefrontal Cortex," *New York Times Magazine*, October 26, 2003, 54.

12. Kevin Helliker, "This Is Your Brain on a Strong Brand," *Wall Street Journal*, November 28, 2006, B1.

13. Stuart Elliott, "A Neuromarketer on the Frontier of Buyology," *New York Times*, January 4, 2009, 30.

Index